WORDTAMER

Imagine a funfair in the classroom...
invite dragons to school...let pupils travel through time!

Written by award-winning children's author Judy Waite, *Wordtamer* offers over fifty ideas for exciting, innovative writing activities and creative workshops. The book explores how authors actually work and what they achieve through their methods. It considers how teachers and children can incorporate these techniques into their own work, and so improve creative writing.

Wordtamer provides easy-to-follow instructions to:

- set up and run inspiring writing lessons and workshops
- cover basic elements such as character and setting
- identify craft skills that link writing with the school curriculum
- develop ideas into contemporary, science fiction, fantasy or time-travel scenarios using tried-and-tested templates that expand on core concepts
- engage reluctant writers by using visual and kinaesthetic approaches
- develop independent and group-work practice
- enrich creative practice and awareness
- explore different writing styles
- improve teaching styles *and* children's writing through a range of innovative and interactive activities
- appreciate why, as well as how, these techniques are so effective.

Underpinned by theory and Judy's own experience of working as an author in schools and running writing workshops for all ages, *Wordtamer* offers step-by-step, inspiring plans for creative writing lessons that will make a buzz in the classroom. Pupils won't just create characters...they will become them.

Judy Waite is an award-winning author and has written over fifty titles ranging from picture books for very young readers, to hard-hitting teenage novels. Having formerly worked in the field of learning support at primary and secondary level, Judy also has extensive experience working in schools as an author and regularly runs writing workshops and residencies for all ages. Judy is Senior Lecturer on the Creative Writing course at the University of Winchester, UK.

'The techniques from this book have inspired my class. The different activities stimulate the children's imaginations, engaging them immediately – reluctant and non-confident writers are putting pen to paper before they even realise. The sessions give a "can do" feel for writing, with no one stuck for ideas. It has transformed attitudes to writing by providing approaches that give the children strategies and skills that they can draw upon time and time again.'

Katie Hadlow, Teacher, Redlands Primary School, UK

'Enticing and engaging by turn, this book is also highly practical, offering teachers a rich array of strategies to support young writers shape their stories. Judy Waite's accessible text reinforces the argument that teachers benefit if they too are involved as writers, profiles visualisation as a form of creative focus and includes a range of examples of creative writing. It will undoubtedly help teachers to develop young wordtamers who take delight in the art and craft of writing.'

Teresa Cremin, Professor of Literacy, Open University, UK
and Past President of the UKLA

WORDTAMER

Activities to Inspire
Creative Thinking and Writing

Judy Waite

Routledge
Taylor & Francis Group

LONDON AND NEW YORK

First published 2018
by Routledge
2 Park Square, Milton Park, Abingdon, Oxon OX14 4RN

and by Routledge
711 Third Avenue, New York, NY 10017

Routledge is an imprint of the Taylor & Francis Group, an informa business

British Library Cataloguing in Publication Data
A catalogue record for this book is available from the British Library

Library of Congress Cataloging in Publication Data
A catalog record for this book has been requested

ISBN: 978-1-138-69457-6 (hbk)
ISBN: 978-1-138-69460-6 (pbk)
ISBN: 978-1-315-52797-0 (ebk)

Typeset in Helvetica and Algerian by
Servis Filmsetting Ltd, Stockport, Cheshire

PROGRAMME

PART III
SHOWTIME: WORDTAMER CREATIVE WRITING ACTIVITIES

PREFACE
The sea of ideas

Once upon a very long time ago, I was enrolled on a writing course led by a poet. This man didn't just write poetry, he breathed it. He could turn anything into a poem. He carried a pen with him everywhere and scrawled poems on the backs of envelopes, train tickets, ice-cream wrappers. On the ice-cream wrapper day he had taken us all to the beach. He gave us each a scrap of paper and told us to write a poem, very quickly, to a stranger. Then he collected the poems without reading them, put them in a green glass bottle, and threw it into the sea. We all watched as our hastily scrawled attempts rolled with the tide, washed back in and then dragged out again. Washed in and then dragged out. Washed in, then dragged out. It seemed like a beautiful thing, these unread poems, all caught by the pull of the moon. I went home full of inspiration; buzzing with new ideas.

Afterwards, I tried to fathom what I'd learnt from it.

It still seemed to be a beautiful thing, but (environmental concerns related to glass bottles aside) what made it so meaningful? Could I recreate a moment like that for myself, or did it only work because the teacher was a poet, and we'd trusted him?

I wanted an underpinning that not only explored why it had been such a powerful moment, but also gave me a sense of the experience leading me somewhere new. I wanted something more than just that one-off event.

This book is the 'something more' that I had looked for on that day.

WORDTAMER
The what and the why

Wordtamer is divided into three sections.

PRE-PERFORMANCE: this first section explores creativity and writing within a classroom context. It includes deconstruction around what works, and why. There is analysis of existing familiar texts from a writer's perspective, with a focus on how successful authors achieve specific effects. The writing strategies of established authors have been adapted to meet the needs of a school-based framework. There is a range of original, interactive and kinaesthetic activities that apply to pre-writing, writing, drafting and editing. Each approach offers samples, and methodology is underpinned with theory and discussion, linking their relevance to school-aged learners. The pre-performance stage further invites teachers to be writers, developing engagement into the writing process. This has been shown to enable teachers to make connections with their own ideas, the creative process of their pupils and the quality of their responses to written outcomes.

THE TRAINING GROUND: drawn from key performance indicators related to writing within education, this section looks at the main elements in writing fiction that are measurable. Outlining the core functions of crafting skills within creative writing, these skills are then explored in isolation. Development of character, setting, plot, suspense, atmosphere, cliffhangers and dialogue are all investigated, explained and underpinned. Specific creative writing activities have been devised that focus on these areas and offer depth and context to their application. These approaches have been developed in primary and secondary classrooms with the support of teachers, pupils and parents.

SHOWTIME: evolving ideas from the experience of a published author in schools, this section offers a selection of extended creative writing activities and workshops that have the potential to run from between 50 minutes and whole days – maybe even whole terms. Designed with templates for teachers to follow, each activity responds to the conventions of specific genres and draws out ideas through interactive and immersive practices that connect with a range of learning and teaching styles. The activities are supported by material that can be easily reproduced or photocopied directly from this book. Suggestions for additional props that might add value to pupil engagement and ultimate learning outcomes are listed, as are extension techniques that educators can apply and adapt.

Each activity also identifies learning outcomes and approaches, offering feedback approaches, based on the focus and content of the activity.

.

ABOUT THE AUTHOR

Think of words as wild creatures. They need handling. Understanding. Taming and training.

www.wordtamer.co.uk

Judy Waite is an award winning author. She has written over fifty titles ranging from picture books for very young readers, to hard hitting teenage novels. She has published educational fiction and fiction for reading schemes, including stories pitched for reluctant readers.

Formerly working in learning support at both primary and secondary level, Judy additionally has extensive experience working in schools as an author. She runs writing workshops and residencies for all ages.

Judy is a Senior Lecturer on the creative writing programme at the University of Winchester, and her research areas revolve around teaching fiction, writing for children, and creativity linked with education. She has devised training for undergraduates who are interested in teaching, and this has a particular focus on those students who are moving onto PGCE or related teacher-training programmes.

ACKNOWLEDGEMENTS

The writing of any book is, ultimately, a solo performance. The author stands alone on the stage of their own potential: scripting, experimenting, rehearsing, reworking. Sometimes (mostly) they practise in the shadows. Sometimes the stage lights glare out, exposing every detail – and all the flaws.

The development of *Wordtamer* has demanded a deep investigation around my own creative processes and responses, and I have likened words themselves to wild beasts: creatures that need taming and training. Throughout this training there has been a backstage but vital cast of experts and supporters who have been particularly significant in helping me wrestle these beasts to the ground. It is this cast I now invite to step forward into the spotlight, so I can thank them all properly.

My first burst of applause goes to Clare Ashworth, in her role as editor at Routledge Education. Clare spotted one of my creative workshops at an annual United Kingdom Literacy Association (UKLA) conference and approached me with a proposal for publication. The possibilities that grew from our early talks and meeting underpinned all my consequent decisions. I must also thank UKLA for letting me loose on their delegates. It is because of my *Wordtaming and the Funfair of Ideas* session at the UKLA conference in Nottingham (2015) that the twinkling potential for a *Wordtamer* book began to glow.

Much of the research that lit the way to *Wordtamer* was underpinned by projects supported by the RKE (Research, Knowledge, Exchange) committee at the University of Winchester. In particular I want to raise my hat and give a wild burst of applause to Dr Inga Bryden, who has been unendingly supportive, encouraging – and patient!

I am deeply indebted to all the primary and secondary level teachers, pupils, educational specialists, authors and librarians who assisted with the research, the activities and feedback. There are too many to list individually, but more wild hat-raising goes in the direction of participating schools Locks Heath Junior School, Peel Common Junior School, Cantell (Secondary) School, Redlands Primary School and Siskin Junior School. And, from Redlands Primary – can Ms Katie Hadlow please step forward. I cannot thank Katie enough for her support and enthusiasm – nor for the consistent loan of her wonderful pupils over several years. Let the stage shake with my thunderous clapping.

Amanda Garrie listened to ideas and introduced me to vital contacts, without whom aspects of research could not have progressed. Amanda is a long-time friend, fellow writer, researcher and experienced teacher who has been generous with advice around a variety of linked projects. She widened the scope of the practical research integral to *Wordtamer*. Please, step into the limelight and take a bow.

The editorial team at Routledge, moving through the super efficiency of Sarah Tuckwell, Christopher Byrne, Fiona Burbage, Lucy Stewart, Olivia Manley, Katharine Atherton, Jan Baiton – and the wonderful Helen Pritt – were all there with professional insight and integrity whenever I needed it. If I have missed any names here, I apologise profoundly. You have all been crucial.

My two amazing daughters were my prompters, standing in an unseen corner, whispering encouragement. Confident (unlike me) that I could ride through all the false starts, and hit the deadlines. I thank you both for listening, with emails, phone calls and on Skype. (You were so far – too far – away.) Rachel Waite and Libby Waite, I call you forward with cheers and frenzied clapping.

When writing this book my home life was sometimes beyond chaotic, and a fresh burst of rapturous applause is called on for my lovely partner, best friend and soulmate – Jason Kaye. Jason tiptoed around an assault course of books, props, paperwork and scrawled notes, knowing that at times the only disturbance I could tolerate was the delivery of endless streams of tea. I celebrate your tolerance and quiet support. For you, I will dim the lights and light a candle.

My final glorious ovation goes to one of the most creative souls I have ever met – the first person to enlighten me to the possibility that teaching could be very different to anything I had experienced. From faded messages on battered postcards, to clay monsters and the silence of cathedrals, I learnt how play is a powerful tool. I also learnt that the passing on of knowledge is best achieved through showing, not telling. Peter Dixon: poet, writer, artist and teacher – it was a long time ago and I'm not sure I knew it at the time, but you set the stage for all my own teachery approaches. Thank you!

Our thanks are due to the following publishers and authors for permission to include materials in the text:

Cambridge University Press, for material printed from Wenger, E. (2013), *Communities of Practice: Learning, Meaning, and Identity*, © Cambridge University Press 1998, reproduced with permission.

Harvard University Press, for material printed from THE CULTURE OF EDUCATION by Jerome Bruner, Cambridge, Mass.: Harvard University Press, Copyright © 1996 by the President and Fellows of Harvard College.

Nature, for material printed from *npj Science of Learning* (No. 1), Hattie, J. and Donoghue, G. (2016), Learning Strategies: A Synthesis and Conceptual Model.

Pennsylvania Association for Adult Continuing Education for material printed from *PAACE Journal of Lifelong Learning*, Vol. 26, Merriam, S., Adult Learning Theory: Evolution and Future Directions, pp. 21–37.

Sage Publications Inc., for material printed from Scott, D. and Hargreaves, E. (eds) (2015), *The SAGE Handbook of Learning*, pp. 353–362; Biesta, G. *Power and Education Journal* (Vol. 5, No. 1), Interrupting the Politics of Learning, pp. 4–15, copyright © 2013 by SAGE Publications. Reprinted by Permission of SAGE Publications.

Wiley, for material printed from Mezirow, J. & Associates (2000), *Learning as Transformation: Critical Perspectives on a Theory in Progress*, pp. 35–70; Mezirow, J., Taylor, E. W. & Associates (2009), *Transformative Learning in Practice: Insights from Community, Workplace and Higher Education*, pp. 18–32; Tennant, M. (2012), *The Learning Self: Understanding the Potential for Transformation*, pp. 17–34.

Jackson, C., Affective Dimensions of Learning, in Scott, D. & Hargreaves, E., *The SAGE Handbook of Learning,* pp. 353–362. Copyright © 2015 by Carolyn Jackson. Reprinted by permission of SAGE Publications, Ltd.

PART I

PRE-PERFORMANCE

School and education

CHAPTER 1

INTRODUCTION

Creative writing and historical context, research and teaching

The fairytale of authors in schools

When I was first published as a children's author, writers were often seen as celebrities in schools. We were invited in to talk about recent books, describe a typical writing day, divulge the mysterious secrets of where we got our ideas and explain the intricacies of the publishing process. We answered questions, sold books and wrote our signatures on the prelim pages with an elaborate flourish.

I was never altogether comfortable with this model. It seemed to be a day when the waters parted; the author rose up from mysterious depths, then later sank back into their watery otherworld. These authors left no discernible traces in the halls of learning. They could only hope that perhaps, sometimes, pupils found a shell, or the bones of small fish, and grew curious about where they'd come from.

I became more interested in exploring approaches that might still resonate once my visit was over. I wanted to investigate how my own creative writing techniques might work even if I wasn't there to facilitate the activity. Consequently, I created bespoke sessions for differentiated activities and outcomes and included extension activities that could run beyond my sessions. Feedback from these was always positive and was often particularly remarkable around pupils who had previously been working at 'below average' in terms of focus, imagination and written outputs.

I was not the first to be thinking like this – it was just that this was the first time I had thought like it.

Creativity, creative process and links to literacy are on a journey that can be traced back to the 1960s and doubtless before that. Educationalist Sir Alec Clegg wrote *The Excitement of Writing* (1964), drawing from peers who were combining art and music to inspire young writers (Jones and Wyse, 2004: 21). The book included samples of pupil work that demonstrated impressive results, and Clegg evolved material that was critical of the divide between mind (something measurable) and spirit (something felt). He articulated this by comparing the differences between writing on a prescribed topic from notes on the blackboard and telling someone in your own personal written words of something that has excited you (Clegg, 1972).

The notion of creative writing as a 'process' rather than a product, attributed to Donald H. Graves, emerged in the 1980s and Graves went on to establish the practice of writing workshops in schools. Writing workshops became embedded within literacy teaching, creating a 'community of writers'. Teachers and pupils wrote alongside each other, creating and sharing ideas and techniques (Chamberlain, 2016). Lucy McCormick Calkins (1994) continued evolving craft approaches alongside writerly practice, acknowledging that 'writing does not begin with deskwork but with lifework'.

Since the turn of the century there has continued to be an impressive flow of innovative pioneers. *Talk for Writing* (Corbett, 2011) takes a collaborative approach: young writers listen to the rhythms and cadences of language in advance of writing their own stories, and teachers share writing practice with their class, evolving and improving ideas through purposeful discussion and example. The National Association of Writers in Education (NAWE) placed writers in nine different schools between 2006 and 2009, visiting once a term over the course of three years and demonstrating measurable progress in the literacy and writing skills of the control groups they were assigned to (Horner, nd). Schools, recognising the impact professional writers could make to the written work of pupils (Cremin and Myhill, 2012: 157–8), brought in writers who would attach to the schools for longer periods, as consultants and as writers-in-residence.

Teresa Cremin, former president of the United Kingdom Literacy Association (UKLA) and Professor of Education (Literacy) at the Open University, has conducted a range of studies and interactive literacy initiatives including schemes that challenge traditional approaches to reading, and has also developed residencies that connect teachers *with* writers, which consequently support teachers *as* writers (Eyres, 2016). These are all models of excellence that demonstrate universal, measurable approaches endorsed by specialists.

Moving beyond the days when I was first throwing poems in the sea, if I now take a group of pupils into the woods and ask them to close their eyes and sense the trees, I understand the 'felt' experience behind the action and the theories that are attached, the value of this activity to writing and how to negotiate the ideas that evolve.

If I transform a whole classroom into an interactive funfair, I know in advance whether I want to link with fantasy, horror, or realism and I steer the connecting activities based on the outcomes identified. I can assess the direct impact of the lesson on the writing, analyse how well character, setting and genre have been utilised, and give in-depth feedback on ways to develop both the language and the ideas overall.

Throughout this book I have 'tamed and trained' my own approaches so they not only have value for others working in education, but also that those same 'others' can take them from me and make them their own. All the material has been researched, adapted and piloted at primary and secondary level in order to assess measurable differences and developments.

Teachers can follow the creative writing in the *Wordtamer Showtime* activities (pages 134– 210) 'by the book' or they can amend and adapt these to suit their own groups' needs and abilities. Although primarily pitched at creative practice within the context of literacy, the activities offer multi-modal and cross-curricular approaches.

It is hoped that *Wordtamer* will be of value to those who hope to learn to teach, those who are learning how to teach and those who are already teaching.

It will also have benefits for anyone who seeks inspiration and the development of crafting skills; those many teachers and professionals I work with who aspire to write stories of their own.

Government reports continually acknowledge the need for more flexible, imaginative practices to be embedded within schools' literacy programmes. Recognition of the value of extended projects that provoke more depth and detail in writing outcomes resulted in a call for teachers to take more risks and to 'be inventive' (Ofsted, 2012). Taking risks and being inventive are the heart and pulse of creative writing, and if new initiatives can continue to support writing at all stages, then models of excellence can literally 'move English forward' into the future.

Wordtaming and the funfair of ideas

A significant number of young people get left behind in the writing race, and this follows them beyond primary and secondary learning, dragging like a ball and chain through all their adult lives. There may be many reasons for this, but some studies highlight issues around an overly intense focus on spelling, punctuation and grammar:

> only just over half of the pupils (KS3) surveyed saw themselves as good writers who valued the opportunity to use their imagination in their writing. The other half did not think they were good at writing and cited their inability to write neatly, spell or punctuate. These young people had clearly not gained the confidence to use writing for their own purposes and expressed a lack of confidence in terms of technical competence rather than in the messages they might need to convey, and recommendations are in place for initiatives to work with teachers and with pupils to address this.
>
> (Horner, 2010)

This is a complex debate, as it is clear that spelling, punctuation and grammar are essential ingredients for good writing. Theories and practice wrestle with alternating approaches. There is the need to establish these skills in advance of evolving creativity, pitted against a desire for creative, engaging sessions that don't concern themselves with more secretarial elements. Either way, at both primary and secondary level skills in writing generally lag behind those with reading. Added to this, studies consistently identify gaps in performance between boys and girls. This is not confined to England, or even the UK: 'Underachievement of boys is a concern broadly paralleled throughout the English-speaking world and beyond'. The gap between girls' and boys' achievement in English is greatest in writing (Ofsted, 2009) and this trend continues (see Ofsted, 2012 and DfE, 2016).

A study of under-achieving primary-age boys aligns with the previous Arts Council survey: boys struggled with punctuation, grammar and sometimes even the practical skill of holding a writing implement, but this didn't mean they didn't have stories in their heads. Many boys indicated that they wrote at home, when they were free to write material that mattered to them, drawing on their own interests and passions (Warrington and Younger, 2006: 146–9).

I have observed from my own school visits that boys (in particular) can rush at me, tumbling out stories that are lengthy, complex and rich with dramatic ideas, but when I respond enthusiastically with 'that sounds great, but don't just say it – write it', they disconnect. If they write at all, the story becomes a dumbed down version of its former self. Storytelling does have a place in the classroom, and is an art in itself, but it has not evolved into a valid, measurable component within the ongoing teaching of literacy. The development of storytelling skills can have positive impacts on the development of language and creativity: aside from its obvious value to the development of talking and listening, it has been described as an opportunity to share 'the soul' of the story. Pupils experience a flow and fluency of ideas, as well as comprehending aspects related to style, voice and structure (Cremin et al., 2015: 18–19). My 'don't just say it – write it' response clearly brings all that energy skidding to a halt, but my experience is that these are different, if related, activities. In addition to the logistics around writing being a more complex, challenging process than talking, a clear disadvantage with articulating a story in full is that any urgency to write it burns away. If I've been driven up the mountain in a four-by-four jeep, gushing about the view and taking pictures as I go, would I later trudge up the same path alone, on foot, in the pouring rain? For this reason, in my own workshops I don't encourage pupils to talk at length about their story per se – we discuss plots and characters, explore potential for settings and consider style and structure but once the idea takes root it is the hand that needs to do the talking, pouring the narrative out through the fingertips into the pen and onto the page. Or, alternatively, into the keyboard and onto the screen.

In considering this disconnect between ideas and the physical act of writing, I became interested in writing as a cross-curricular activity. Despite being a techno-phobic, I started thinking about the integration of creative writing combined with information technology. Ofsted (2009) identified that best practice in English should include 'video stories, web sites, electronic communication with authors and the development of animations' and more recent studies continue to recommend that modern technology should be utilised much more within the English curriculum (Ofsted, 2012: 22). It was also noted that the best schools were extending the links between English and other subjects (Ofsted, 2012).

Cross-curricular education helps develop adaptability, and an extension to this can be seen to be blended learning – a form of e-learning that combines computer technology with more traditional 'classroom' styles of training. Robinson (2010) in the RSA Edge Lecture states: 'how do children take their place in the economy of the twenty-first century, given that we don't know what is going to happen next week?'

It is worth noting here that although most writing in schools is still initially produced as handwritten, there is a move towards writing ideas directly onto the screen. For a variety of reasons, some pupils (including adults) prefer it. In the context of my research, those participants who have written using keyboards rather than pen and paper appear to have still experienced the same benefits and values from the creative activities.

Debates still rage as to whether or not writing will survive the revolution brought about by electronic media and consumer placement. Headlines such as 'Is Google making us Stupid?' (Carr, 2010) provoke knee-jerk reactions. Mobile phones are melting our brains. The internet causes autism and ADHD. Our friends are mere tricks-of-the-light, beamed to us through hyperspace. We're losing our memories. We've lost our minds. There are probably as many myths as truths regarding the reality around internet hysteria, and it may be that the current misgivings are born more from historical trends that whip up panic around gizmos and gadgetry (Jarrett, 2015: 217–19).

Studies have shown that many pupils – and very often more reluctant learners – are motivated by literacy lessons that make use of modern technology. Their own equipment at home is often far more sophisticated than that available in schools and reports suggest there is a strong case for greater uses of ICT resources that can be linked with English, particularly when it is adapted to meet the needs of specific pupils, or classes. Many people fear change and are suspicious of technology. We might put this in context if we think about Socrates' (471–399 BC) warnings about the impact on memory through the worrying new trend of 'writing things down'!

Change is inevitable. The ability to invent, to create and to move forward are all central to what makes us human. By opening discussion around what is working and what isn't, we stay alert and in control. We can adapt and amend advances and approaches: that worrying new trend of 'writing things down' will find new ways to reinvent itself.

In 2010 I saw potential in the linking of my own creative writing knowledge with all that gizmo and gadgetry. I wanted to connect with the strugglers and stragglers identified in various studies, and to aid the development of ICT skills with regard to Robinson's (2010) questions about a future we can't yet predict.

I needed to find a way to capture my own processes and re-interpret them for this computer-crazed audience, and my first consideration drew from the value of deep thinking, meditation and visualisation – activities that may initially seem diametrically opposed to ICT methodologies.

I use visualisation and meditation as a form of creative focus. I adapt the process, moving away from what is personal and utilising instead an immersion in creative ideas. The concentration is applied to problem solving related to stories and emotions that connect with character. In interpreting the broader concept of creativity into something I can visualise I often use an image of a fairground. This is a fairground of ideas, with carousels and a Ferris wheel and candy floss and music.

Drawing from this imagery and as part of University of Winchester research into writing in education, I developed a free schools' resource, which is an interactive animated website that develops craft skills in writing. The funfair is both colourful and surreal, partly to connect with this target user and partly to reflect the meditative dream-like qualities of my visualisations. Pupils are invited to become apprentice wordtamers. They 'capture' words as they move around the fairground activities, then take them into a circus ring to train them or, in other words, to begin their stories (Waite, 2015). The website is free, writing produced on it can be saved and developed offline, or initial ideas can be printed and continued by hand. There are also downloadable achievement certificates and a writing tutorial option.

Blank in the mind

I continued my research beyond the *Wordtamer* website (www.wordtamer.co.uk), working initially with a small focus group of primary-level low-achievers. These pupils did not engage well with writing tasks, did the minimum they could get away with and were performing at levels that put them at least a year below the national average in both reading and writing (T. Rich, Head of English, Locks Heath School, in Waite, 2014).

I initially asked the pupils their opinions about writing, and received the following responses:

I can't think what to write.
I hate the blank page because I'm scared to get started in case it's not good enough.
I do try but I am always told to try harder.
When I'm asked to write a story my mind goes blank.
If I have to do writing, I get distracted.
I don't really like stories. I only like things that are real.

I then set them a task, giving them an opportunity to write about 'anything they liked'. Without any peer discussion or influence from me, they all chose autobiography, producing a selection of titled responses:

- Family and Friends
- My Holiday
- Something that Really Happened
- My Day Out
- Christmas Day
- When I Went to the Doctor

They could all clearly write with conviction about their own experiences – they'd been there, they'd done it – they knew how to fill the page because they knew what happened. What these children didn't have was confidence around their own imaginations. They didn't know *how* to cross the boundary between 'real' and 'imagined' and go somewhere new (Waite, 2014).

On Tuesday I thought it would be a normal day but after lunch I got a unexpected note. It sayd I had to go home at 15.00, because my mum wanted me to go to the doctor ... she did a form for me to have an X-ray. Yesterday I had an X-ray so again I left at 15.00.

Tom, Locks Heath School

On Sunday my mum, Alisha [sister] and I went to my Aunty Sally's house to meet my whole family. I hadn't seen my whole family in ages! 10 minutes later we were walking my aunt's dog carlose in the park we all had a good chat and had been talking about school I was talking a lot about school.

Jessica, Locks Heath School

My conclusion from this first week was that my focus should be to help them discover that their imagination was alive and well. They just needed the belief that they could access it. Moving beyond the initial *Wordtamer* activities, pupils went in role to a whole-class funfair and evolved stories through acting out scenarios inspired by a hall of mirrors. They later flew on magic carpets to mysterious and exotic fantasy lands, and brought dragons, wizards and other imagined wonders into the classroom. (The examples which follow are first draft and un-edited).

As I was flying throwe the hot, Sunny sky. In the distance was a small land that looks like theres life! I flow down to check on it. The first thing to catch my eye was the crystl Blue Sea with rainbow fish and silver dolphins.

Lauren, Locks Heath School

At the back of the maze was a huge long mirror she ran up to it and closed her eyes ... then opened ... weres her reflection were did it go 30 seconds later a tall girl with blue hair and blue eyes even Blue wings. It looked at her then smiled ... the fairy swirled around Beth then nothing happened wait she can hear the fairy saying 'you belong here!'

Jessica, Locks Heath School

Although the project only lasted six weeks, the impact was measurable. I visited the school three weeks later for a final meeting with the Head of Year. Ms Rich had assessed the 'before' writing levels of these pupils, and was then able to present me with the 'after' (Waite, 2014). All the pupils had moved up between one and two sublevels within the measured grading system, and were sustaining these levels.

I did not address grammar, punctuation or spelling as part of my study as there was no time in the brief period that I had, and as my previous extract from the NLT survey (Horner, nd) demonstrates, standard assessment criteria measures these beyond and above creative content. However, I was able to offer feedback on the writing content. I responded to characterisation, setting and descriptive detail, and build-up of tension. Even though the creative development itself seemed to be impressive, I accept that the 'leap' cannot be described as huge. However, I only had four weeks, which amounted to six hours contact time in total, so it was felt a movement of one to two levels for each child was encouraging. What might be achieved in a whole term? A whole year?

Perhaps the real evidence for the potential of projects such as this came from the letters the pupils wrote at the end – this extract particularly resonated, and made me feel that not only had there been a difference left behind for the school in general, but also I had hopefully left behind something valid for individual pupils too.

Dear Mrs Waite

Thank you for coming in you really helped me with my writing I've enjod learning so much from you. you have inspired me. My favioute bit was When we did the flying carpet and you got to design your own carpet and then described what it looked like I also enjoyed the mirror maze When we went into the mirror and and me couldn't get out. I want to become an author When I'm older becauce I'm not blank in the mind anymore, I know what to write,

your sincerly Lauren.

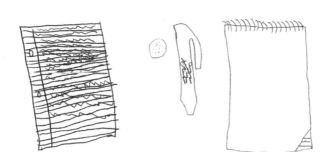

A similar approach with older (secondary age) pupils yielded similar, if darker, results:

> When I was nine years old, my Mum and Dad brought me a puppy – a golden labredor. After she had her jabs, we were finally able to take her for a walk. We went to a place in Winchester where there were lots of rivers.
>
> Bethany, Cantell School

> As I walked through the corridors of the asylum, I saw that the white walls weren't so white. The walls had dimmed into a darker grey – at least the part that I could see had. Over the grey walls were red handprints – still fresh and dripping.
>
> Bethany, Cantell School

Although comparisons between non-fiction and fiction were not the focus, it is easy to see the enhanced detail and complexity of thought applied to the creative samples for both age groups. The above (secondary level) extracts each involve 'going for a walk' but the visual detail and build-up of tension in the second is gripping, yet still coherent.

There is a case, of course, for applying creativity to non-fiction, but for the purposes of my particular study I was concerned with developing confidence for the writing of fictional, imaginative work. The outputs demonstrate the difference a belief in the imagination can make.

Once young people believe in the magic of their own ideas, they connect with writing that feels worthwhile. Creative writing *is* worthwhile. Stories matter.

Can creative writing be taught?

In past times, it was believed that creativity was born of some sort of magic dust that only the chosen few had been sprinkled with. You either were creative, or you weren't.

My own schooling is perhaps an example of this; it was recognised that I was 'good' at writing stories and regularly praised – my parents were even told at an open evening that 'she'll be a writer one day' but there was no attempt to extend or enhance any innate ability, nor was there any expectation from either my parents or myself that this should happen. The inspirational approaches of Sir Alec Clegg and Donald Graves clearly never made it as far as Fareham, in Hampshire. However, the praise and endorsement had enormous value in itself. It is something I have been able to hold onto whenever the demon-of-doubt takes hold, as I battle through some unwieldy draft that just isn't doing whatever it is I need it to do.

Beyond this early whispering of potential, I was never 'taught' to write, but found my own way through the process, experimenting with approaches with a beautiful freedom that I still draw from today. I used art as inspiration, I walked, I cut up old books and I wrote using random scatterings of words. I discovered freewriting and automatic writing. I started ideas with characters. I started ideas with settings. I indulged in 'method writing'. The truth is, it all worked. There was no single way that it had to be done.

Once I became published, I inevitably rubbed shoulders with other authors at conferences and events. Additionally, I listened to author interviews and read autobiographies. Both then, and now, the element I always found most intriguing was that they too had all experimented with similar approaches; it felt as if somehow we were all wired up and working subconsciously in some sort of universal approach.

This suggested to me that, by capturing techniques and re-envisaging them for emerging learners, these approaches could be a way of engaging with those who had either had less opportunity or minimal inclination to explore their own potential as writers.

Creative writing is a discipline that has fed down to schools from MA university level; it is possible to gain a degree, an MA and even a PhD in the subject. The discipline spans a range of 'writerly' options. Fiction is one of these, but most programmes offer a mix of alternative but equal subjects including poetry, non-fiction, screen-writing, writing for theatre and writing for the community. Courses generally combine creative content with academic rigour: the process and output of a piece of writing is supported by some form of critical analyses related to process, primary sources and secondary technique. However, an important detail here is that all the students that enrol for these programmes are doing so by choice: they want to ultimately earn their living (if they can) through the written word.

In a typical school environment this is not the case, and nor should it be. Society doesn't need, or want, every child to grow up to be a best-selling writer: what it does need is for every child to grow up having the skills to communicate ideas and consider choices, to be able to empathise with others and to respect alternative points of view. This is what fictional writing (in particular) does. The moral development of young people – not merely following adult rules but learning to value and understand the significance of their own opinions – can be evolved through story (Fisher, 2015: 63–80). These stories are very often drawn from existing familiar books by established authors, but this can be pushed further. In my experience, when young writers evolve their own creative, original narratives they gain ownership of ideas, and can reflect on the politics of their individual viewpoints in more meaningful ways. Writing becomes both relevant *and* exciting.

But the excitement and motivation alone is, ultimately, not enough. The teaching of writing is partly about what is popularly described as craft, learning to use a toolkit of writerly devices as ideas are sculpted and revised. It is also about what is felt, what is known, and what can be imagined. By stirring what is felt and known into the mix of all those saws, chisels and hammers, it becomes possible not only to raise standards in writing, but also to engage with innovative approaches that help re-shape literacy in the twenty-first century.

Why *do* stories matter?

With so much emphasis put upon assessment and literacy levels, I have often heard teachers claim they don't mind what their pupils read, as long as they are reading something. Bus timetables, warning labels and ingredients on a cereal packet have all been provided as evidence for reluctant readers' engagement with process, and earned pupils points in various classroom reward initiatives. These have their place. The literacy curriculum specifies that pupils identify audience and write in a range of forms, both fictional and non-fictional. In the Big Wide World everything is written by someone. It's all valid.

However, the strongest form of communication is through stories. The bus timetable in itself doesn't help us see the world from a timetable's point of view (although it would make for an interesting creative exercise). The warning label doesn't provoke discussion about the implications of taking risks (once again, I can feel a story coming on). They both work as devices for communicating information but there are no levels and layers at play. No big questions about right and wrong. Stories tell us things we need to know, either overtly or covertly. Even the simplest fairytales have determined the ways Western children have been socialised (Zipes, 1997). Roald Dahl's writings draw on fear and longing (Treglown, 1994: 11), subverting status and empowering young readers through disempowering flawed adults; Michael Morpurgo (2003) takes readers through the mud and sludge of battlefields, provoking debate about the pointlessness of war.

Real life is a complex business and stories enable us to discuss deeds and dilemmas at a safe distance. The communication of experience lies at the heart of all storytelling (Zipes, 1997:

137) and the scope for pupils to engage with themes and messages through their own writing enables them to reflect on, challenge and face up to the complexities of life, as well as explore the delights of the imagination.

With its focus primarily on fiction, this book will weave established authors' creative approaches through everyday classroom practice. It will offer big ideas for fully fledged stories, and consider both practical and experiential approaches to punctuation and grammar. It breaks down what 'craft' means in the context of writing, and how to nurture both practical and emotional responses to literacy and language. You can't get all that on a bus timetable.

References

Carr, N. (2010) *The Shallows: How the Internet Is Changing the Way We Think, Read and Remember.* New York, W. W. Norton

Chamberlain, L. (2016) *Inspiring Writing in Primary Schools.* London: Sage

Clegg, A. (1964) *The Excitement of Writing.* London: Chatto and Windus

Clegg, A. (1972) Oxford Education Authority *The Creativity of Children* (1981), https://sites.google.com/site/teachchoice/siraleccleg (accessed 12 December 2016)

Corbett, P. (2011) *Talk for Writing.* Maidenhead: Open University Press

Cremin, T. and Myhill, D. (2012) *Writing Voices.* Abingdon: Routledge

Cremin, T., Reedy, D., Bearne, E. and Dombey, H. (2015) *Teaching English Creatively.* Abingdon: Routledge

DfE (Department for Education) (2016) National curriculum assessments at key stage 2 in England, www.gov.uk/government/uploads/system/uploads/attachment_data/file/549432/SFR39_2016_text.pdf (accessed 5 January 2017)

Eyres, I. (2016) Call yourself a writer, *Teachers as Writers.* www.teachersaswriters.org/general/call-yourself-a-writer/#more-342 (accessed 3 January 2017)

Fisher, R. (2015) *Teaching Thinking* (4th edn). London: Bloomsbury Academic

Horner, S. (nd) Class writing, www.nawe.co.uk/writing-in-education/writers-in-schools/research.html (accessed 7 July 2014)

Horner, S. (2010) Magic dust that lasts, www.artscouncil.org.uk/media/uploads/Writers_in_schools.pdf (accessed 8 July 2014)

Jarrett, C. (2015) *Great Myths of the Brain.* Chichester: Wiley Blackwell

Jones, R. and Wyse, D. (2004) English, in R. Jones and D. Wyse (eds) *Creativity in the Primary Curriculum.* Abingdon: David Fulton

McCormick Calkins, L. (1994) *The Art of Teaching Writing* (2nd edn). Portsmouth, NH: Heinemann Educational

Morpurgo, M. (2003) *Private Peaceful.* London: Harper Collins

Office for Standards in Education (Ofsted) (2009) *English at the Crossroads.* London: Ofsted. www.ofsted.gov.uk (accessed 12 December 2016)

Office for Standards in Education (Ofsted) (2012) *Moving English Forward.* London: Ofsted. www.educationengland.org.uk/documents/pdfs/2012-ofsted-english.pdf (accessed 12 December 2016)

Robinson, Sir K. (2010) RSA animates edge lecture changing paradigms. www.youtube.com/watch?v=zDZFcDGpL4U (accessed 21 March 2013)

Treglown, J. (1994) *Roald Dahl: A Biography.* New York: Farrar, Straus and Giroux

Waite, J. (2014) Blank in the mind, *Writing in Education* 64: 15–21

Waite, J. (2015) Wordtaming and the funfair of ideas, *The International Journal for the Practice of Teaching and Creative Writing* 12, 1. www.tandfonline.com/action/doSearch?AllField=Judy+Waite&SeriesKey=rmnw20 (accessed 12 December 2016)

Warrington, M. and Younger, M. (2006) *Raising Boys' Achievement in Primary Schools.* Maidenhead: Open University Press

Zipes, J. (1997) *Happily Ever After: Fairytales, Children and the Culture Industry.* New York/London: Routledge

CHAPTER 2

WRITERS IN SCHOOLS – THE HYBRID CLASSROOM

How to connect writerly practice with school demands

Chapter contents

What shall we do with the grumpy author?

He arrives, looking shabby in a beaten up old car. The caretaker challenges him. This visitor looks decidedly dodgy. Surely he can't have a genuine reason for entering the school? The stranger mutters something about the librarian booking him for 'Book Week'. The caretaker nods and moves out of the way.

Pupils eye the intruder with suspicion as he shambles towards reception. Five minutes later the lovely librarian comes to get him and he shuffles after her. She tries to make him feel at ease and asks about his journey. He growls back, "Terrible. A criminal use of my time, stuck in traffic all the way." The librarian's heart sinks. She has a group of disruptive boys coming to the first session. She leads him to the library and shows him where he will be working. He grunts, dumps his bags down and looks around the room as if he's planning to set fire to it at a later date.

The pupils arrive. The librarian introduces the author by name, and lists his better-known books. (In her head she has labelled him 'Mr Grumpy'.) The pupils don't hear the introduction because the disruptive boys are playing 'catch the lunch box', one of which splits open and an apple, a squidgy sandwich and a pot of yoghurt spill out. The disruptive boys find this hilarious and a game begins where they compete to see who can balance the apple on their head the longest.

The librarian wonders if she could pre-empt the 'later date' fire and set the fire alarms off right that second. Clear the library. Apologise to Mr Grumpy. The Book Week event is unavoidably cancelled.

From behind her, she hears a throat clearing. Mr Grumpy steps forward.

The pupils turn to look at him. "This library," he says, "appears to have a lot of wall space, but the truth is, it is a room full of bridges."

The pupils glance at each other nervously. The apple, currently teetering amongst a flame of curls on the head of a freckle-faced boy, rolls to the floor. Mr Grumpy nods. "What goes up must come down." He looks around, making eye contact with each and every pupil. "If we want to see further than others, we must stand on the shoulders of giants. Does anyone know who said that?"

One pupil puts up her hand. "Er … you did, sir."

A few pupils snigger. Most stay quiet.

Mr Grumpy smiles and his smile is warm, like the sun breaking through clouds. "Sense of humour. I like that. Yes, I did indeed say it, but someone else said it first. Someone wiser than me. Someone taller in wisdom than the tallest giant. I'll leave you to try and find the quote. Goggle it later, or whatever it is you young people do. Today, we are not going to look at screens. We are going to learn from the giants who live in this room."

Pupils glance round nervously, as if there might be giants lurking in every corner. "Young man," Mr Grumpy points to curly red-head. "Fetch me a book from a shelf. It can be any book. Perhaps one you've borrowed before, and enjoyed. Perhaps one that just grabs your attention."

Curly red-head fetches a book. It has a roaring fire-dragon on the cover. "Stories," says Mr Grumpy, flicking through the pages, "are words that grow from the apple-pips of ideas. I am going to find you a scattering of apple pips from inside this book, and we will plant them and water them right now, in this session. You will each grow a unique and wonderful tree of a story today. You too can be giants."

The librarian sighs with relief. Other than that sigh, you could have heard an apple-pip drop.

The above piece evolved from a study I undertook, exploring the value of authors in schools through the experiences of other writers, teachers, librarians and relevant educational specialists. One librarian who regularly brought in authors for Book Week told me 'overall my experience of authors has been good. Even one particular grumpy old gent, who made me think "what have I done?" turned out to be great when he had an audience of students' (Helen Smith, Brookfield School, Hampshire, pers. comm., 2016). My response is a demonstration of how real-life can become fiction, but also leads into the impact authors can make in a single session. From the responses to my research questions it seems clear that authors can make exciting, innovative and measurable differences to ongoing approaches and outcomes.

Not all authors are grumpy; hopefully not many of us are grumpy, and hopefully authors are usually perceived as 'great' when they visit schools, but 'being great' in itself needs further exploration.

What do authors do in schools? What do they contribute on the day, and can they leave any lasting legacy?

The initial value makes a direct connection to the enhancement of reading. Authors have all written books, and pupils can read those books prior to the author's visit, preparing questions not merely around process generally, but specific to the book. Not just 'where do you get your ideas?' but 'where did you get *that* idea; why did you tell the story from *that* character's point of view? Why did you choose *that* ending?'

Reading whole books prior to a visit is not essential, and for lower set pupils mostly unfeasible unless the books are pitched for reluctant readers, but the impact of an author visit is still perceived as valuable:

> On the day, having an author in school can generate some excitement, although perhaps not with all pupils. It does for those who are already readers. However, I have received feedback from pupils who are struggling or disengaged readers, who are surprised and pleased that they have been selected to attend something like this. A successful author visit can have a long-lasting effect though. Pupils are often still talking about them for quite a long time.
>
> (Fiona Crowther, Romsey School, Romsey, pers. comm., 2016)

Less able readers can still engage with the material, even just discussing the title or the blurb, or perhaps reading a selected extract prior to the event. Authors generally liaise with schools and will be willing to discuss approaches so that the needs of more reluctant readers are embedded in the delivery on the day. Experienced agencies (such as Authors Aloud UK) offer excellent advice as well as handling bookings, or many authors can be booked via their own websites.

Authors, then, often trigger a creative release that resonates long beyond the actual visit. Pupils can be liberated from inhibitions brought about by a too intense focus on punctuation, syllabifying and spelling. When young people see themselves as authors rather than just writers, the thinking process enhances self-discovery through written expressions. Writing can also be fun (Rowe and Humphries, 2001: 164) and playfulness is integral to developing new ideas and has long been recognised as effective in any learning context. Even for established adult writers 'play' seems an essential ingredient – we don't need to be child*ish* but we do need to be child*like:* getting messy with possibilities and sloshing around, not caring about the mud because we are chasing the butterfly of an idea.

However, not all schools have the budget for an author visit, and even for those that have, the visit is (usually) a one-day event. Even considering the positive reverberations of a school visit, there are still 189 days when it is teachers themselves who need to keep the energy and inspiration around reading and writing alive. Are there ways that teachers can capture the essence of an author and, like the *BFG*'s jars of dreams, mix together 'gigglehouses' and 'boggleboxes' (Dahl, 2016: 106) of lessons? In raising aspirations around writing and school standards, it seems there is a strong argument for hybrid alternatives that connect creative process with teacher practice.

> If I have seen further than others, it is by standing on the shoulders of giants.
>
> (Isaac Newton, 1676)

Author creative process

I am sitting by the window. It is raining outside. I am thinking about a chapter in a book I need to write. The chapter considers the ongoing value of authors in schools. What conflicts might arise in terms of process, and practice?

The leaves are down from the trees, lying in soggy heaps of gold and brown and ochre. The colours of rust.

I must get on with writing that chapter.

There is a lot of colour in my front garden, even on a rainy day. The brick wall is all roughened red and a brave white rose seems to have survived the first frosts. It doesn't look happy, but it's holding its ground. The sky is a flat wash of grey, like metal.

Metal rusts.

I must get on with writing that chapter.

I am sitting by the window. It is raining outside. I am thinking about a chapter in a book I need to write. Thinking. Not writing. What might I look like to a teacher, or a class of pupils? Sitting so still. Just thinking. "We thought she was a writer," they might say. "She can't get much done in a day."

It occurs to me that creativity might be something we could discuss. What it means. How it works. Creative process is something authors learn to trust.

I must.

Sitting and gazing at the rain may not seem like a valid process for commencing a day's work, and it most definitely doesn't seem like something that can be readily endorsed in a school environment but the rest of this chapter, and indeed this whole book, considers the creative journey juxtaposed with school-based approaches. Writers are always, in some sense, staring out of the window. It's time to go outside, and look in, instead.

Virginia Woolf once said that writing a novel is like walking through a dark room, holding a lantern that lights up what is already in the room anyway. Perhaps, through looking in through the window of the classroom, we can raise our lantern to those processes and practices that we hadn't illuminated before. We might realise they are already there. It may not be beyond our scope to keep those areas lit.

Hearing voices

Roald Dahl, when once asked how he could write so well for eight year olds, replied 'because I *am* eight years old' (Powling, 1994: 67).

All fiction needs a voice but it involves more than one; it is actually closer to a clamour of voices. The voice of the individual – the person we are – is the first voice. If I were with you now, and we were talking, you would be forming an idea about me through tone, body language and the content that is implicit in what I say. Although we can't 'hear' writing, something of this personality transfers itself to any individual's writing style, and makes it distinct (Boulter, 2007: 58–63). It is the unique mark on a writer's work, imprinted as deeply as any brand. Second, we create characters and we find a voice for those characters. What types of beings are they? How do they move around in their world? What are their motivations? Third, there is the voice of the story, and this evolves from subject, style, theme and genre. A horror story will 'sound' different from a romance, for instance.

To this clamour I now introduce a fourth voice: this is the voice that distinguishes the challenges for children's and young-adult writers from writers for adult fiction; the former need to capture the voice of the age group they are pitching for.

It's hard to imagine a children's or young-adult author who doesn't connect with children or young adults. Readers need to climb inside stories; the character's worries and overall scenarios should be something that any age of reader can relate to. This is what Dahl means when he says he is 'eight years old'. Dahl is not only drawing from his own childhood experiences (Treglown, 1994), but he is also able to translate these into an age-appropriate voice. The plots may be fantastic, scenes may be magical, language is often quirky or complex, but there is a childlike simplicity running through every one of Dahl's best-selling works. Dahl's writing is never scaled down for his child readership (Powling, 1994: 67) but it seems as if he is a child writing for children; perhaps he captures the way children would write for each other if they had the skills (Powling, 1994: 79).

Dorothea Brande (1996: 152–4) talks about the need to control the mind in order to let our writing voices truly be heard. She refers to this process as 'writer's magic' but like all magic it is really sleight of hand. The dove that appeared from nowhere has been in the magician's pocket all along. We can follow the trail of feathers and work out the trick for ourselves.

The heart of the matter

In applying techniques that connect convention with more varied approaches, even reluctant writers can realise they have something to say, and that their way of saying it has value. When writing is being drawn from the outside in – perhaps by responding to and emulating a published author, pupils (particularly those who are reluctant readers and writers) may feel little motivation to respond with enthusiasm. The story they are battling their way through feels external and remote. There is no resonance. Ray Bradbury, talking about voice and inspiration, reflects on how real love – or real hate – can 'slam the page like a lightning bolt' when emotion hits the paper (Bradbury, 1996: 4). This doesn't mean that the most impassioned writing is expressive (Cremin and Myhill, 2012: 18) and autobiographical. Writing can be reflexive *and* fictional. I tell my students that as an author you don't ever need to harbour grudges or react badly to anyone who upsets you. Strong emotion gives us energy, and writers use this energy to drive stories.

Let me tell you a true story.

When I was ten, I painted a picture of a pony called Benjy. It was to be a Christmas gift to the lovely lady who ran the local riding school (I was horse mad). As Christmas came closer, my courage failed me. My painting was rubbish. Not worthy of the wondrous riding-school lady (Linda) who lit up my Saturday afternoons. A friend of mine (another horsey geek type) took over. 'I'll give it to her for you', she said. That weekend, we took my now framed and festively wrapped nervous offering along to the stables.

'Is that for me?' asked Linda, smiling as she took the gift from my friend. Her eyes widened as she opened it. 'A painting of Benjy. It's incredible, and so kind of you. This must have taken ages. Did you paint it all by yourself?' And my friend said 'Yes.'

I felt shocked, hurt and betrayed, but didn't know how to deal with it at the time. Years later I wrote the novel *Cheat* (Waite, 1998), which is the story of a ten-year-old boy who steals a blind man's painting, passes it off as his own and wins a prize. That little book turned out to be a best-seller and has remained in print for over twenty years. I send thanks through the years to my long-ago friend. That shock and outrage transformed itself into a powerful energy that gave life to *Cheat.*

A writing task that draws from material the pupil isn't personally engaged in, and that merely bows and scrapes to the assessment criteria, is never going to elicit energised, exciting outputs

(Ofsted 2009: 25–6). The most persuasive writing 'feels' something and that can only happen if the author has felt it too. This comes from writing from the inside out. Writing from the heart.

Writing from the heart can be approached from a myriad of angles in a school's environment, enhancing activities that are initially influenced by the processes of established authors, yet still acknowledging more standardised teaching methods and outcomes. A hybrid methodology explores ways to make this happen.

Sometimes, it is as simple as gazing outside at the rain.

The sad case of the missing muse

I was once one of a group of authors invited to work in a school to celebrate writing. The invitation was exciting and the concept was to be applauded. One of the tasks was to design a school library. Pupils were told to imagine the library was stripped of books, furniture and equipment. Money was no object. In their wildest library-longing dream, what would make this the best library in the world? Pupils worked in groups and were instructed to be 'thoughtful and creative'.

This was all promising, except that no one had told these pupils what creative thinking actually meant. There was no background underpinning. They were given pens; big sheets of paper; could sit anywhere they wanted. Many struggled. They didn't fill the paper. They drew small, serious charts and diagrams. At one point in the session the teacher who instigated the project became exasperated. 'Be creative', he shouted. 'Use COLOUR!!! What's the matter with you all?'

Ah yes, lots of colour – that would do it.

The problem here was not only that the pupils hadn't been told what creative thinking was, but also neither had the teacher. Creative subjects demand creative teaching (Joubert, 2001: 22), and embedding techniques that will draw out original solutions requires a combination of purposeful thinking and something that comes close to daydreaming. With limited time-frameworks it can't be left to chance.

The lack of guided thinking and time afforded to enable it (Fisher, 2015), coupled with a misunderstanding about creativity and its process, undermined the potential for true engagement with the above activity. We can consider the implications of this same lack of grounding and comprehension to writing in education.

Getting messy

Creativity itself is described as something akin to 'a mess'. Through combining random elements and striking up new associations, a new 'something' that was not there before is evolved (Bono, 1996: 3).

Creativity is not an ordered process and it cannot be reached through a planned series of actions (Bohm, 1998: 26). In addition to this there is no fixed way to write, and so consequently there is no fixed way to teach others to write. That doesn't mean that anything goes, but it is more a reflection on the needs of the individual. Authors need routines and patterns of working but they vary from writer to writer. Young people are also not only individuals but they need to explore a range of creative approaches, discarding some and embracing others in order to see what works for them. Some writers plot, some don't. Some need silence, some don't. Some start with character. Some with setting. In an environment that seeks to standardise and apply formulas for appraisal, how could teachers embed these inconsistent approaches into a plan for literacy?

The first step might be to fully understand the way the mind orders itself through the creative process. The explorations through ideas may feel muddled and incoherent, but if we could float upwards and look down on the mess, we would see that what is going on is following a recognisable pattern.

Creativity has five distinct stages. The first of these is the preparation: an immersion in ideas that stimulates curiosity. The second is the period of incubation, as this initial curiosity combined with gathered knowledge 'churns around' and is processed by the subconscious mind. This second stage is vital to the quality of the eventual output, as it is during this stage that unexpected connections and combinations of thought evolve. The third stage is the 'Aha!' moment of revelation, which brings new insight and moves through the fourth stage: evaluating and questioning whether this spark of new awareness is worthy of pursuit. The fifth stage is when the work starts, and the ideas are followed through into conscious application (Czikszentmihalyi, 1997: 79–90).

In the specifics of creative writing, the first three phases of creativity suggest starting points that can be adapted to work within classroom practice.

Established writers write for publishers, and publishers have clear specifications. Is this perceived outcome to be a work of horror fiction, or fantasy? What do publishers of horror, or fantasy, look for? What else has been published in that genre? Is the idea original or even groundbreaking? How long might the completed novel need to be?

This writerly approach can be replicated through exposing young writers to the most relevant stories that grip their imaginations, discussing ideas and pinning down a sense of what makes that story what it is. Beyond this, if pupils are truly to write like authors, they need to forget the conscious detail of what was discussed (Rowe and Humphries, 2001: 164). The knowledge goes to the subconscious mind to get stirred around. The act of not thinking results in greater creativity (Bradbury, 1996: 143). Established writers may not consciously return to the idea for weeks, or months, but the possibilities are being 'fused and welded' (Brande, 1996). If you are a teacher, you may already be packaging up this book to sell as used and new on Amazon. You don't have weeks or months. You probably only have days, and even then you don't have whole days. You have half a day – maybe even only half an hour. Despair not! There are adaptive approaches that *can* work within educational timeframes: approaches that don't involve sending pupils home for six months of creative incubation.

Engaging with stage two might mean fitting the project into a larger unit of study. It can tie itself to other aspects of the curriculum, and involve real-world research. For instance, I have developed a session that draws from research around endangered species of animals. The stage one element of this involves reading books where this particular animal is featured, looking at visual footage of endangered species and related issues, and discussing what it might be like to *be* that animal. Habitat, geography, weather patterns and flora/fauna are established, and all the while the subconscious keeps adding this knowledge to the earlier discussions about books that feature endangered animals.

The subconscious workings are, of course, invisible. Teachers can't be sure they are really happening. There is nothing to mark after school, nothing to put in the tray for parents at open evening, nothing to parade before an inspector. But without them, the quality of thoughts can't evolve. Pupils will be crammed through a factory-line thinking process – we might get Supa-Value ideas at knock down prices but there is the danger these will be throwaway thoughts; easily found, easily discarded. Schools tend to put higher values on the conscious aspect of the mind but harnessing and stimulating creativity in school needs to attach value to non-conscious as well as conscious explorations (Craft, 2015: 165–6).

The roots of a tree are not evident from above the ground, but were we to dig them up we would find they are equal in spread, depth and quantity to the branches that stretch visibly towards the sky. The same principle applies to creative thinking. The more deeply and thoroughly the ideas are rooted, the more expansive the branches and the foliage.

Loo rolls and literacy

As the process moves on, it is time to experiment with words and ideas that might become stories. For established authors this can be an obsessive experience. I've scrawled on napkins in restaurants. I've scribbled on the backs of envelopes. In times of desperation I have resorted to writing on toilet paper. The more insubstantial the paper, the more freedom just to splurge down thoughts. No one will see them. No one will ever judge. For pupils, collect old envelopes. Scraps of cardboard. Backs of birthday cards. It might feel strange at first, but if the activity is linked to writer's process, the way *real* writers work, it can be invigorating. We are back to 'fun' again.

Story sacks are a popular resource at primary level, used to support class-readers or popular published works, bringing these to life through models of characters, paper, games and activity cards (National Literacy Trust, nd). This model can be re-interpreted as part of a pupil's creative journey.

In my own creative process I collect 'things and stuff' – a heart-shaped pebble on a beach. A postcard in a junk shop. The lyrics from a song. Meaningless to anyone else, the pebble was collected not by me, but my character. It connects to the postcard that says simply 'Miss you'. The song lyrics are from a haunting love song: someone has gone away. The obvious implication is a teen romance, but in fact these collections triggered a story about a much loved toy bear, left behind on a beach: a story pitched for five to seven year olds.

This process – despite the misgivings of my close family and friends – is not merely eccentricity veering towards madness. Novelist Linda Newbery reflects on her own writing and endorses that the collection of 'things' marks the beginning of any new, evolving idea. Newbery also lists postcards, music and stones as being core to her 'collectables' (Cremin and Myhill, 2012: 167–70). An afternoon in a junk shop is as exciting to an author as a day out to a theme park might be to someone else.

Pupils can gather a portfolio of 'things and stuff'. The scrappy writings, an apple-pip, a drawing of a fire-red dragon or the title of a relevant book are all valid, and provide evidence (to anyone that wants to see it) that the growing idea is being watered. Scrapbooks can be made of 'things and stuff', and they will become artworks in themselves. This tangible display of process can have profound value, especially for young writers whose ideas may be vivid but for whom the final written activity may not reflect the depth of their process. If the pupil 'gatherings' don't feel viable given the groups involved, then teachers can have their own boxes of beginnings. Collect buttons, a pressed flower, a scrap of fabric, an old photograph. Because these items are cheap and easy to find they won't *feel* too precious to be touched – pupils can handle them, draw them, glue them into books. Used effectively the things in themselves still won't be precious, but for young writers they can be as valuable as diamonds.

Get 'dabbling'

As the process moves forward, authorial 'dabblings' (Chamberlain, 2016) can be discussed and reflected on. They are a way of broadening the scope of the idea; creating combinations of thoughts (Bohm, 1998: 157). More focused responses will come forward when they are called. Making space for creativity means creating an overt mental climate (Craft, 2015: 162) and this can mean not just the space in the classroom, or on the timetable, but also time 'in our heads'. Chamberlain (2016: 40) discusses 'dabbling' as part of a linear process that includes initial saturation of existing texts, followed by deconstruction of these around structure and style, and from this pupils can explore and experiment with language features before making their final choices around the ultimate composition. The components, therefore, in Chamberlain's model are:

- Saturation
- Deconstruction
- *Dabbling*
- Composing

The 'dabbling' here stretches potential, drawing from existing knowledge and playing with possible approaches before moving these ideas forward into a format that suits the writing task.

For fictional writing we can take this further, using this period of experimentation as a playful yet creative element that embraces a range of approaches.

Pre-writing is another term for this period of 'gathering' (Boulter, 2007: 120–2). As well as notes and doodles, pre-writing can include plans, illustrations and strange charts. There can be maps and role plays and the hot-seating of characters. Everything advances the idea, but it is not yet clear what the idea is going to be. This approach embraces the needs of visual and kinaesthetic learners as well as those who are more competent at reading and writing tasks.

For example, during a research project that involved pupils who didn't trust the potential of their own imaginations (Waite, 2014), the group first discussed fantasy and magic realism in fiction, looking at the books they had enjoyed and being clear about the genre and potential story styles. I then introduced my 'magic carpet' – in reality an old and somewhat faded specimen that had been brought back from a market in the Middle East. (I appreciate not everyone will have such a delight in their prop-box, but at primary level even a large glittery, silky scarf from a charity shop will do the job.) Producing a selection of silky waistcoats and – yes – more glittery scarves – these Year 5 pupils were invited to slip into one of the costumes and have a go at flying on the carpet. As each pupil took their turn, they closed their eyes and described to me what it was like to fly, and the descriptive ideas included the carpet being 'buffeted by the wind and hard to keep a grip of'. Beyond this interactive role play, which still was embedded with a discussion about description and language choices, they then made notes about how it had felt. Pupils jotted ideas down in a notebook that was purely for 'dabblings' and gathering ideas. This notebook was an integral element of the project and pupils were free to interpret their experiences in images, random words and maps. They then designed their own magic carpet in this notebook.

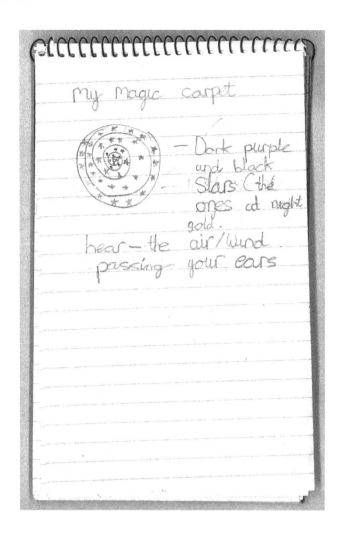

This led into the development of stories involving magic carpets and faraway lands.

The carpet is flying higher and higher with its fringes flapping in the air some coming off. It was dark so I could hardly see but when I could see I saw a storm raging towards me ... when I look down I saw darkness nothing to be seen. The flashing of lightning made me see that fences were there surrounding grass the crashing of thunder got louder and louder. Grew closer and closer.

Tom, Locks Heath School

For secondary age pupils (in fact any age learner, but secondary level pupils seem to respond well here), the development of characters can form part of these dabblings and gatherings. Again, they can be developed in notebooks or sometimes character profile sheets help the activity to feel more focused. These characters can then role play, or be placed in a 'hot-seat' game (getting pupils to introduce their characters to each other in pairs, or in a group circle, expanding their knowledge of that character as they talk).

Create a Character

You are going to 'grow' a character, just by learning a few details about someone in your imagination. I want you to think of someone your sort of age – a boy or girl who isn't based on anyone you know, but who lives in this country and goes to school in this country – they don't need to live in a house like yours though – they might live in a tiny village or big city. They might live in a huge posh house or a very small hut. Please bring your notes about this character to the workshop – but DON'T write story about them. All we need at the moment is to know who they are, and what they are like.

Name (of character)

Andrea   cleo is

Description (what do you think they look like?)

She wears shorts and T-shirts most of the time and has pitch black hair that is very long. goes to a school for people in the village. is 10 years old and loves animals she owns a dog and a cat. got crickets.

What sort of person are they most of the time? (choose one MAIN one).

Moody   Grumpy   (Friendly)—(Kind)

Anxious   Shy   Confident   Mean   Happy   Sad

(Adventures)

I 'dabble' ideas myself in these ways, and this has included making a collage and creating a whole street where my characters live, working out their stories from the visual stimulus. This evolved into a published series for young-adult reluctant readers, based on four teenage characters – best friends – who live on *The Street* (Waite, 2017).

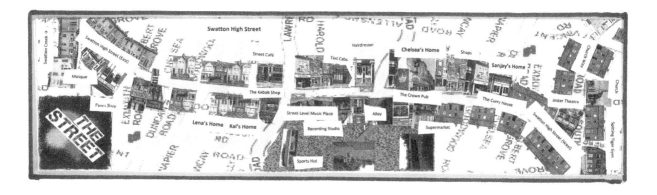

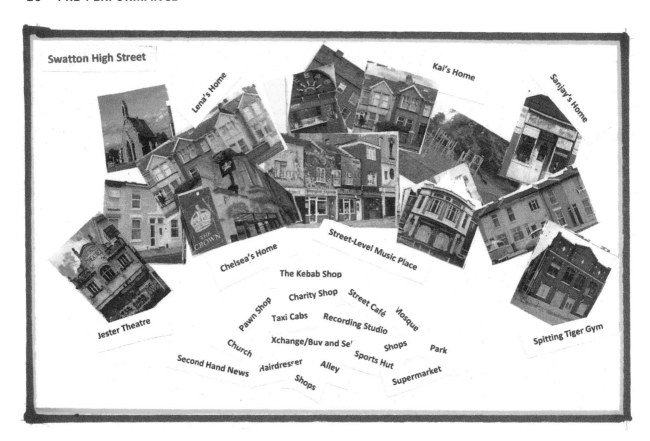

Using these collages, I mapped out where each of the four friends lived. I next identified specific settings – a music venue, a derelict theatre, a kick-boxing gym and a run-down local park. I then developed street-culture scenarios based on social media, self image, relationship issues and moral dilemmas. The resultant series offers short, but edgy, contemporary story-lines that have appeal for secondary age readers (Waite, 2017). Fictional ideas evolve through all these activities. 'Dabbling' and 'gathering' can be as simple as making notes, mindmapping and brainstorming. It can be as elaborate as role playing characters to see how they react to different circumstances. It offers up creative, interactive and visual experiences that support ideas and planning. It weaves in the magic, experiments with patterns and helps stories to fly.

Literacy in unlikely places: experiential learning

Once, on researching a horse story, I visited an auction very early in the morning. I stopped to watch a nervous white pony with strange blue eyes, and, because I felt drawn to it, I sketched it in my notepad. A woman tapped me on the shoulder. 'Are you a journalist?' she said. 'No, um, I'm an author', I replied, slightly embarrassed. I'm always slightly embarrassed in these situations – somehow the phrase 'I'm an author' sounds pretentious, or as if I might be making it up. She regarded me for a moment and then nodded in the direction of the blue-eyed pony. 'That one will go for meat', she said. My heart twisted. 'Why?' 'It's the blue eye', she explained. 'No one wants ponies with blue eyes. See that man over there … that's the meat man. He buys up all the horses that sell for fewer than twenty-one guineas and this poor mare won't reach more than that.' The meat man looked as if he'd actually stepped out from a book of horrors. He was broadly built, with a large head, heavy eyebrows and bulbous lips. It seemed to me as if he was already licking those lips, mentally sharpening a giant carving knife as he scrutinised the horses.

He made it into my book, stalking a pearl white horse rescued from an auction and trained by my main character, Nicky:

and it wasn't just the tense, watchful way the horse was standing that made Nicky want to get closer. It was the horse's eyes. Even in the early morning mist, Nicky could tell they were different from anything he had ever seen before. They were blue … a rich deep blue that made the animal look somehow alien and magical all at once.

(Waite, 1999)

Ray Bradbury (1996: 58) recalls a time when he came upon a collapsed roller coaster half buried by sand and washed over by the sea. He described the decay of struts, tracks and ties as looking like a dinosaur, and later added to the idea when he heard the mournful cry of a foghorn. The dinosaur was lonely. It believed the foghorn was a kindred dinosaur, calling to it. In trying to find this kindred creature, it swam to the beach and died. The resultant story was a book *The Beast from 20,000 Fathoms* (1951), later adapted into the film *The Fog Horn* (1953). Bradbury incubated the concept of the dinosaur on the beach, connected it to something unrelated that could be attributed to synchronicity or coincidence (Cameron, 1997: 20), and had the 'Aha!' moment of making something that hadn't existed before.

Schools can't take bus loads of pupils to auctions, nor to collapsed funfair rides, although there could be scope, depending on subjects and themes, to incorporate a school trip or even just a walk outside. Experiential learning is gaining a voice within mainstream education, and theories and philosophies that draw from the world beyond the classroom connect well with creative thinking and writing (Smith and Knapp, 2011). Local history and environment topics built into the school create cross-curricular opportunities, or it may be possible to link up with newsworthy events. I used a plague of starfish washed up onto a local beach after a storm as a literacy lesson, collecting ideas following a class visit to the beach. On another occasion a local area class-walk took its focus from street names and signs, which were jotted into notebooks and then reworked into stories. The pupil's random collections were later cut up and reshuffled, forming new associations in a process that was a visible reflection of the creative incubation period itself.

There may also be a multitude of influences away from the school day. Pupils have out-of-school activities. They watch films and television programmes. They interact with their families and their friends. In incubating ideas away from school, pupils will be thinking like writers. Many writers keep notebooks or journals, jotting down ideas about everything and anything. Lucy McCormick Calkins (1994: 28) talks about writing not being about lists and subjects and mapping out ideas in class, but a way of life. A brief glance at my own notebook of inspirations shows me that I wrote, at different times:

1: Dragons can Happen. (working title)
2: Land of the Lost – an abandoned village on a Greek mountainside. Two children go there. One doesn't come back.
3: A Way with Wolves (boy who is a 'wolf whisperer' on quest to find rare (?) magic (?) last (?) silver wolf).
4: Crocodile Tears (based on true story of croc sighting in UK – poss for reluctant readers series).

Any one of these ideas might be explored further – it's not unusual for me to be experimenting with several possibilities at once. At some point, one idea will usually become more gripping, or more urgent. The others then go on the back-burner to be returned to at a different time. Very often I will draft out a few interpretations of each storyline, and an editor will step in and select whatever feels strongest for that particular publisher's list.

My notebook collects experiences, moods, images and ideas, and for pupils this might be worked into homework with a myriad of benefits that link to observational skills as well as direct connections with writing. Ownership of ideas is important too, and this can be enhanced when a group, or a whole class, respond to the notebook collections of their peers. For example, I set a task for a group who were reluctant writers. They were each asked to keep a notebook for a week. The notebook didn't just need to collect words – 'things and stuff' were acceptable too. At the beginning of the next week the 'collectors' were grouped with peers, some of whom were able writers, and groups discussed the potential for stories from the notebook. These collaborations then evolved into stories. This approach enabled the reluctant writers to have a key role in a literacy lesson; a subject that many had previously perceived themselves as failing in. The whole group may have chosen their contribution. Their shell, or stone, or button might be at the centre of everyone's story ideas. They have earned their place in the development of a piece of fiction, and gained the respect of their peers by a choice that *they* made. When this happens, you can almost see those pupils puff up with pride.

Consider what types of items pupils might add to their writer's notebook. A bus timetable? A poem (either original or copied)? A few notes about the weather? A warning label? A photograph (or written description) of a lizard? A list of ingredients from a cereal packet?

The ensuing discussion doesn't need to use everything: the flow of a developing story can be seriously hampered by trying to cram too much in, but the rule of three is always a good guide. Let's take the timetable, the warning and the lizard.

What if a strange lizard is spotted? *What if* a young boy misses the school bus because he is intrigued enough to follow it? *What if* the lizard leads him somewhere he shouldn't go?

Pupils might not always find something as direct as a story, but they may snag onto feelings or experiences that make the ultimate output truly theirs. Jealousy towards a younger and annoying sister is as valuable as outrage over a stolen horse painting (see page 19). Characters in stories can be motivated by jealousy. Fire dragons have feelings and histories and reasons for their behaviours. We find things when we are looking, but we find them when we are not looking too. Very often the things we find by chance give us our most magical treasures.

References

Authors Aloud UK www.authorsalouduk.co.uk (accessed 1 October 2017)

Bohm, D. (1998) *On Creativity*, ed. L. Nichol. London: Routledge

Bono, de E. (1996) *Serious Creativity*. London: Harper Collins

Boulter, A. (2007) *Writing Fiction: Creative and Critical Approaches*. Basingstoke and New York: Palgrave Macmillan

Bradbury, R. (1996) *Zen in the Art of Writing*. Santa Barbara, CA: Joshua Odell

Brande, D. (1996) *Becoming a Writer*. London: Macmillan Reference Books

Cameron, J. (1997) *The Vein of Gold*. London: Pan Books

Chamberlain, L. (2016) *Inspiring Writing*. London: Sage

Craft, A. (2015) *Creativity, Education and Society: Writings of Anna Craft*, comp. K. Chappell, T. Cremin and B. Jeffrey. London: Institute of Education Press

Cremin, T. and Myhill, D. (2012) *Writing Voices*. Abingdon: Routledge

Csikszentmihalyi, M. (1997) *Creativity*. New York: Harper Perennial

Dahl, R. (2016) *The BFG*. London: Puffin Books

Fisher, R. (2015) *Teaching Thinking* (4th edn). London: Bloomsbury Academic

Joubert, M. M. (2001) The art of creative teaching: NACCCE and beyond, in A. Craft, B. Jeffrey and M. Leibling (eds) *Creativity in Education*. London and New York: Continuum

McCormick Calkins, L. (1994) *The Art of Teaching Writing* (2nd edn). Portsmouth, NH: Heinemann

National Literacy Trust (nd) Story sacks. www.literacytrust.org.uk/assets/0000/3210/Story_sack_guide.pdf (accessed 27 November 2016)

Office for Standards in Education (Ofsted) (2009) *English at the Crossroads*. London: Ofsted. www.ofsted. gov.uk (accessed 12 December 2016)

Powling, C. (1994) *Roald Dahl: A Biography*. London: Puffin Books

Rowe, S. and Humphries, S. (2001) Creating a climate for learning at Coombes Infant and Nursery School, A. Craft, B. Jeffrey and M. Leibling (eds) *Creativity in Education*. London and New York: Continuum

Smith, T. E. and Knapp, C.E. (Eds) (2011) *Experiential Education*. Abingdon: Routledge

Treglown, J. (1994) *Roald Dahl: A Biography*. New York: Farrar, Straus and Giroux

Waite, J. (1998) *Cheat*. Oxford: Heinemann

Waite, J. (1999) *Sapphire*. London: Scholastic Children's Books

Waite, J. (2014) Blank in the mind, *Writing in Education* 64: 15–21

Waite, J. (2017) *Chelsea's Story: The Street*. London: Bloomsbury

Waite, J. (2017) *Kai's Story: The Street*. London: Bloomsbury

Waite, J. (2017) *Lena's Story: The Street*. London: Bloomsbury

Waite, J. (2017) *Sanjay's Story: The Street*. London: Bloomsbury

CHAPTER 3

ROOM FOR WRITING

Creative literacy in a classroom setting

Writing the wrongs

Creative subjects are generally considered to be art, music and drama and many schools find innovative ways to embrace these within cross-curricular activities (Rowe and Humphries, 2001:

159–62) but writing itself, although often enhanced by these innovations, is not always seen as a discipline that requires creative nurturing in its own right. Literacy, after all, is alive and well, balancing balls on its nose and honking as it flaps its flippers. It may have to leap through hoops but it is at least still respected in the context of assessable learning. Art, music and drama are more often set free to wander away into the woods and fend for themselves. Their anguished howls can be heard on many a moonlit night.

Added to this, writing is a complex task. Language and speech have been shown to occur as a natural process but writing, like reading, is an unnatural activity that needs to be taught (Abbott and Burkitt, 2015: 67–83). Thoughts are transferred to paper but thoughts, in essence, are often random or uncertain. There is a process; a rearrangement of ideas that is necessary for context and clarity. Then there is the practical application. Holding a pen. Forming letters. Making it legible. Writing demands focus and concentration. Pupils are exposed through writing in a way that doesn't happen when they are merely reading:

> No one really knows that reading is a struggle … however; with writing it is all too clear that you find it tricky. The second your pen hits the page your secret is out.
>
> (Chamberlain, 2016: 1–2)

Margaret Atwood (2002: 48) considers the act of writing in a similar vein, describing the written word as 'evidence' that a writer might be judged against. Unlike speech, writing is a physical entity. All our writerly flaws and flourishes are vulnerable. They can be held up to the light, scrutinised, then banished to the Land of the Bad.

At school level the 'getting it wrong' is more easily applied to misuse of grammar and spelling. A pupil may write a compelling, original and exciting story only to find it marked down because they haven't used sufficient semicolons or subjunctive clauses. This may, in part, be because it is still considered that creativity is some kind of invisible force that cannot be assessed or commented on critically (Cremin and Myhill, 2012: 25) – it's so much simpler to apply a 'right and wrong' response to something that is easy to identify. However, it may also be that not every teacher is confident enough to give valuable feedback on the content, as opposed to the mechanics, of a piece of writing. Not all teachers are specialists in English (Ofsted, 2012: 31). They won't all have the skills to connect with writing other than at surface value. This is absorbed by pupils too. Often, young people consider that what makes a good writer is good handwriting and the ability to spell (Chamberlain, 2016: 19).

Using a layering of immersive techniques can re-motivate pupils, and as ideas evolve through emotional connections there is less emphasis on what is right or wrong: the focus can be shifted to how well the pupil is communicating their ideas through words. This will include paying attention to grammar and spelling, but the context will be on skills that combine the two. Technical aspects of the writing can be measured within the context of their relevance to the content, and ways this could be improved.

For instance, the following extracts evolved through pupils researching endangered species, identifying animal traits and understanding habitats. These elements established character, setting and action related to plot that then evolved into a work of fiction. The feedback focus therefore responds to how well the research has informed the fictional elements:

[Bear – 'Harrison' is a bear and research included diet, hunting and hibernation] It was in the middle of the day when Harrison stomped to the river off salmon. Harrison had to do all off the hunting himself because he lived on his own. The big bear thrashed its paw at a salmon when it jumped out off the water and ate it whole from wear he had been starving.

Jack, Redlands Primary School

[Chimps – 'Dave' is a chimp and research included group behaviour, play and external threats] I run on and on and on until finally I manage to catch up with him. "Your it now." I shout, but then stop. David looks at me with scared eyes. "What is it?" I ask, puzzled. David slowly points behind us. I look. "Theres nothing there for miles!" I say. "Exactly. Think about it." So I do. And then it hits me. I can't see home.

Emily, Redlands Primary School

[Wolf – 'Casper' is a wolf and research included setting, hunting and threats from humans] Deep in a forest in Europe there lays a wolf pack sleeping under the moonlight. There was a sound. A sort of scampering sound a moose or a deer might make. Casper woke up at the sound and steadily stood up in attention worrying that it might be a human hunting them. He started to walk closer to the sound.

Molly, Redlands Primary School

All three pupils drew excellent ideas from the research of their animals. They built stories with viable characters, believable settings and dramatic endings that are easy to identify and could be described as 'measurable' in an assessment context. All three could benefit from stronger visual elements – what is the terrain the bear stomps through? Where are the chimps playing? What is the landscape they look back on? How well can a wolf see at night and can his walk through the woods be built with greater suspense? These additional questions give clear ideas for continued development and further research by the pupils, as they strengthen the fiction through description and detail drawn from their non-fictional investigations.

Keeping 'active' (and being interactive)

'Active approaches' have been seen to make a significant difference to the motivation and engagement of pupils, and have potential to close the gap between boys' and girls' writing attainments (Ofsted, 2009: 44). Active approaches can include drama and role play, with pupils writing in role as characters, or writing spontaneously from 'seize the moment' activities which don't attach to specific genres or writing styles (Cremin et al., 2015: 99).

This also encompasses collaborative work and sharing ideas. I often begin with a group proposal, but move this to independent work. For example, I sometimes create a spooky house as a whole-class activity and then break the class into groups: the different groups have a room each to develop. From this each member of the group creates a character – it could be a ghost or someone real – and gives them a backstory. Groups act out scenes from their room, then write a first person monologue from their individual character's point of view and read it aloud to their groups.

For genre-specific approaches, I frequently utilise images and/or music. The images trigger the development of settings, while music is used for subconscious manipulations suggesting mood, suspense, or genre-focused narratives. The creative mind is an open place, so the choice of material needs to be considered carefully. Images are more effective if they provide a background to build from, rather than suggesting a whole story. Showing exteriors of old, abandoned houses is a starting point for my 'House of Rooms' activity, enabling the pupils' imaginations to then build their own house, and discuss the possible interiors. For music, if the aim is to evoke a spooky atmosphere, then the composition needs to reflect this, although I would avoid anything that is too specifically Halloween as this tends to create clichéd responses – unless of course the session is about Halloween, in which case that choice would be perfect. A futuristic piece of music inspires science-fiction scenarios. Fantasy writing calls for – well – something fantastic and otherworldly.

This collection of techniques can be defined under the VARK learning style. Derived from the acronym VAK, the VARK approach was born from the belief that all individuals have preferred learning styles: Visual, Aural, Reading/writing and Kinaesthetic. By building profiles of individual pupils' learning styles it was thought that lessons could be pitched towards preferences and therefore engage learners more effectively (Warrington et al., 2006: 169–70). The rationale for this has moved on now, and research demonstrates that learners respond to all teaching styles (Jarret, 2015: 208), but for me the 'all approaches' approach seems like a happy place to be.

I aim to integrate all four teaching/learning styles into any creative session, and this layered methodology seems to please 'all of the people most of the time'. Pupils don't get bored or distracted because each segment triggers a fresh response and the energy of the session remains consistent. The House of Rooms includes discussion about language and image, sound (music), collaboration of ideas, role play, writing and reading. Even within the four walls of a classroom I try to offer experiences, and when pupils connect with experience their emotions are engaged. Emotion is a central force in the drive of writing.

Emo☺☺☹tion and creative writing

While running an adult-education creative writing group I introduced an activity that involved the development of characters in real-life scenarios. For some students it was their very first encounter with the world of creative writing. One such student was forty-year-old 'Dave' who owned two overseas businesses, a local business, plus various rental properties in the south of England.

In this adult-ed session I had asked students to indulge in a touch of method acting (Stanislavski, 2013), which would transfer to the process of method writing (writing in role).

Students initially chose their new persona from a collection of photographs of (anonymous) people at work. These included a policeman, a plumber, a nurse, a taxi driver and a farmer. They were given names and students invented a family history to attach to their character.

The students then role played over coffee, giving their characters a voice and opinions as they responded to a series of newspaper articles. This enabled the students to deepen their understanding of their character's drives, motivations and personal issues. Dave 'became' a newly qualified policeman who was desperate to see the world from a 'right'/'wrong' perspective. Beyond the role play there was a freewriting session, with students writing an inner monologue in role. Dave's policeman described an anguished ethical dilemma when he discovered the perpetrator of a crime was his best friend from schooldays.

The day after the session Dave rang me and told me in an awed voice about the impact the process had had on him. On his way home he became so overwhelmed by a rush of emotion that he actually pulled his car into a lay-by and sobbed. It is not the sobbing that is important, but that Dave hadn't been taught – or had forgotten how – to feel. The act of writing triggered the release.

Triggering feelings through combinations of drama and visual stimulus are ways to engage with more artistic approaches to literacy, as well as emulating genuine writerly processes (Baker and Cremin, 2017: 110). Experienced writers grab at emotion, drawing from 'big' and 'small' experiences; it is all valid and valuable. Grabbing at emotion doesn't mean authors have to make a visible display of deep passions; to some extent feelings are better contained as the power then comes out in the writing (Highsmith, 2014: 225). Writing itself is therapeutic. Diaries, morning pages (Cameron, 2016) and journals all have jottings that writhe with emotion, but these are invariably evolved from freewriting approaches. There is generally no expectation that these outpourings will be read by anyone else. They are private, secret, overflowing with the 'inner-self'.

Yet, writing what we feel, as a way to explore and express reality (Cameron, 2016: 114), is also a powerful current that authors redirect into their fictional work. I once even drew not from my own direct emotion, but from my grandmother, who had experienced the tragic loss of her eldest daughter who was just fifteen. My (would have been) aunt was knocked off her bike by a car in 1936 and died. My grandmother, drawn to a crowd in the street, realised her own daughter was the victim. Over sixty years later I wrote a scene where a child has drowned in the sea, and the mother sees a crowd on the beach and goes to see what has happened – I knew as I wrote it that the powerful, impassioned drama that was spilling painfully onto the page came from a whole lineage of grief that had been triggered by this event (Waite, 2001).

Emotion, then, can be channelled through young writers in these same ways, to emerge as fiction. All young people are sometimes angry, sometimes sad. All young people feel fear. Feelings don't, of course, need to always be dark. Writing can also capture joy, excitement, yearning and love; the important point is that it needs to be felt, and experiencing ideas through alternative interpretations is a powerful medium. A case study which focused on evolving young people as writers reinforces the value of emotion by looking at writing as a form of expression (Baker and Cremin, 2017: 110), as opposed to writing that is drawn from 'codes and conventions' (Cremin et al., 2017: 34), and these expressive techniques can be adapted to evolve exciting, meaningful fictional ideas.

Feeling through words

The value of feelings can be drawn from discussion as well as actions. The outputs can then be re-interpreted as a piece of creative writing.

I have created a mood box, using fonts that give a visual clue to the word:

ANGER   happiness   *Despair*

The words are cut and placed in sealed envelopes. With the class in a circle, volunteer pupils take a card from the box and take care not to let anyone else see it. They then mime the emotion, while the watching pupils suggest the word that must have been on the card. Once the mimed responses have been discussed, this can move on a stage further. What is the colour of anger? What might happiness look like? These more ambiguous responses can deepen creative thinking, as pupils respond through instinct and memory, and the activity also has the potential to open up a community of enquiry (Fisher, 2015). Why might anger be perceived as red? What is it about yellow that makes us associate this with happiness? The class can then move to ideas that enable them to incorporate colour into writing, as well as evolving more dramatic outputs stimulated by the energies of moods.

I have created the following activity to enhance visual aspects of writing, alongside deepening the content. I use the image of bottles as a metaphor because people often talk about 'bottling up' emotion, and the sense that something is bottled in a clear container also enables us to 'see' it: to visualise how it might behave when it has nowhere else to go.

Explore this exercise with different emotions in bottles, then expand the captured emotion into a descriptive paragraph but without using the mood-word itself.

Anger in a bottle

Spiky. Jagged. It seems to jolt and twitch. Red sparks glow and flash up from black coals.

Jealousy in a bottle

Slides and slithers. Is thin, like a worm.

Oily, slimy. Green.

It writhes slowly.

Happiness in a bottle

Yellow and gold. Shining. It is shaped like the sun.

The jar feels warm to touch.

Kindness in a bottle

Rainbow colours – sometimes soft, sometimes faded so you can hardly see them. The colours drift like a soft mist. They press up against the edges of the jar, then float away again.

Wordtamer sample model: what bottled emotion is this creative paragraph evolved from?

A small cluster of jagged black coals lay at the bottom of the jar. Sparks of fierce orange glimmered out from the coals. A red mist appeared in the centre of the bottle. It twisted and writhed. The sparks turned into flames that hissed and spat, before hardening into spikes. The spikes exploded outwards, smashing against the edges of the glass. They cracked and spluttered, then hurled themselves again and again, and again.

Moving on

There have been a series of national discussions that focus on the role and identity of English in the twenty-first century (Ofsted, 2009: 22), and these include the *At the Heart of English* (Looking for the Heart of English, nd) booklet and the Looking for the Heart of English website, which makes suggestions as to how teachers can creatively integrate curriculum specifications into classroom practice.

There are schools with 'flipped classrooms' where pupils learn about the subject *before* they go to class and then apply the knowledge by contributing to group discussion during the taught time (Robinson and Aronica, 2016: 113). There are schools that integrate Carl Honoré's (2004: 235–6) 'slow movement', which advocates more fluidity and freedom in education. There are schools where pupils choose their own timetables (Sands School, nd) and even whether or not to attend lessons (Summerhill, nd). Some of these more alternative approaches may seem radical but then that is the point of an alternative approach. The existing one isn't working, or at least not for everyone. If fresh methodologies around established systems can be seen as valuable in a creative classroom context (Craft, 2015: 86) then this can be subject specific too. Writing itself can be explored from a range of innovative activities.

With creative thinking, vibrant imaginative outcomes can be attained even within the present systems. The moods will escape from their bottles. They will ooze, whizz, whirl and splatter. We'll watch what they do and scribble down notes on the shapes and colours of the future.

References

Abbott, R. and Burkitt, E. (2015) *Child Development and the Brain*. Bristol: Policy Press

Atwood, M. (2002) *Negotiating with the Dead*. Cambridge: Cambridge University Press

Baker, S. and Cremin, T. (2017) Teachers' identities as writers, in T. Cremin and T. Locke (eds), *Writer Identity*. Abingdon: Routledge

Cameron, J. (2016) *The Artist's Way*. London: Macmillan

Chamberlain, L. (2016) *Inspiring Writing in Primary Schools*. London: Sage

Craft, A. (2015) *Creativity, Education and Society: Writings of Anna Craft*, comp. K. Chappell, T. Cremin and B. Jeffrey. London: Institute of Education Press

Cremin, T. and Myhill, D. (2012) *Writing Voices*. Abingdon: Routledge

Cremin, T., Lillis, T., Myhill, D. and Eyres, I. (2017) in T. Cremin and T. Locke (eds) *Writer Identity*. Abingdon: Routledge

Cremin, T., Reedy, D., Bearne, E. and Dombey, B. (2015) *Teaching English Creatively* (2nd edn). Abingdon: Routledge

Fisher, R. (2015) *Teaching Thinking* (4th edn). London: Bloomsbury

Highsmith, P. (2014) *Plotting and Writing Suspense Fiction* (Kindle edn). Sphere

Honoré, C. (2005) *In Praise of Slow* (2nd edn). London: Orion

Jarret, C. (2015) *Great Myths of the Brain*. Chichester: Wiley Blackwell

Looking for the Heart of English (nd) *At the Heart of English*. https://heartofenglishblog.wordpress.com (accessed 13 December 2016)

Office for Standards in Education (Ofsted) (2009) *English at the Crossroads*. London: Ofsted. www.ofsted.gov.uk (accessed 12 December 2016)

Office for Standards in Education (Ofsted) (2012) *Moving English Forward*. London: Ofsted. www.educationengland.org.uk/documents/pdfs/2012-ofsted-english.pdf (accessed 12 December 2016)

Robinson, K. and Aronica, L. (2016) *Creative Schools*. London: Penguin

Rowe, S. and Humphries, S. (2001) Creating a climate for learning at Coombes Infant and Nursery School, in A. Craft, B. Jeffrey and M. Leibling (eds) *Creativity in Education*. London and New York: Continuum

Sands School (nd) www.sands-school.co.uk/choosing-what-to-learn/ (accessed 3 January 2017)

Stanislavski, C. (2013) *Building a Character* (5th edn). London and New York: Bloomsbury

Summerhill School (nd) www.summerhillschool.co.uk/an-overview.php (accessed 3 January 2017)

Waite, J. (2001) *Shopaholic*. Oxford: Oxford University Press

Warrington, M., Younger, M. and Bearne, E. (2006) *Raising Boys' Achievement in Primary School*. Maidenhead: Open University Press

CHAPTER 4

GOOD, BETTER AND BRILLIANT

Ways of working, drafting and editing ideas

> One night a girl saw a moonbeam in her garden. It made a special glow. She went outside into the garden and caught the moonbeam in a bottle.

My invisible friend

Sometimes students enrolled on creative writing courses are unable to attend a session. They generally email their apologies. If a writing task has been set as a homework, they often attach their contribution and ask if the group can discuss this in their absence. When this happens I find that the students who read the work open up with their opinions and responses. Without that writer in the room, there is more freedom, and more honesty.

I wanted to explore this in a school's context but was hampered by the fact that many of my school-based workshops are one-off events, and the opportunity doesn't arise. In addition to this, a school's set-up is not normally one where this could be easily implemented.

I decided, instead, to create my own imaginary friend – a fictitious pupil that I could ask a class of young writers to give guidance to. I call my friend Stanley, and he is generally introduced as a pupil from a school I have recently visited. Stanley has emailed me, or sent me the beginning of his story, and we (myself and the class I am working with) are going to help him develop the idea. This approach has proved very effective, perhaps because the pupils have a sense of wanting not only to help me, but also to help Stanley. They become mini-teachers, and this gives them a layering of control over their learning. They can have meaningful input in someone else's development. This method connects with many new models of alternative education already in existence (Robinson and Arnica, 2016) and pupils seem to embrace the responsibility it affords them.

I generally photocopy an extract of 'Stanley's' writing for pupils to work on independently, or alternatively take the *Talk for Writing* approach (Corbett and Strong, 2011) and improve the piece in front of the whole class, incorporating ideas and redrafting through discussion.

The development of Stanley's early idea demonstrated at points in this chapter was achieved through the latter approach, and drew from conversations about character and setting (who was the girl who caught the moonbeam, and where was she?), and descriptive writing (what words could Stanley use to help the reader imagine the glow? What are similes and metaphors? Why might one description work better than another?). Once the characters and early scene are established, pupils suggest a range of plot possibilities I can send to Stanley, then work independently on the continuation of the story with the idea they feel the strongest connection with.

> It was night time. The moon shone brightly. Its beams seemed magical. Lucy went into the garden so she could see them more clearly.

Fizzy thinking

It can be challenging (for teachers) to draw out creative energy from a lesson where so many 'tick-list' requirements around grammar and spelling might be a core focus. Creative 'fizz' can go flat in the process, but in my experience the two don't have to be mutually exclusive. If writing tasks are approached with energy and motivation, then much of the 'tick list' of curriculum objectives can still be measured; they will be evident at the end of the process and form part of the essential editorial process. Over and above correct usage of punctuation, spellings, subordinating conjunctions etc., the discussion can also be around quality of ideas, depth of content and creative integrity. However, an experienced eye is needed to truly identify what works, what could be improved and – perhaps the most important of all – why. The 'why' is arguably the greatest gap between the way a teacher will respond to a piece of writing and the way an experienced author will view it. Understanding the 'why' is a way to shake up the bottle with the lid still on; all the lovely fizzy thinking won't just spill out randomly. The bubbles will be stimulated and easier to see. The following sections in this chapter examine the teacher/author differences and explore the 'why' within a feedback context.

The good, the bad and the in between

What, first, is 'good' writing? A common response is that 'you know it when you see it', but that is little help to anyone trying to teach, or learn, the craft. I have often quizzed those who enthusiastically tell me that the latest book they read was 'brilliant' or '*so* powerful' and they can discuss what happened at length but when I ask them how the author achieved specific effects, even very advanced adult readers don't always know.

'Good' writing is generally not actually about writing at all, it is about rewriting. It is rare for a first draft to be anything other than experimental, and even those few writers who claim they don't rework acknowledge that this is because they may have spent months, or even years, just 'thinking' about the idea – and this thinking may include significant research (*The Writing Life*, 2011). Professional writers have stores of memories they can draw from, and time to research and inform their ideas. Their 'stores' can be filled to bursting: when the doors to this subconscious bunker are opened, all the boxes and parcels come tumbling out. Younger writers will not have sufficient knowledge or life experiences for such a rush of possibilities (Fisher, 2005: 94). There is little expectation that there can be an abundance of potential ideas, and when the writing starts, it is inevitably raw and unshaped. Discussion and relevant research around early drafts can sculpt and expand the initial attempts, deepening content. For instance, the following sentences (an extract from a fantasy-based piece) can become more visual and descriptive with research.

> He stood slowly. He heard noises coming from nearby. It was chirping and tweeting of the tropical, vibrant birds.
>
> Jess, Peel Common Junior School

> *Research tropical birds. Build in words that describe them, and let the reader know where they are.*

> He stood slowly. He heard noises coming from nearby. It was the chirping and tweeting of hundreds of colourful birds. As they swooped amongst the towering tropical trees Liam saw vibrant flashes of yellow, green and sapphire blue.

Even those young writers perceived as above average (Chamberlain, 2016: 19–20) can – and should – elevate the content of their work through rewriting.

Most established writers make no attempt to assume their first draft will be their last. For me, the only value of a first draft is that it gets it out of the way. The content usually consists of a baggy, confused and shapeless splurge of possibilities. The second draft is not much better, and the third might have me making decisions that alter the course of the story altogether. It is generally not until the fifth or sixth reworking that I hit that creative process 'Aha!' feeling – perhaps I know where this is going after all. I generally at this point make a fresh start, but the fresh start is somewhere beyond those six drafts, taking echoes of the initial idea but making my starting point a deeper, more interesting and more relevant place. It is not unheard of for me to have written up to forty drafts as I work my way further and further into a narrative.

This could be my own madness, but the testimony of other published writers suggests otherwise. Anne Fine (*The Writing Life*, 2011) writes drafts again, and again, and again – sometimes printing a new version of a single page twenty or thirty times. Fine can 'fill boxes rising to two or three feet off the floor' with drafts. These early deliberations have enormous value as they often capture the energy of the idea, whilst consequent drafts are attempts to shape and tune so that 'at least the reader has a shortened version' (Michael Holroyd in *The Writing Life*, 2011).

The concept of a shortened version highlights one of the significant differences between writing in schools, and writing professionally. Research suggests young writers generally consider that changing text is about adding things, as opposed to taking the 'designer's knife to the writing' (Cremin and Myhill, 2012: 77–8). Adding in extra lines, descriptions and short sentences is often a pupil interpretation of what needs to be done to improve (Myhill and Jones, 2007). In my own school-based workshops I regularly experience pupils thrusting their books at me, bursting with pride not because of any sense of glory about a turn of phrase or a brilliantly conceived twist-in-the-tail, but simply because they have filled pages with words and they believe quantity is what I am looking for.

There is a further quandary here. Drafting is very often 'freewriting', and this approach inevitably results in unshaped, unformed outpourings. This is vital to mining the diamonds of possibilities, but the practice of sending young writers away to rework pages of writing can be interpreted as punishment for having engaged so vigorously. Why write so much if it's all going to be changed? What's the point of so much effort?

Teachers can cultivate attitudes that nothing is ever wasted, that mistakes have value and every amendment improves the quality (Bowkett, 2014: 103) but young writers may still interpret constructive criticism as a secret message: 'you've thrown your heart and soul at this, but it still isn't good enough'.

If a young writer has poured their identity into pages of expressive writing (Cremin and Myhill, 2012: 18), or spilled down ideas they believe are original and exciting (Fisher, 2005: 36), they naturally want everyone to be thrilled by their brilliance. In order to feel engaged and motivated, young writers need to experience a connection to their writing; a degree of ownership and authorial agency (Cremin and Myhill, 2012: 86), but insensitive or over-zealous critiquing can trample over emerging energies. The point of intrusion, the time when the writer would most benefit from a fresh opinion, needs careful consideration.

Sometimes this intrusion might come at the point when the writer isn't sure how else to improve. Sometimes it might mean an intense focus on just one area or paragraph, enabling the author to 'see what happens' when they respond to advice about a specific section. Once they experience the differences, pupils can make their own decisions about the remaining writing. Another technique is to work collectively, improving an anonymous piece, and then seeing how writers can apply these details to their own work. This third technique is my 'Stanley' approach.

> It was a dark night. The moon rose high in the sky. Its beams seemed magical. Lucy crept into the garden so she could see them more clearly. She was so busy looking at the moonbeams that she nearly tripped over an empty bottle laying in the grass. Lucy picked the bottle up, and held it high. A moonbeam floated inside.

From daft to draft

So, what is happening in the minds of professional writers as they work feverishly through their endless drafts?

In general, at this advanced level writers are not only deepening the idea, but they are experimenting with plot. They are making decisions about style and structure. Alongside structure come decisions about character, voice and point of view. First or third person? Past or present tense? (Bell and Magrs, 2001).

These writers are also 'feeling' the story. This element of feeling is as important as the more tangible, measurable approaches that link to craft, and it draws from the concept of 'felt sense' (Gendlin, 1982: 32). The felt sense refers to individual reactions to characters and places, situations and circumstances. A writer may not articulate them fully, but because they draw from internal rhythms, moods and instincts then this sense finds its way onto the page. Felt sense is what we know about someone, or something, before we actually apply thought to that feeling. If I 'feel' the idea of my cat, I get a sense of something small, grey, shadowlike. I experience the strange green glow of his eyes as they watch me from the top of the stairs. Something feral. Somehow out of reach. I know my cat to be unpredictable, and sometimes wonder what his perception is of me. What would he do if he was my size, and I was his? But if I were to write my cat into a story, I wouldn't need to say all this. *The grey cat crouched on the top stair; a shadow with a green burn of gaze. It waited, and it watched.* Writers don't need to pin down every detail of what is happening. The additional detail is implied through what is *not* said (Boulter, 2007: 107).

Helping young writers to redraft and retain only what is needed brings us closer to what good writing might be. If the writer has drawn from a felt-sense, then the reader will feel it too, but this is a skill to be learnt. Taking risks with writing means teachers need to reward the experiment as much as the result. If there is a chance of an approach not working, and therefore not celebrated, this could be perceived as failure and pupils will learn it is safer not to take risks in language – or in anything else (Joubert, 2001: 21–2).

Morpurgo describes his early draft writing process as writing by hand, initially up to 2000 words, which he writes 'extraordinarily fast, letting it flow', knowing he will go back and 're-jig' later (*The Writing Life*, 2011).

On being asked what sort of person a child might need to be in order to become an author, Roald Dahl gave a list of responses that included 'you must never be satisfied with what you have written until you have re-written it again and again, making it as good as you possibly can' (Dahl, in Powling, 1983: 68).

But still then, what is the 'good' that even Dahl strove to achieve? In order for pupils to redraft effectively, they need to know what it is that makes a piece of writing better. The first discussion needs to establish that quality, rather than quantity, comes top of the list.

Professional writers generally agree that for quality writing 'less is more'. The term 'purple-prose' is perceived as derogatory; coined by the Roman poet Horace (65–8 BC) it was initially used to compare this overly lavish writing with patches of purple sewn onto clothes. In Horace's period, purple was a sign of wealth and pretentiousness; comparisons with writing apply to prose and poetry characterised by the extensive use of adverbs, adjectives and metaphors. The writer of purple-prose is so immersed in their writerly feasting that they have forgotten their primary intention is to communicate. 'Rich, ornate prose is hard to digest, generally unwholesome, and sometimes nauseating' (Strunk and White, 2000: 72).

> The wonderful, magical glow of the moonbeam from Lucy's bottle shone vibrantly and brilliantly. It kept shining vividly and brightly. The glistening shine was like a light from a giant lorry's headlights on the motorway on a dark, gloomy, black as coal night.

Yet – and yet – adverbs, adjectives and metaphors are all fundamental in terms of teaching literacy in schools.

Purple-prose has value in expanding language and enriching ideas, while even at a professional level raw outpourings might have significant impact on the crafted result. In untamed, expansive prose we sometimes uncover those diamonds that illuminate what we are saying. If, like Morpurgo, we can give ourselves permission to write badly, then many of us could write 'very well indeed' (Cameron, 2000: 23). The skill lies, perhaps, in relation to greed. Instead of scooping up barrows full of gemstones, let's just choose a few – those that catch the most rainbows. Those with the strongest glow. Those whose colours match the eyes of our main characters.

How, then, can teachers help pupils search for such treasure without blowing up the mine?

The study of style

Teachers' familiarisation with genre has raised awareness of conventions that enable more valid and focused feedback on pupils' writing, and this has been born of the DfEE's (2000) developing emphasis on *writerly knowledge* that puts a focus on craft and genre, moving beyond the more basic discussions around spelling, punctuation and grammar (Chamberlain, 2016: 31).

For instance, has the writer built suspense and atmosphere in a horror story? If so, how specifically has this been achieved? If not, what techniques could the writer try to enhance the impact? Is the fantasy setting evolved through language that depicts somewhere strange; perhaps magical? Does background detail in science fiction writing feel like a glimpse of the future?

Teachers can also recognise what is superfluous. The clusters of words, or even sentences, that have the same meaning or do the same job. Similes and metaphors need to be relevant, and to connect mood and place. Language choices can evoke genre and atmosphere: a battle with machines in a science-fiction scenario could encapsulate a more mechanical style than a creeping danger moving through a house of horrors.

Once again, there is no need for pupils to redraft pages and pages of writing.

Small scenes, just several sentences, can be focused in on and honed. This way pupils can still be praised for effort in their early draft outpourings, but the rewrites can be applied to favourite sections or those that offer the most potential. Scrutiny can be around not just language and sentence structure, but the overall flow of the chosen scene.

Consider Stanley's piece, evolving through my class full of 'mini-teachers':

> The magical glow of moonbeams shining out from Lucy's bottle shone softly and gently. The glimmering shine was like a light from a giant lorry's headlights racing along on a motorway in the fog.

In the example above the style and content suggests fantasy and magic realism, so these elements can be praised, but Stanley can improve further by making deeper connections with the language choices. He could edit out 'softly' because it does the same job as 'gently'. 'Glimmering' and 'shine' are also similes, and one can go. The metaphor about the giant lorry on the motorway is distracting, takes the reader somewhere completely different, and infects the mood of the piece.

My mini-teachers' more advanced version evolved like this:

> The bottle glimmered gently, like lamplight in fog.

The redrafted piece has not merely been edited. It has been reworked and achieves more powerful and relevant imagery. It says the same thing but applies a more complex use of language, yet it is shorter. Stanley can learn an important lesson in effective writing, gleaning wisdom from Hippocrates (471–399 BC) who said 'The chief virtue that language can have is clarity.'

Knowing what to say

I have often run workshops where writing is being critiqued. Many times it is clear when students have not properly engaged with another's creative offering. The feedback is bland: 'I loved the bit where you described the moonbeam', 'Lucy seems really interesting', 'I can't wait to hear what will happen next'. These empty gushings are generally accompanied by enthusiastic nods and encouraging smiles. The writer being critiqued is no better informed as to what it is about the moonbeam's description that works so well, nor what is so compelling about the whole piece that their peer 'can't wait to read the rest'. Overall, the group are generally reluctant to give negative feedback. Of course, this is all beautiful. Everyone stays friends. No one gets hurt. Nobody dies.

But for writing to improve, the critique needs to have a value and that value needs to be as constructive about what doesn't work, as well as what does.

I generally dislike the word 'rules' in connection with creative practice, but they do seem essential in a workshop environment. My 'rule' around critiques is that everyone tries to think of one aspect they enjoyed, and one aspect they were less certain about. Then, within these opposing responses, what is it about the former that resonated so well, and what is it about the latter that needs development?

Purposeful talk is an essential ingredient, and the workshop can initially be teacher-guided with the aims (such as a focus on character, or setting, for instance) explained. The process can then move to more child-initiated responses as pupils work in either pairs or small groups. They discuss the content of each other's writing in the context of the stated aims. The steered discussion not only enables the writers to hear their ideas over and above the act of reading aloud, but also responders learn how to be good listeners (Myhill et al., 2006); if responders are to give insightful feedback, they need to have listened carefully.

In order to ensure first effective listening, and second the confidence to give feedback, my own approach is to clarify content related to anticipated outcome. Ultimately a story needs characters, plots, settings, genre, etc., but each element has its own distinct approaches and trying to crowd too much into tight timeframes results in writing that doesn't explore its own potential.

A typical session might take just two elements: fantasy (genre) and setting (place). I foreground both through an initial discussion of what this means in writing, extract examples from published texts and model an early draft of my own. Pupils then evolve fantasy settings through a range of possibilities (see Chapter 7) and produce a piece of fantasy writing with a specific setting.

The true benefit of this is realised at feedback stage. It is not about how good the writing is overall, but how well the setting has been evolved. How well can the reader/listener *see* that place? Does the environment feel relevant to the fantasy genre? Characters, actions, pace and plot all play their part but for the purpose of *this* lesson we have fallen in love with fantasy settings and will rejoice in all the wondrous opportunities this has spread before us.

For teachers for whom writing creatively is not 'their first language' this offers up an instant engagement with the writing. They know they taught 'fantasy' and 'setting' to their pupils, so they don't have to fall back on scrutinising adjectives or the correct placing of an apostrophe. That can come later. Bland, polite or layman level 'I love the bit where you described the moonbeam' responses can be banished to a land of smoking volcanoes and belching bogs. The teacher response can be all about the setting and its relevance to the genre, and how well it has been evoked and embedded into the writing.

These two freewriting extracts were evolved through an initial 'under the sea' (Act 3, Sea World, p. 152) setting and character development activity:

Aleah swam in. The rock face she swam past almost glistened like her baby blue scales on her tale. The dark blue sea rippled as she sped through it. She took out her brush made out of a clam and old hedgehog spines and lifted herself out of the water in the moon pool and started brushing her long brown locks.

Molly, Redlands Primary School 2016

Splish splash splash. The jelly fish was floating about in the sea wead with the glittering sun shining over it. Nearby was an old, mouldy shipwreak which on top of it lay an old chest with jewls and jelwery spilling out of the sides. There was then a moon pool and it looked as if there were tuns of different lights shining down on it. Then I saw a beautiful Mer-boy, painting a picture.

Lydia, Redlands Primary School 2016

The focus for this part of the session was the visual quality of the writing alongside characterisation, so over and above basic punctuation this can also be the focus for the feedback. How well can the reader 'see' the scene? Do we gain a sense of character yet? As the story moved on, the taught focus changed to drama and action in amongst this characterisation and setting scenario:

[W]hen he opened his eyes, it seemed that everyone had vanished. He strolled forwards confused. A beam of sweat begun to dripp down his face as he grew more and more nervous. As he searched the school, cluelessly, a door was left open, leaning back and forth. As he shut the door it creaked but, only then did he here a 'swosh' behind him.

Louie, Redlands Primary School

Suddenly she spotted a gorgeous shell bracelet. Without hesitating she immediately swam down to the bottom and slided it onto her hand. She started to feel unstable and fainted on the spot! A few minutes later she stood up and gazed down at her tail...

"Aaaaaaggghhhh. What's happened to my beautiful tail," shrieked Merlia.

Charlotte, Redlands Primary School

"Hurry up Helga!" exclaimed the impatient King [Neptune]. "Yes your majesty Helga said in an eerie tone. "HELGA!" shouted the head cook angrily in her despret need for money "You bernt the bread again! If you pay atention you will not need to make more dough every half an hour! If his majesty doesn't get his feast I don't get paid!!"

Georgina, Redlands Primary School

Feedback can become even more meaningful here. Not only can the work be discussed in the context of setting, character and suspenseful writing skills but scrutiny into language choices can aid future drafting – is 'strolled' the best word for someone confused and nervous? Can the tail be gazed down on if it's gone? Could the cook in Neptune's palace prepare something more 'fishy' than bread – this author could have a fantastic time creating delicious jellyfish jellies, seaweed soup or inky octopus sauce. Keeping the theme consistent is important, and is a stimulating challenge for the imagination. We can also see exciting positives with plots pushing through. What is behind the door in that mer-school? Did the greed for the necklace harm the much-admired tail? What are the consequences for the penniless cook?

Feedback on a piece evolved through clear creative writing objectives can be precise, and responses qualified.

The pupils have this same focus too. For younger or less experienced writers a reader-response aid guides them through relevant questions, and has the additional benefit of the writer having something physical to redraft from.

Reader as editor form

Listen carefully to the story being read, and notice what detail the writer has given about the setting. Can you see the place in your own mind?

Once you have listened to the story, jot notes down onto this form.

Where do you think this story is taking place?

....

Is it day or night? Do you know what season it is? What is the weather like?

....

Is the place beautiful, or scary? What main things do you know about it?

....

Feedback to the writer how you imagine their setting to be: they can use your feedback as a starting point for redrafting their idea.

As pupils respond to the writing of their peers, be they real or imaginary, they advance their own self-editing skills.

Rhyme, reason and words that sing

Poetry pre-dates writing, and one early purpose of poetic form was to make it possible for the performer to remember long narratives about battles, or history, or current affairs (Burroway, 2003: 309). Rhyme and patterns in both poetry and prose help us to remember the words themselves. We can easily sing along with the lyrics of a favourite song, but how easily could we recite, word for word, a standard passage from a favourite book? Rhyme is a memory aid for the listener too. Small children learn to read through language patterns and rhythms and many picture books either rhyme, or have a beat that works like a song, structured with a recognisable verse and chorus.

The same applies to prose. The most evocative writing somehow 'sings' on the page, and when writers hear the voice of their work captured through being read aloud, they can revise and develop for rhythm and effect.

Reading aloud, then, should form part of the redrafting process, particularly as it moves towards the final edit. Classroom activities which enable writers to read aloud at relevant points not only help them pick out the rhythms and cadences of their own work, but also refine the reader's sense of identity as a writer. Reading aloud does not always need to be about performance, or for the purpose of another's critique. When young writers read aloud 'in their head', or read aloud to themselves at key points of development, the writing is strengthened (Cremin and Myhill, 2012: 197). I can often be seen hunched over my computer, muttering as I amend and reshape my work. I am hearing my novel in process, developing patterns and making connections with what has come before and what I might evolve next.

Furthermore, I never send a book off to a publisher without reading it aloud. It is a sometimes lengthy process as I have written fiction amounting to over 70,000 words, but I consider it a vital stage. Only through reading aloud do I pick out clumsy syntax, repetitions (of both words and ideas) and confused paragraphs.

In a classroom context, where work is being critiqued prior to redraft, it is important to establish the value related to the activity. Writers and listeners should have differing agendas. For the writer, the benefit can be related to content: Did I stumble over words when I read that paragraph? Is that sentence too long? Is there enough drama or action? For the listener, it might mean clarification of detail around what's happening, or an emotional response to an event. Both sides will be able to listen for rhythm or flow, and this is also a golden opportunity to consider punctuation as present in the process.

That pesky punctuation

Most writers, on reading their own work, will apply the stops and pauses within the piece regardless of whether they have punctuated correctly. They are hearing the shape of the piece, and performing it; they know innately where the breaks should come.

An 'ear' for grammar, evolved through constant language interactions, needs to be actively developed to become implicit in writing as well as speaking. Punctuation both underpins and enhances the power of the written word (Corbett and Strong, 2014: xi).

Awareness of pause and effect may be innate in oral storytelling, and indeed in everyday conversation, but it is not an innate ability when transferred to writing. Punctuation needs to be taught, alongside spelling and grammar, but it often results in liberal smatterings of apostrophes, commas and punctuation marks. Young writers know they need to use them, so if they put them in everywhere, perhaps some of them might be in the right places.

Talk-based games and activities help pupils *feel* the difference that punctuation makes, and drama can play an important role in making punctuation meaningful. Young children engage well when the punctuation in an existing text is acted out, and through the performance they develop a sense of its real value (Corbett and Strong, 2014: 150–72).

Young writers can experience how punctuation works by experiencing it with their whole body (Fisher, 2015: 193) and also by learning it in less traditional environments. I explored the application of this when supporting a disabled child in primary education, back in the days when the possibility of my ever being a published author was just a twinkle in my mind's eye. 'Jack' had cerebral palsy. He struggled with motor control, spatial awareness and concentration. I worked with Jack for seven years, and often needed to move beyond the classroom, experimenting with a broader range of approaches more appropriate to his learning needs.

I found that by chalking giant letters and numbers across the playground we could walk the shapes, and get a physical sense that was then recaptured in a subsequent 'learn your letters' task. I adapted the methodology for a group of Year 4 pupils identified as below average in terms of literacy skills.

We not only chalked and walked, but we also made living sentences. 'Who goes where?' was a game where pupils became a human sentence and offered a kinaesthetic approach to children who were struggling with basic literacy skills. Each pupil took a word or punctuation point and stood in order.

the ran . lizard ground along The
The lizard ran along the ground.
. its shouted " look ' lizard Seb ! a "Oh ,
"Oh look, it's a lizard!" shouted Seb.
Body green , a tongue eyes , black a . had The flickering and lizard
The lizard had a green body, black eyes and a flickering tongue.

The emphasis is on the sentence making sense, and the group discuss the implication of alternatives. The first example offers no options, but the second would work equally well as: *Seb shouted, "Oh look, it's a lizard!"* and the third invites deeper investigation into the build of tension alongside the punctuation. For instance, what changes if the 'flickering tongue' is the first clause? The sentence is still correct, but does it work so well in terms of suspense and creative application? The trick here is to build through the levels suggested by the information. The least interesting aspect is the green body. The black eyes give it life. The flickering tongue suggests a reaction, and danger.

After pupils had arranged themselves in the best logical order, we would read these living sentences aloud with pauses and dramatic intonation to emphasise punctuation.

Other groups of learners who struggle with punctuation may be those for whom English is not their first language, or those struggling with learning issues such as dyslexia or dyspraxia. For teenage learners within this group there are additional peer pressure and self-esteem values associated with the inability to grasp the basics. I was commissioned to write a series of four interweaving books set on a fictitious street, drawing from four main characters with different ethnic backgrounds (Waite, 2017). In order to write this series I liaised with literacy specialists skilled in working with this group of learners. These readers read slowly, without intonation or expression. They also ignore most punctuation (Reid, pers. comm.). In my experience they write this way too. At eleven-plus it is generally not considered 'cool' to form living sentences or play punctuation games, yet this group may have powerful imaginations or have experienced life events that give them wide knowledge or observational skills. I have found this group often identify with script ideas that can be pitched for film or TV. This starts with discussion and then a summary. Group scripts can be written, showing pause and effect through punctuation. These are then acted out, responding to the punctuation. The script below has deliberately not used contractions (see page 112), but these could be inserted, depending on the reading level of the group.

Exercise: Read pitch

Put pupils in groups of four.

Crocodile Tears: This is a film about four friends who mess about by a river near where they live. It is a sunny day and the weather is calm. They are watching swans and skimming stones. Then one of the friends spots something weird – a swan disappears. No one believes him/her. The others wander off. He/she is left alone, still trying to work out what happened.

Each pupil takes a role (names can be inserted based on gender of the group).

Pupil 1: I wish I was a swan. They look *so* cool.
Pupil 2: You would be more like an ugly duckling.
Pupil 1: You are *so* annoying!
Pupil 3: Stop it, you two. Can you see that swan by the far bank? It looks lost.
Pupil 4: Where?
Pupil 3: Over there. Oh no...!
Pupil 4: What?
Pupil 3: Something grabbed it. It has pulled it under the water.
Pupil 2: You are crazy, mate. There is nothing there.
Pupil 1: He is right. There would be feathers left behind.
Pupil 4: We would have heard it squawking. It would sound like this – **SQUAWK! SQUAWK!**
Pupil 2: We would see blood.
Pupil 3: It looked like something grabbed it from underneath.
Pupil 1: I am bored with this rubbish. Anyone up for getting a burger from that new place in the street.
Pupil 2: Cool.
Pupil 4: YES! I am starving.
Pupil 3: I will catch you up. I want to check there are *definitely* no feathers first.

The group can now decide what happens next to the remaining friend *or*, depending on ability, write ideas or continue the story individually.

For average and more able pupils of any age, reading each other's work aloud provides a multi-layered value. The young writers listen to their own work through another's perspective – have they communicated content? Is it punctuated accurately, sending messages around *how* it must be read?

Physically reading aloud, or reading aloud silently, is another way to learn the patterns and pauses. If punctuation is embedded as a form of mental whisper, like a ghost on a shoulder, young writers might always be able to hear where it needs to go.

Supershine me

The final edit is an act of 'super shining'. It is the last stage and the point where the writing gets its final polish.

There seems little value in checking the spellings and grammatical elements of work that is going to be altered or deleted. Over-emphasis on editing during rewriting can give a message that the work is finished, when it could still be developed for better effect.

This supershine polish draws on crafting skills and a keen eye. As writers move through the drafting stages, there is a shift in process from the more organic to the more analytic. Errors can appear like weeds between the foliage of words. Generally small and simple to remove, they need pulling up by the roots.

Repetition is one of these weeds. Used skilfully it is a sophisticated tool. It can bring in echoes and patterns, and be used for impact and effect. Used lazily it presents as sloppy writing, and makes a sentence or paragraph awkward and uncared for:

Tola saw the wolves running towards the river. The water was running fast, smashing across the boulders. Tola knew that time was running out.

This sort of repetition is easy to alter, simply by finding a synonym or a different phrasing.

Tola saw the wolves running towards the river. The water surged as it flowed, smashing across the boulders. She knew there wasn't much time.

All writers repeat words without good reason from time to time. Re-reading, and reading work aloud, usually weeds these out.

Tense changes are another unwelcome dandelion. The wrong tense may seem like a small detail but it undermines any sense of control: writing littered with tense changes is messy and under-nurtured.

Tola saw the wolves running towards the river. The water is running fast, smashing across the boulders. Tola knows that time was running out.

Other final checks include seeking out logical inconsistencies; bland words that might be replaced with something more dramatic, or dramatic words that have been plucked from the thesaurus and intrude like a giant thistle in a field of summer flowers.

Checks around spelling, grammar and punctuation are the last action to take. With every 'i' dotted and every 't' crossed, young writers can finally step back, basking in the polished glow of their own achievement. Now, it is time to…

CELEBRATE!

As the Writer-in-Residence for Hampshire Museum Service, I co-ran a project connecting children to history through creative writing. The project was set in the seventeenth century, and involved a visit to a local castle. Pupils created characters who became seventeenth-century prisoners through role play, and sent letters 'home' to loved ones. These young writers gathered ideas while on location and redrafted in the classroom.

Pupils worked on 'super shining' and edited their work, then worked on illustrations, which included designing book covers. After this they performed an evening of celebration, where myself and members of the museum service were special guests, alongside parents. The young writers read extracts from their published works and were recorded and from this a CD was made available to buy at Christmas.

Publishing or celebrating the final writing in some form not only provides an audience for the pupils' work, but also offers added meaning throughout the process itself (Corbett, 2009: 113).

The celebration doesn't always need to be a grand affair, but some level of recognition is important. Artwork can be hung on the wall. Music gets heard. Drama gets watched. Writing, unless someone takes the time and trouble to pay attention to it, can disappear. Over and above marking, a balanced creative writing session should ideally be book-ended so that attention to the final product is as visible and enthusiastic as the introduction. This might mean making books for an open day, or collecting favourite sentences and creating a collage for the classroom wall. Pupils can read their best paragraphs to the class, or in smaller groups to each other. This is no longer for feedback purposes but for closure; with writing it can be hard to know when to stop. Whatever form this end-game takes, teachers will have moved their pupils through 'baggy draft' to 'revised and tightened edit': everyone will be closer to knowing what 'good writing' actually is.

> *Good evening ladies and gentlemen, my name is Stanley and I would like to read you an extract from my story:*
>
> ### The Magic Moonbeam
> It was a dark night. The silvery moon rose high in the sky. Its beams cast a magical glow. Lucy crept into the garden so she could see them more clearly. Still dazzled by the moonbeams, she nearly tripped over an empty bottle. Lucy picked the bottle up. She held it high.
>
> One moonbeam floated towards her. It drifted across the lip of the bottle then curled softly inside. Lucy gasped with delight. She pressed down on the top of the bottle, scared the moonbeam would float back out again. The bottle glimmered gently, like lamplight in fog.
>
> It shone up through Lucy's fingers. The shine warmed her hand, but it made her shivery too. She had captured a moonbeam. What would she do with it ... and what might it do to her?
>
> (With thanks to my invisible friend Stanley, and
> Creative Writing Club pupils at Locks Heath Junior School)

References

Bell, J. and Magrs, P. (2001) *The Creative Writing Course Book*. London: Macmillan

Boulter, A. (2007) *Writing Fiction: Creative and Critical Approaches*. Basingstoke: Palgrave Macmillan

Bowkett, S. (2014) *A Creative Approach to Teaching Writing*. London: Bloomsbury

Burroway, J. (2003) *Imaginative Writing: The Elements of Craft*. New York: Longman

Cameron, J. (2000) *The Right to Write*. London: Pan Macmillan

Chamberlain, L. (2016) *Inspiring Writing*. London: Sage

Corbett, P. (2009) *Jumpstart! Storymaking*. Abingdon: Routledge

Corbett, P. and Strong, J. (2011) *Talk for Writing*. Maidenhead: Open University Press

Corbett, P. and Strong, J. (2014) *Jumpstart! Grammar*. Abingdon: Routledge

Cremin, T. and Myhill, D. (2012) *Writing Voices*. Abingdon: Routledge

DfEE (2000) *Grammar for Writing*. London: DfEE

Fisher, R. (2005) *Teaching Children to Think* (2nd edn). Cheltenham: Nelson Thornes

Fisher, R. (2015) *Teaching Thinking* (4th edn). London: Bloomsbury Academic

Gendlin, E. (1982) *Focusing*. London and New York: Bantam

Joubert, M. M. (2001) The art of creative teaching: NACCCE and beyond, in A. Craft, B. Jeffrey and M. Leibling (eds) *Creativity in Education*. London and New York: Continuum

Myhill, D. and Jones, S. (2007) More than just error correction: children's reflections on their revision processes, *Written Communication* 24(4): 323–43

Myhill, D., Jones, S. and Hopper, R. (2006) *Talking, Listening, Learning*. Maidenhead: Open University Press

Powling, C. (1983) *Roald Dahl: A Biography*. London: Puffin Books

Reid, D. (2017) training@catchup.org Thetford, Catchup. www.catchup.org/ (accessed 11 March 2017)

Robinson, K. and Arnica, L. (2016) *Creative Schools*. London: Penguin

Strunk, W., Jr and White, E. B. (2000) *The Elements of Style*. Upper Saddle River, NJ: Pearson Education

The Writing Life: Authors Speak (2011) Author interviews with Sarah O'Reilly (CD ROM). London: British Library Board

Waite, J. (2017) *Chelsea's Story: The Street*. London: Bloomsbury

Waite, J. (2017) *Kai's Story: The Street*. London: Bloomsbury

Waite, J. (2017) *Lena's Story: The Street*. London: Bloomsbury

Waite, J. (2017) *Sanjay's Story: The Street*. London: Bloomsbury

CHAPTER 5

THE RIGHT TO WRITE

Confidence, creative thinking and evolving a 'writer's mind'

Job Vacancy: School Teacher (only the Very Brilliant need apply)

Description Must be highly skilled in numeracy and literacy. Must have good working knowledge of cross-curricular subjects, including a high level of competency with ICT. An excellent communicator, the successful candidate will be able to liaise with both adults and young people on a day-to-day basis. Good team-work skills are essential, as is the ability to connect and respond to specialists and experts on a range of issues. Applicants will need to appreciate complex elements of psychology related to learning, behaviour and social sub-texts. They should have awareness of First Aid and be able to respond to the medical needs of those in their charge. The post demands sufficient strength of character to enable them to control and direct large groups. They must display sensitivity and empathy towards those who struggle, and also rise to the challenge of stretching and nurturing the abilities of the very gifted. High-order strategies for time management and personal motivation are essential, and it is assumed applicants will be able to work evenings and weekends. Applicants must be punctual, reliable, honest and fair-minded. Flexibility is expected to be a key component in both their approaches and responses. Oh, and they also need to be creative.

Genius ideas

Creativity is often understood as belonging to those who have been gifted with the ability to see the world in unusual ways. Individuals first have a *genetic predisposition* for a particular domain, and beyond this they are endowed with personality traits that seem to be common in highly creative personalities. Curiosity, a sense of wonder, openness to experience and a fluid attitude to problem solving make up some of the innate traits that have become recognised as integral to the creative persona. They are also complex, control their own energies and can be paradoxically 'smart and naïve' at the same time (Csikszentmihalyi, 1997: 51–76).

International authority on creativity in education, Professor Anna Craft (2015: 39–43), explores important differences between what she labels big 'C' creativity (BCC) as distinct from little 'c' creativity (lcc). Those with BCC belong to Csikszentmihalyi's genius level individuals, and these are defined as a minority group who change existing domains of knowledge, or invent new ones. However, this does not mean creativity is the exclusive domain of those in possession of genius traits. Lcc is within the scope of everyone.

Lost thoughts

If everyone is deemed capable of being creative, it seems puzzling as to why so many adults do not perceive themselves to be innovative, imaginative individuals. Most children are 'buzzing' with ideas and the inference is that something must happen to them as they grow up; an underlying problem must exist (Robinson, 2001: 2).

Ian Rankin (*The Writing Life*, 2011) described his own childhood as a world of pretence, where 'exciting things happen'. Rankin's belief is that writers never grow up; they are still, in some sense, always playing with an imaginary friend.

In opposition to Rankin's experiences, by the time people reach adulthood, many have lost all connection with their original creative spontaneity. The creative, curious, open-minded and 'let's pretend' elements of the personality have been stifled behind the need to 'stop all that childish nonsense and grow up'. It has been argued that this process happens during education. Divergent thinking includes the capacity to think laterally and see multiple answers to questions (De Bono, 1995). This seems innate in young children, but very often deteriorates through an education system that tests young people against criteria where there is only one 'right' answer. Children who score 98 per cent in divergent thinking skills at pre-school level are down to 50 per cent by the time they reach of 8–10 years old (Robinson, 2010).

If the results of the divergent thinking tests demonstrate such significant deterioration at primary level (Land and Jarman, 1998), then the potential for adults to have shut their minds off from creative possibilities seems a viable explanation as to why so many don't have the confidence to believe in their own innovations. In fact, in my experience it runs deeper even than this. I have worked with a significant number of adults who don't consider themselves capable of spawning an idea, let alone consider whether it has value or not.

Education is not the only factor impacting on the lack of creativity in individual belief systems. There has been a cultural revolution in the arts generally, resulting in 'two different castes' of thinking. This revolution resulted initially in those people who (it was assumed) understood art, and those who did not. Presumptions were made that only the educated, or the intelligent, or the artistically gifted, could have a view about what art actually was. As a result, large sections of the population did not feel connected to the subject in any form. This in turn led to subdivisions separating 'high art' from 'popular art', which played out through a counter-culture that has impacted on music, literature, drama and other creative disciplines (Carey, 2005: 21–35). We have classical music and punk rock. There is theatre and pantomime. There are literary award-winning novels and fan fiction.

What is happening overall seems to be that art itself has become a debate. Is it art, or isn't it? Can a renaissance painting have any connections with the conceptual relevance of Tracey Emin's (1999) 'unmade bed'? Does the eloquent prose of a literary award-winner have more value to society than a best-seller about vampires in love? Who is qualified enough to know?

These reflections carry relevance in many spheres of life. Attitudes to art, particularly with reference to the subjective elements that make it more difficult to assess, are concerns within education (Robinson, 2001: 156). If a system requires teaching to be packaged around standardisation and conformity (Robinson and Arnica, 2016: 6–9, 68–9), then those subjects that don't have clean, neat edges need to be shoehorned into the pre-prepared boxes, the excess trimmed off and thrown into the bin. Creative writing is one subject that has been forced into the wrong-shaped box in order to make it easier to manage and understand.

The trouble with tick-boxing

The challenges partly lie in attitudes to creativity, and partly in perceptions that still linger around the creative/not creative debate.

For those teachers who do not believe they are creative, then the focus on essential skills and grammar is easy to fall back on. I have, on many occasions, stood with a teacher and delighted in some powerfully visual or energised piece of pupil writing, while the teacher has gone into rhapsodies about their correct usage of a subordinate clause.

Teachers who don't believe themselves to be creative per se are less likely to write creatively too, which means they will struggle to recognise such ability in their pupils. They will fall back on approaches that yield results that they *can* respond to. They may also not see the value of risk taking in writing (Craft et al., 2001: 57): ideas that don't develop; structures that don't work; approaches that are unusual, may all be considered a waste of time or even regarded as failures. In reality, exploring and rejecting possibilities are essential to evolving creative work. In addition to this, highly creative young people can present with challenging behaviours due to independent and non-conformist attitudes. They may not perform well in statutory tests, and are more likely to grow bored and consequently disruptive (Airs et al., 2005: 72). Being able to recognise the creativity in individual pupils, and having the ability to nurture it, is an extra advantage for teachers who engage with writing themselves.

There is no 'tick box' template to writing, but the more we try to force creative process into that box, the more it kicks and squeals. Or sometimes – and worse – it goes silent. Deprived of the air drawn from exploration and curiosity, the hapless creativity creature cannot survive. Yet, the ability to raise levels of creativity within a writing activity doesn't need to be challenging or difficult. Inspiration is the fun bit, and without inspiration there will not be motivation; motivation is what drives writers on through the trickier areas of crafting and reworking.

Blossoming ideas

I once ran a writing activity with a group of gifted children from the NAGC (National Association of Gifted Children). The task was to describe what it felt like to sit under a tree. We worked in the classroom on a Saturday afternoon, and the group – all capable and motivated – wrote enthusiastic purple-prose about leaves and birds and blue summer skies.

I then took them outside to the school field, sat them beneath real trees, and repeated the task. The results were a vivid account of the journey of an ant across bark, musings over the metal fish that was floating across 'a water-grey sky', a conversation with a tree about advancing diggers. When the parents came to collect the children, one mother spoke with tears in her eyes. 'He got so much from this', she told me. 'I'm a scientist. I can't do things like this with him. I'm just not creative.'

All I had done was to take the children outside, into a simple and familiar setting, and asked them to respond – in writing – to their observations whilst sitting under a tree.

Lcc is achievable for all (Craft, 2015: 39–56) but inventive approaches – new ways of seeing – need to be the starting point. Booker Prize-winning author John Berger (2016) explores how we have 'habits' of seeing, and that these habits tie in with convention. Very often we don't take in the detail of our surroundings because we assume we know where we are; even somewhere new consists of things we recognise and it is only when confronted with something outside our conventional experience that we actually stop and look.

Visual artists, with their need to record spaces, colours, lines and shapes, have what is described as 'thoughts without words', reacting to visual stimuli in innovate ways (Fisher, 2005: 15). Leonardo da Vinci (Gombrich, 1962, in Fisher, 2005: 15) offered up ways of re-interpreting existing shapes to create new images in the mind:

> You should look at certain walls stained with damp, or at stones of uneven colour … you will see there battles and strange figures in violent action… an infinity of things: Leonardo Da Vinci (1452–1519).

Anyone who has ever seen creatures in the clouds, dragons in fire or faces looming out of random patterns is drawing from the perceptual cognition of visual stimuli (Fisher, 2005: 15). Writers tap into that mysterious power called 'imagination' in this same way. They connect existing realities and alter them, collide them and re-shape them, looking at the world of possibilities through unusual and unpredictable connections. *What if…? How could…? Why would…?*

In order to think in more unpredictable ways, the brain needs to change focus. Looking harder and longer at something in the same direction will only produce predictable ideas. If the focus is changed and something unrelated is brought to the mix, more unusual patterns of thought are activated.

Connecting ideas

These unusual patterns of thought have relevance to connecting the unconnected. A major component in the processes of creative genius (BCC) lies in the ability to generate associations between dissimilar objects. The same can be achieved within an Icc application; this technique of connecting may not be innate in this second category, but it can be learnt.

During one of my very first school visits, I was in a resources room taking an author Q&A with a group of pupils. I was asked the usual gold nugget of a question 'Where do you get your ideas?' and did my best to explain that I see the potential for ideas everywhere. It is a channel I never tune out of. Challenging myself, I told pupils to pick out anywhere in the room and I would show them how an idea could grow from it.

I evolved various connecting possibilities around graffiti on tables, an eraser that had fallen to the floor, and a bird that flew past the window.

'Oh', said one of the boys, clearly fascinated by the process, 'so that's how your mind works.' This boy's response was equally fascinating to me. Until he had said that, I had not fully comprehended that other minds weren't naturally finding stories lurking in every corner.

One of the girls then pointed to a rather ugly box-like contraption on the ceiling. It was an electrical power base; wires and leads sprung out of it. Some led nowhere, whilst others travelled messily along the ceiling and through the walls. 'Can you tell a story about that?' she asked. I was momentarily flummoxed. The box-like contraption was not visually appealing, and the wiring systems of the school seemed both too technical and beyond my comprehension. Then I spotted a poster on the wall, advertising Book Week – the reason why I was there at all. At once the box of mad wires became part of a science-fiction scenario. It was the Brain of Ideas, evolved from a future technology that enabled the preservation of super-brains from deceased best-selling authors; an alternative to buying in 'living' authors such as myself. The concept had such an impact on the pupils, and the subsequent writing that they evolved, that I have since re-envisaged it as one of the creative exercises within this book.

However, I am more than aware that my own anecdotes are drawn from a lifetime of watching the world through what Roald Dahl describes as 'glittering eyes' (Dahl, 2013). Maybe glittering eyes have no appeal for you. All that glitter might just be annoying, like grains of grit that need to be rubbed out with a tissue. Seeing everyday things from a creative stance does not need to be so magical, or so fanciful.

I have tried the following, with positive results, with those who just feel an overtly creative view isn't something they are comfortable with.

Exercise 1: Drawing the curtains

Take a notebook and sit in a room that has a window with curtains. Write down

- The colour of the curtains.
- The pattern.
- The fabric type.

Based on those three basic observations, ask yourself the question 'If these curtains were a person, what sort of person would they be?' Gender? Personality type? Give them a name.

Wordtamer sample model

Curtains creamy beige, leaves and flower pattern, silky — have a silvery sheen. These curtains as a person would be female, someone very floaty — a bit of a dreamer. They are gentle but at times almost too delicate. Too sensitive. This person is called Isabelle.

Imagine they are writing in a diary or journal. What would they write?

Thursday (Isabelle): I can't go back to work today. Not after what happened yesterday. It's not that I'm ill, but the things John said affected me. Badly. It's all got inside my head and my thoughts keep spinning. In fact, I feel as if my whole body is spinning. Perhaps I'll go for a walk in the fields. The trees will be in bloom. Fresh air might help. At the moment I feel I could walk, and keep walking. What if I did that – what if I kept walking, and never went home…

If ideas have evolved from this, then brilliant. Even if you choose not to continue the story, you can now see that you could.

Exercise 2: Off their trolley

Choose a queue in the supermarket that is longer than usual.

Take a moment to look, surreptitiously, at the contents of someone else's trolley or basket. Also, note whether this shopper is male or female and estimate their age.

Make notes if you can (but be careful – 'super-spy' subterfuge is required) to remind yourself later of your observations. You could pretend to be annotating your shopping list, or even send yourself a text.

Based on what they are buying, what do you know about them? What sort of home do you think they live in? Can you give them a brief recent history?

Wordtamer sample model

Male, mid-thirties. Two bottles of wine — one red, one white. A bunch of rose-pink tulips. Muesli. Pack of white toilet rolls. Grapefruit. Wholemeal bread. Lives in a small modern house or maisonette. Clean, smart — nicely furnished but nothing elaborate. Is divorced or separated, and moved out of the family home to this new, more modest dwelling. Has had a couple of dates with a woman he met via a dating site and has now been invited for a meal.

Next, imagine this character arriving home at the abode you have associated them with, where they will be greeted with one of the following scenarios:

1   They have won a sizeable sum on the lottery.
2   A crime has been committed.
3   Their home has disappeared.

More ideas may have evolved from this approach. Even if you choose not to write a story beyond the character development, you can now see that you could.

Ideas about ideas

The 'Where do you get your ideas?' question is something authors are frequently asked; perhaps the questioners are hopeful of being directed to a special compartment in their own minds where all creative possibilities live. A place where the hatch can be opened and a fledgling story plucked out. If only it were that simple.

All authors will cite differing approaches to igniting ideas. P. D. James' preference is to begin with a place – a setting – from which the story evolves. Michael Morpurgo often takes an autobiographical approach, drawing inspiration from his childhood experiences. Ian Rankin finds that themes are his way into stories, generally instigated through 'BIG' stories that are making world news. Maureen Duffy considers her ideas start life as 'a little bit of grit' collected from something else she has read (all four writers discussed in *The Writing Life*, 2011).

For teachers, it can be daunting to be faced with such a multitude of starting points. What would work best? Which might be easiest to achieve?

Poet Paul Bailey (*The Writing Life*, 2011) discusses the various approaches to starting a writing task by stating 'what suits you doesn't suit me', and in my view this is not only the essence of the issue, but also a delightful positive. With such a spectrum of choices, sources of inspiration and applied technique can be specific to individuals. The 'what suits me' approach can form part of the teacher's creative toolkit too. Teachers can interpret and explore traditional and contemporary options, applying these to their own methodologies and preferences. Instead of so many alternatives feeling like mountains to climb, they can be paths to dance along. Stories can be started using characters, or plots. Even inexperienced authors can write the last line and consider what the beginning might be. They can pluck first lines from a bucket. There can be objects, props or images. There can be dramatic settings to look at, or story-moods triggered by a CD of sounds. Try everything. Something will suit you, and it might be the thing you would never, ever have thought of. Creativity happens through the unexpected. The only requirement is to be open to all possibilities.

The model teacher and the 'own goal' goof

Teacher confidence becomes increasingly important in the analysis of texts. It can be challenging to talk with authority about hooks, language choices and (perceived) author intentions, without having had personal experience of the process. I could liken this to my attempting to give a running commentary about a football match. Not only do I understand little of how the game is played, but also I have never even been to a match. No one would pay much attention to my opinion of what went wrong for the losing team. Teachers who don't write are equally unlikely to be able to offer insightful deconstruction of work by professionals.

If even spelling causes anxiety for some (particularly newly qualified) teachers (Adoniou, 2014: 144), then how much more daunting must the process of effective redrafting and editing appear?

True confidence comes from the practical understanding of what works and what doesn't (Chamberlain, 2016: 42–4). Or, put more simply: 'We can't just expect children to write a poem about a seal, unless we've written a poem about a seal ourselves' (Katie Hadlow, Redlands Primary School, Fareham, pers. comm., 2016). The requirement for reluctant teachers to turn to writing may be perceived by some as an excuse to turn instead to drink, but evidence supports the benefits not just to subsequent pupils' writing, but also to the teacher themselves.

In discussing the success of a two-year project working with teachers' identities as writers, Teresa Cremin (Eyres, 2016) states:

> As they [teachers] have explored ways of integrating elements of writer identity in their own classroom, my strong impression is that their confidence to see themselves as writers has increased along with their willingness to fold this aspect of their identity into their pedagogy. And somewhere along the way the binary distinction between 'writer' and 'not a writer' becomes irrelevant.

A teacher's tale

As teachers grapple with their own writing, they work their way through creative process, climbing inside their own stories.

English at the Crossroads (Ofsted, 2009: 5), in identifying the differing standards between reading and writing, saw significant improvement when teachers wrote themselves:

> In the primary schools visited, standards in writing were considerably lower than in reading. Teachers who were confident as writers themselves, and who could demonstrate how writing is composed, taught it effectively.

Teachers who write not only gain insight into technique, but also identify better with the struggles all writers encounter. Along with all the highs, lows and in betweens, they experiment with ways to trigger ideas, appreciate the value of the incubation period and understand the demands linked to drafting and editing (Morgan, 2017: 49).

The notion of teachers being writers is being built into professional learning experiences for teachers (Street and Stang, 2017: 63) and this supports teachers' identities as writers but there are still a range of ways to engage with writing: should it be a solitary occupation performed at home with 'secret' stories that get hidden in drawers or stuffed at the back of bookcases? Should teachers embrace the practice and work in groups, sharing ideas with each other? Should teachers always be modelling writing, working alongside pupils?

My own rule of thumb is that I would never ask a pupil or student to take on any task that I haven't trialled myself – but I'm a writer. I've tried everything and I've got a lot to draw from. I also get a thrill from writing. Any sort of writing is a happy place for me.

Pupils who are reluctant writers grow up. Some of them become teachers. Becoming a teacher doesn't mean they magically transform and see all the thrills and spills of writing as a worthwhile way to spend their time. Added to that, teachers may not have much spare time. Being overly busy with planning, teaching, marking and managing can dampen creative process like a downpour on firework night. Even those who enjoy writing may struggle to nurture the sparks of their imagination.

However, teachers might catch glimmers of hope from the revelation that even Michael Morpurgo (*The Writing Life*, 2011) does not believe himself to be gifted with imagination. Morpurgo explains how he makes creative connections between everyday experiences and applies this to another passion – that of history, which in his case particularly relates to themes around war. Morpurgo's marrying of everyday experience connecting with historical interests was a key trigger for one of his most successful novels. Morpurgo (*The Writing Life*, 2011) had watched a shy boy talking animatedly to a horse on a farm. The horse appeared to be listening. Morpurgo created a narrative from the point of view of a horse. This story has its origins on a farm. The boy and the horse have a special friendship – a bond – that pulls them through the horrors of war. The resultant novel, *War Horse* (Morpurgo, 2007), has been adapted for both stage and screen.

This brilliant best-seller of an idea came from connecting something Morpurgo knew (war history) with something he observed (the horse and the boy) and then lighting the touch paper by asking *what if* a horse told his own experiences about what it was like to be used by the army in the First World War.

Writing at home enables a less confident teacher to work without judgement or criticism, as well as moving them closer to a more 'real' writer's experience. In thinking like a writer, teachers can find a methodology that suits them. Initial scribblings and early drafts can later be shared with pupils. This more 'real' approach will suggest adaptable activities that might be viable within the constraints of a classroom.

As confidence develops, teachers can move to modelling their ideas and early drafts in front of a class, so that pupils can see that writing is something the teacher does too. This then evolves to teachers being able to work alongside pupils, working on new ideas with their groups. Writing creatively becomes collaborative, and achievable (Cremin et al., 2015: 93–5; Cremin and Locke, 2017).

Teachers' writing doesn't need to be an awesome display that explodes colours across the sky. The solitary sparkler at the back of the garden glows with just as much delight.

Try this at home

The following activity utilises creative approaches discussed in the previous sections. It includes triggers for inspiration drawn from:

- memory (autobiography)
- an existing published work of fiction (work perceived as 'good' and therefore credible)
- a random element plucked from non-fiction (an existing reality).

The three elements are connected together in ways that might not previously be considered, moving away from predictable outcomes and enabling divergent thinking. Taking the earlier concept of creativity with a lower-case 'c', this can be applied to writing. Teachers can start out as writers with a lower case 'w'. I have trialled the approaches and worked through them myself. My imperfect offering is followed by the actual activity.

Trialled approach (approx 40 minutes)

I sat on the sofa, writing on rough paper (for the purpose of the exercise it will be better to use rough paper of some sort, rather than official-looking writing books – this is partly because ideas will be cut up and partly because the more formal or 'special' the paper, the more daunting the starting point can be).

Autobiography – evoke a memory from childhood; a time around the age of the pupils being worked with. Don't edit or angst over this paragraph. It is merely a starting point.

My childhood memory was a time when I lived in Singapore. I was ten years old and my brother's friend, Malcolm, had decided to throw my beloved puppet, a dragon called Dennis, over a high fence into the field beyond our garden. This field was forbidden to us children. The long grass was a potential hiding place for a stealth of snakes, lizards and other bitey sorts of beasts. Should I save Dennis, or let him fester forever in the field of fiends? Loyalty got the better of me and with no thought for my own wellbeing, I scrambled over the fence. Miraculously, I found Dennis amongst the long grass, and climbed back to the safety of our garden. Only then did I discover that I was covered from head to toe with giant red soldier ants.

My favourite sentence from this written childhood memory:

The long grass was a potential hiding place for a stealth of snakes, lizards and other bitey sorts of beasts.

Descriptive sentence from a favourite children's or young-adult book (depending on age group teacher works with):

My chosen book was *James and the Giant Peach* and the sentence from a random page was: 'It hit the water with a colossal splash and sank like a stone' (Dahl, 2016: 55).

Random non-fiction phrase, taken from an object or article in the room:

My non-fictional phrase or sentence came from the packaging on a fire-log in the front room where I was working, and it read: KEEP OUT OF REACH OF CHILDREN. Choose from labels, newspapers, packaging etc.

The story-starter that emerged, written without editing. Again, just the beginning of a beginning:

> **KEEP OUT: CHILDREN**
> Seb stood by the river's edge, puzzling over the sign. It seemed to have been stuck randomly at the edge of the field. And why just children? If the field was dangerous for children, it would surely be unsafe for adults too? He looked across at the long grass. It was beautiful, tinged with soft golds and greens. Seb didn't think it looked dangerous, although, of course, it could have hidden a stealth of snakes or lizards. At that moment something whirled towards him, moving in a high arc across the sky. He dodged sideways and it plunged into the river, hitting the water with a colossal splash. Someone had hurled a rock at him. Before he had time to consider who, or why, Seb saw more movement. A gang of children moved stealthily towards him. They seemed

beautiful, like the grass, tinged with soft golds and greens. As they grew closer, Seb got the sense that he knew them, but he wasn't sure where from. The leader smiled. Seb saw her sharp fangs and strange scaly-patterns across her skin. He suddenly knew what the sign had really meant.

In my sample, I didn't simply repeat the three sentences I'd 'collected' (underlined in the above example) – I altered them to work with the emerging story, but what has remained are the key elements, particularly in terms of setting from the childhood memory. There is a still a field with long grass. There are still references to snakes and lizards. The addition of Dahl's 'splash' gave me an inciting moment (the point when something triggers a change and things begin to happen). The KEEP AWAY warning, randomly chosen and copied from my fire log, turned out to be the premise for the whole idea and has become the title. It is the children themselves who are dangerous. They are dragon children (inspired by the lizards). Who knows what such children might do?

Exercise

You will need pen, paper, scissors, and a favourite book written for the age category in which you teach.

Write down a (brief) childhood memory on rough paper. One or two paragraphs will be sufficient, and just draw from memory, not fact. No one is checking you for accuracy. Highlight one significant sentence, either because you like it, or because it feels important.

Rewrite the highlighted sentence on a separate sheet.

Take a favourite fictional children's book and open it at random; flick through a few pages if desired. Choose a descriptive sentence (not dialogue) that entices you, and copy it down beneath your highlighted 'memory' sentence.

Take a sentence or phrase from something non-fictional in the room you are in. This might be an extract from a news article, a television guide, or even a sign or label. Copy this down beneath the other two sentences.

Cut out the three sentences then move them around, considering how they might connect, and what order they might best connect in.

You don't need to make any decisions, just ask yourself questions. *What if...? How could...? Who might...?* If you can't get all three to connect but an idea is coming through by combining two, then that's fine. There are no rules, only possibilities.

Take a new sheet of paper and let a story idea start. The idea should be inspired by your three sentences, but it doesn't need to repeat them in either specific form, or any form at all. I personally use a freewriting technique; just writing without stopping or editing and this is generally the most effective for the majority of people, but you may be someone who prefers to edit as you go. If that's the case, work like that. The idea will be growing as you pause and reflect.

You might find yourself wondering, or worrying, about where the plot is going. It doesn't matter. If your intention is to use it to show *your* work to your pupils, then you have enough. If you want to take it further and try to shape and structure, then apply plot and character techniques. For plot, perhaps experiment with evolving the idea using mindmaps, and then plot a timeline:

Seb Williams: age 11 – Story set small town, river (where children have been disappearing). Backdrop mountains Inactive volcano. (Ancient). Genre fantasy/quest/magic realism.

For character development, ask the character who they are, then write down what they tell you:

> I am Seb Williams. I am 11 years old. I'm no good at ANYTHING. My big sister Bella is really smart and I know my baby sister Daisy will grow up to be AMAZING!!! The only thing people notice about me is my red curly hair, which I HATE. I'm into lizards and want one as a pet but Bella says that having dead flies in the fridge would be disgusting and Mum says it would mean me and Bella would fight even more. Mum can't stand the fighting, especially now she is so busy with Daisy. I expect that's why Dad left, because of all the fighting. He doesn't say that, but then he doesn't visit much either, so there's not much chance for speaking.

Trust me. And if you can't trust me, trust the process.

This is the subconscious mind at play. Everyone who can write, and access their own memories, can write creatively. It is not time, or circumstance, but our own lack of belief that causes our biggest blocks. Now, has anyone seen that packet of sparklers?

Job Vacancy: School Teacher (only the Very Brilliant need apply)

Description Applicants will have the confidence to access their own imaginations and evolve original, innovative writing. They will have an active understanding of creative process and sufficient skills to encourage pupils to experiment with approaches in the context of stories and writing outputs. Must be highly skilled in numeracy and literacy. Must have good working knowledge of cross-curricular subjects, including a high level of competency with ICT. An excellent communicator, the successful candidate will etc., etc., etc.

References

Adoniou, M. (2014) What should teachers know about spelling, *Literacy* 48(3): 144–58

Airs, J., Wright, J. Williams, L. and Adkins R. (2005) The performing arts, in R. Jones, and D. Wyse (eds) *Creativity in the Primary Curriculum*. Abingdon: David Fulton

Berger, J., presenter (2016) *The Art of Looking*. BBC4 television, 6 November

Bono, de E. (1996) *Serious Creativity*. London: Harper Collins

Carey, J. (2005) *What Good are the Arts?* London: Faber and Faber

Chamberlain, L. (2016) *Inspiring Writing*. London: Sage

Craft, A. (2015) *Creativity, Education and Society: Writings of Anna Craft*, comp. K. Chappell, T. Cremin and B. Jeffrey. London: Institute of Education Press

Craft, A., Jeffrey, B. and Leibling, M. (2001) *Creativity in Education*. London: Continuum

Cremin, T. and Locke, T., eds (2017) *Writer Identity*. London: Routledge

Cremin, T., Reedy, D., Bearne, E. and Dombey, B. (2015) *Teaching English Creatively* (2nd edn). Abingdon: Routledge

Csikszentmihalyi, M. (1997) *Creativity* (2nd edn). New York: Harper Collins

Dahl, R. (2013) *The Minpins*. London: Puffin

Dahl, R. (2016) *James and the Giant Peach.* London: Puffin

Emin, T. (1999) Tracey Emin: My Bed. www.saatchigallery.com/artists/artpages/tracey_emin_my_bed.htm (accessed 14 March 2017)

Eyres, I. (2016) Call yourself a writer, *Teachers as Writers.* www.teachersaswriters.org/general/call-yourself-a-writer/#more-342 (accessed 3 January 2017)

Fisher, R. (2005) *Teaching Children to Think* (2nd edn). Cheltenham: Nelson Thornes

Land, G. and Jarman, B. (1998) *Breakpoint and Beyond.* Scottsdale, AZ: Leadership 2000 Inc.

Morgan, D. N. (2017) 'I'm not a good writer': supporting teachers' writing identities in a university course, in T. Cremin and T. Locke (eds) *Writer Identity.* Abingdon: Routledge

Morpurgo, M. (2007) *War Horse.* London: Egmont

Office for Standards in Education (Ofsted) (2009) *English at the Crossroads.* London: Ofsted. www.ofsted. gov.uk (accessed 12 December 2016)

Robinson, K. (2001) *Out of Our Minds.* Oxford: Capstone

Robinson, K. (2010) Changing education paradigms, *RSA Animate.* www.ted.com/talks/ken_robinson_changing_education_paradigms (accessed 28/12/2016)

Robinson, K. and Arnica, L. (2016) *Creative Schools.* London: Penguin

Street, C. and Stang, K. K. (2017) Addressing resistance: encouraging in-service teachers to think of themselves as writers, in T. Cremin and T. Locke (eds) *Writer Identity.* Abingdon: Routledge

The Writing Life: Authors Speak (2011) Author interviews with Sarah O'Reilly (CD ROM). London: British Library Board.

CHAPTER 6

CREATIVE PLACES AND CREATIVE SPACES

Visualisation and the power of purposeful thinking

The sound of silence

Our lives are full of electronic babble.

TV   video   music   radio   text-tones   mobile-phones   bleep   tweet   never-sleep

Then there is the human contribution.

SHOUTS and prattle, songs and gabble, laugh, jabber, screeeam, blabber, murmur
whisper snore zzz

Most children have been bombarded with noise from the moment they added their own primal scream to the mix. Maybe the television is always on. Maybe someone is always talking on their mobile. There are toys that burp and screech and whirr. We encourage it. It stimulates and excites.

Schools are noisy places too (Cremin and Myhill, 2012: 197). The chatter of young voices. Instruction from the teacher. Questions. Answers. That happy buzz is generations away from the long-ago land of more formal teaching when learning meant sitting still, listening and following instructions. Silence, in this long-ago sense, is taboo in contemporary learning. The emphasis now is on pupils speaking out and speaking up, sharing ideas and having the confidence to be heard.

Yet, as a writer I sometimes crave silence. Silence helps me to think more deeply – to gain clarity and focus. To an outsider, I am gazing out through the window, watching the autumn morning. Inside my mind I am being channelled through a changing landscape, strange-shaped leaves floating and settling, every new leaf ready to be turned.

Internationally acclaimed filmmaker and writer David Lynch (2006) describes the process of meditating on ideas through the metaphor of fishing. If you only want to fill your net with minnows, then stay in shallow water, but for the big fish – the powerful possibilities – you have to go deeper.

Silence enables insight. Through silence, we can hear ourselves thinking (Cameron, 1997: 172–4).

To achieve this deepened focus for young writers I have devised a mix of meditation and visualisation, swept up into leaf-mounds of creative techniques for schools.

Meditation has something of a bad press within a school's context. Alongside mindfulness, both are sometimes perceived to be associated with religion. In a secular society this can suggest letters home, permission to attend and all the ensuing complications. I once set up a series of meditation classes, expanding imaginations with first-year creative writing undergraduates. A student dropped out because she had strong Christian beliefs and was worried any 'new ways' of thinking might wreak havoc with her views.

Although the fostering of new ways of thinking seems the central value of creative endeavour, worries around outcomes need acknowledgement and respect. The above student's concerns were valid based on her beliefs associated with meditative practice. My response needed to both acknowledge and accept her concerns, whilst additionally encouraging her to explore her own responses.

Education can be seen to be organic: evolving. Change is always possible. The essential function of schools is to facilitate learning (Robinson and Arnica, 2016: 62–70) but some approaches assume the basics must become second nature before learners can move into unknown territories (Langer, 1997: 2). However, these 'basics' can also stifle interest. Who would want to be led towards unknown territories that they don't care about in the first place? Elements of meditative learning could become intrinsic as methodologies, not bypassing the basics but weaving along them like ivy on a red brick wall. If meditation, and the practice of silence, can be embedded into the school day, then the act of reflection both before and after a task can become as normalised as picking up a pen to write with.

The space for spaces

Silence, used effectively, is a valuable pedagogic tool. It is also free. Dr Helen E. Lees (2012) separates silence into two types: 'weak silence' and 'strong silence'. Weak silence is about power and domination, achieved by the 'be quiet, I'm in charge' approach. Strong silence has its own power and its own recorded benefits in the context of schools and learning (Lees, 2012: 59). One practical approach to integrate silence into school practice has been the implementation of designated tranquil spaces. These can take the form of sheds, or pods. There might be 'silent tents' or 'thinking gardens'. Schools who find room for such spaces report they have seen improved self-esteem, higher test results and enhancement of the overall school ethos (Lees, 2012: 101).

Developing space and a physical place for thinking is deeply appealing in the context of incubating ideas for writing projects.

Roald Dahl famously had a shed where all his writing was achieved. Other contemporary children's writers hide out in barns (Berlie Doherty, pers. comm., 2016), or adapt pods and portable studios (Ali Sparkes, pers. comm., 2016). Others stay in bed, energise themselves with copious amounts of muesli, and write until the muse is sated:

> What I hate most is being interrupted when I am fully in the zone and working hard. I do not even interrupt myself to eat or go to the bathroom until it is really quite urgent. I call this the muesli phase of editing. This is because I just keep a pack of open muesli beside me and that is all I eat – in handfuls as I am editing (I can't deal with bowls or spoons as that breaks my flow. I find the oats gives me the energy I need to continue and the fruit a little bit of sugar boost which keeps me focused. When I come out of the editing process perhaps after five–eight hours, there is a big mess all around me! But a bit of hoovering sorts that out:)
>
> I always write in bed on a laptop. So obviously the sheets often need to be shaken onto the floor before the hoovering starts! I find writing in bed is the best. This is because it stops blood pooling in my ankles if I am in a sitting position. Also I can support my back with big cushions – best of all it stops me from getting cold. Because I am immobile for such long periods of time I get very very cold.
>
> I'm sure writing is awful for one's health – but I try to walk for an hour or more every day to offset this :(
>
> (Sarah Mussi, pers. comm., 2016)

Established authors are generally highly motivated with an innate talent for writing. They also have time demands, and a deadline, all pushing and pressing up against their processes. Any retreat into silence will be embraced as a gift. The mere provision of such space for school-age pupils – particularly reluctant learners – wouldn't, in itself, unleash volcanic eruptions of brilliance. 'Space time' needs to enable structured, guided silence that focuses on, and enhances, the initial idea. And it doesn't always need that special physical place. The most special place of all is inside our own minds.

From my own experiences, going into schools and engaging pupils with silence, there are constant interruptions. Enter my world, for a moment, whilst I'm using silent visualisation as preparation for a writing task. The classroom lights have been dimmed and LED tealight candles are lit to evoke atmosphere. The pupils are imagining a key scene from the beginning of a proposed story. It has been suggested that they close their eyes, to help them concentrate: A hand goes up. 'Excuse me, I have to leave now for my music lesson.' The classroom door opens. 'Oh, Hi, sorry to interrupt … I just need to pop these books on the shelves there.' Another hand waves in the air. 'Please Miss, can I go to the toilet?' Outside a year group are practising (loudly) for sports day. Two staff members are (loudly) discussing the end of term play at the back of the class. A boy with curly red hair fidgets and frowns as he announces, out of the blue, 'I've lost my lunch box.'

It might sound impossible to create a true silence experience in schools, but in fact it is often very easy. The 'secret' is to be clear about the expectation, and guide pupils to focus as they retreat into their imaginations.

My aim, then, is not to create an external space for silence, but to instil a mindset that enables silence within the individual. Pupils enter their own zone.

Even established authors may not always embrace that gift of silence. Some like to write with music playing because it cuts out extraneous noise (Diana Kimpton, pers. comm., 2016). Others enhance the 'background music' approach and have the music itself as a trigger:

> I also use music. The entire Slated trilogy and much since then have been written to the same Mark Knopfler sound track: the first few bars of music begin and it seems to tune my brain in that it is writing time.
>
> (Teri Terry, pers. comm., 2016)

Others choose commuter trains, or bustling cafes, and I have written perfectly happily on a crowded beach on a summer's day. The essential element is to be in 'the zone' – something Czikszentmihalyi (2002) describes as 'the state of Flow'. When in Flow, the mind is not running around madly with no focus or purpose, but is instead so immersed in a specific task that it is able to cut out background chatter and all interruption. I am writing this in my office at the University of Winchester and a door has just banged. A banter of students is spilling out from a lecture. They are laughing and talking – now they have gone. I heard them, but I didn't hear them. I only shifted my focus slightly to invite them into this paragraph.

But 'zone'
should be honed...

It seems extra-ordinary that we expect young writers to explore creative depths without any mental preparation. My approach combines 'strong' or purposeful silence with visualisation. Developing a visual imagination is a powerful learning tool, and it produces particularly vivid results for creative writers. 'Memories' can be created in the mind, and used as a powerful stimulus for writing (Fisher, 2005: 193). I guide pupils through a place, asking them to notice sound, movement, and visual detail from the point of view of a pre-created character.

'Your character is at the foot of a mountain, an extinct volcano. Look around. Is it day or night? Hot or cold? Is the ground rocky, or smooth? Are there any sounds? Is there a path up this mountain, or some way to climb it? Does the place feel welcoming, or menacing? How are they feeling?' As pupils picture their character in a specific place, they gather descriptive detail just as powerfully as if they were beside the mountain with a notebook in hand. In fact, they gather more. We react to image faster than either the spoken or written word; many of the greatest minds of our times, including Einstein, have had their most genius inventions dancing through their minds as images rather than words (Michalko, 2001).

The subject of the session I am running, and the intentions and outcomes, are always established at the start. This generally includes confirming genre, setting and character. Pens, pencils, erasers, sharpeners, rough paper and 'neat' paper (or writing books) all need handing out. For a true visualisation lesson to work effectively it needs to run as a seamless flow, with as little possibility for distraction as possible (Waite, 2014). If there are blinds, I pull them down, and I use LED tealight candles to calm the room. I sometimes use music, although only music that can act as 'wallpaper'. The sound mustn't intrude on the imagery or suggest action.

Structured visualisation offers a multi-modal approach to writing, with its combination of thinking, discussion, planning, strong silence, visualising, writing and sharing. It also guarantees ownership of ideas. Drawing from the subconscious through focused imagining sparks originality. Those volcanoes can erupt at last. Great fires will explode from their centres. Molten lava will rain down from the ceiling. Crystals will form on all the desks. Can that really be happening? Or is it all in the mind?

Exercise: Guided visualisation script

Ensure all pencils, books erasers etc. are on the desks. I generally have both scrap paper for planning, and writing books or lined paper for the story elements that occur after each visualisation.

Props: LED tealights, ideally sufficient for one per pupil, or at least one per table.

Introduce writing topic and associated material (for instance, if the piece of writing is to be derived from an idea about dragons and heroes, then this should be foregrounded through either class or group discussion). Provide relevant word choices and/or images to provoke imaginative responses.

Pupils consider main characters and settings and make rough notes around possible story ideas. Agree a 2 minute silence.

Hand out LED candles; ideally pull down blinds and turn out lights.

Pupils put down pens etc., let go of all distractions. They may choose to focus on a candle, or close their eyes.

Guide pupils verbally through the scene, help them see what they need to be seeing.

Allow the silence to 'happen' then, at the end of the prescribed time, quietly tell pupils to write the scene they have just imagined.

Feedback on what was written – look for descriptive details and visual qualities in the writing.

As pupils get more tuned to the technique, they become able to visualise independently at any point when they get blocked or need to enhance their idea.

References

Cameron, J. (1997) *The Vein of Gold*. London: Pan Books

Cremin, T. and Myhill, D. (2012) *Writing Voices*. Abingdon: Routledge

Czikszentmihalyi, M. (2002) *Flow*. London: Rider – Random House Group

Fisher, R. (2005) *Teaching Children to Think* (2nd edn). Cheltenham: Nelson Thornes

Langer, E. J. (1997) *The Power of Mindful Learning*. New York: Perseus Books

Lees, H. E. (2012) *Silence in Schools*. London: Institute of Education Press

Lynch, D. (2006) *Catching the Big Fish*. New York: Tarcher Penguin

Michalko, M. (2001) *Cracking Creativity*. Berkeley CA: Ten Speed Press

Mussi, S. (2016) email extract

Robinson, K. and Aronica, L. (2016) *Creative Schools*. London: Penguin

Teri, T. (2016) email extract

Waite, J. (2014) Blank in the mind, *Writing in Education* 64: 15–21

PART II

THE TRAINING GROUND
Learning the craft

In the writing of established authors, everything on the page will have been chosen deliberately. Every word, every sentence, every paragraph, every pause is scrutinised. Nothing is there by chance. The author has focused on technique, using crafting skills to shape their sculpture of words. That's why the writing works. By identifying the specifics of these skills, teachers (and pupils) can explore how stories are made.

There is no established order for these skills to be introduced. In an ideal writerly world they should all be viewed at the same time. Like a troupe of dancers, each element is part of a choreographed piece. They flow together even when someone steps forward to dance solo.

But the joy is, when viewed separately, the dance still makes sense.

Let me introduce you to the solo performers:

- setting
- character
- plot
- dialogue
- suspense.

Sneak in, and enjoy the rehearsals in the training ground.

CHAPTER 7

SETTING THE SCENE

How to write effective scenes as backdrops to fiction

Every picture tells a story

Visual thinking is not the sole domain of the artist. Theoretical physicist Albert Einstein (1879–1955) created metaphors through visualisation and used these to 'problem solve' his ideas. He also invented imaginary worlds with different rules, which enabled him to see new perspectives that he could then re-envisage within the real world. This was how he came up with the theory of relativity (Michalko, 2001: 216–25).

The value of training young minds to think in pictures has an obvious cross-curricular value, but its impact on writing can be dramatic. Words themselves are not visual, but when writers translate powerful imagery into words effectively, they pass these pictures into the minds of their readers.

Visual art – a painting or a sculpture, for instance – requires a personal response, but too often viewers make assumptions about the art they are responding too. They don't look for long enough. They see what they think they are seeing (Fisher, 2015: 211–12). The mind needs to be trained first in how to look at art, then how to respond to it. From this, we can make the links between image and writing.

'Every picture tells a story' is a cliché most of us are familiar with, but I want to draw ideas from an opposite approach: 'every story tells a picture'. Using setting as the starting point, the written painting of the place will have impact on all aspects of the emerging story.

Where am I?

Characters don't exist in empty spaces. Everybody has to *be* somewhere and if the author doesn't paint this 'somewhere' with words, then the reader has to fill in the gaps with images from their own experience. If their interpretation doesn't connect with the author's intention, at some point the reader is going to get horribly surprised. The lane they imagined to be sunlit and leafy turns out to be a twisty, sordid and sinister track. The castle with its crumbling towers that evolved in the reader's mind's eye suddenly has a character skipping confidently up the golden staircase.

Authors need to supply as much information as is necessary in order that the reader can be on the same journey as the character. Whatever the character can see, the reader needs to see it too, but there is more than that. To write a convincing scene that includes setting, the author should know everything that is around; they don't then use everything – they use as much (or as little) as is necessary to invite the reader into their own created backdrop. The best way to achieve this is for writers to draw from their visual imagination.

What you see is what you get

We can start with just simply learning how to look.

The use of visual art as a stimulus for writing can be traced back to the 1960s, when Alec Clegg (1964) devised an approach using a piece of visual art, which pupils studied and then made an immediate response through descriptive writing. Clegg offered a similar approach using music. In recognising this as an early attempt to link writing with the arts (Jones and Wyse, 2004: 21) this was considered successful, but at the same time was seen as restrictive in terms of the activity being 'teacher designated'. In a project focused on fostering creativity, it didn't embrace the multitude of ways that young learners find inspiration. Andrew Green (2004: 47–8) suggests guided writing frames for weaker writers, set against a more open approach where pupils respond to the characters in pictures. *Who are they? What might they want? What are they feeling, and how do you know?*

These oppositional standpoints can be brought together, capturing both the guided writing approach and simultaneously enabling more open responses. I have evolved a session that aims to achieve this, starting with a black and white image of a setting – no characters.

Without colour, pupils are challenged to discuss in more detail what this setting might be like, and gradually 'paint in' the colours with their own suggestions. I also add sound, sometimes weather sounds (BBC Sound Effects Library, 1993), sometimes something more suspenseful (Schulze, 2016) depending on the genres, styles and atmospheres that need to be evolved. As with Clegg's early connections with writing and art forms, this combines music, sound and image. This method restricts initial responses by attaching my own focus, but then applies an 'open-framed' (Green, 2004) approach through the addition of colour, which is then followed by the introduction of characters created either collaboratively or independently.

Fisher (2015: 212) talks about using art to provoke philosophical debate in schools, and this form of extended questioning can also impact on writing, giving a depth and morality to the ideas drawn from visual responses. Fisher suggests pupils take 3–5 minutes just looking, then make scribbled notes, moving away from the image and viewing it from different perspectives. The teacher then asks questions, and lets questions emerge. What emotions are being stirred? What is curious, or puzzling? In what ways could this be the scene for some sort of action, and what narrative forms could be evoked from it?

What is happening here is that the mind is being fed by the imagery (Fisher, 1996), and stories can evolve while the imagination is in this hungry, receptive state.

Well-chosen pictures provoke ready questions that stimulate discourse. However, responding to strong imagery is not the same as thinking visually and doesn't necessarily give the ownership and originality that motivates young writers. It also doesn't mean that the writing itself offers visual impact to the reader. That is where craft skills, and control of writing, come in.

Dumping-down

The term 'info dump' applied to writing means, literally, that the scene has too much information. Everything has been dumped in, and the reader has to wade through this forest of detail, hoping for glimpses of blue sky between the branches. Young writers can get lost in their own purple-prose, but they are generally more discerning with the material they choose to read. In conversation with the children's commissioning editor of a major publishing house, she reflected on how feedback from young writers showed them as becoming bored, restless and complaining that 'nothing is happening' when a piece is overly descriptive (Beverley Birch, pers. comm., 2011).

A beautiful stage set with no actors would soon have the audience shuffling in their seats, but this sense that 'nothing is happening' has sometimes been re-interpreted as stories for young readers needing to have very little description. It is worth casting a glance in the direction of one of the masters of children's storytelling, Roald Dahl.

Dahl's vivid visual imagination paints extraordinary scenes with words. The extract below is actually taking place against a backdrop of sunrise, but the characters don't stop to enjoy the view. They are moving past it, above it, through it. This is setting, in children's fiction, at its very best:

> He leapt over a dozen rivers. He went rattling over a great forest, then down into the valley and up over a range of hills as bare as concrete, and soon he was galloping over a desolate wasteland that was not quite of this earth. The ground was flat and pale yellow. Great lumps of blue rock were scattered around, and dead trees stood everywhere, like skeletons. The moon had long since disappeared and now the dawn was breaking. Sophie, still peering out from the blanket, saw suddenly ahead of her a great craggy mountain.
>
> (Dahl, 2016: 13–14)

If Einstein was a genius in physics, Dahl was a genius at writing. In this scene it is clear he has visualised his setting just as much as Einstein must have visualised his own fantasy lands. Dahl knows exactly where his character is, and how his character is experiencing her environment. He has given just enough setting detail to enable the reader to go with Sophie and The BFG on their journey. He hasn't info-dumped, but he hasn't dumbed it down either.

A sense of place

If we physically visit a real place, we do not react to that scene all in one go. We experience it in small details. Perhaps the smell hits us first. We may have a sense of colours. A dart of movement near a pile of autumn leaves catches our attention, although it is gone before we can be sure what it is:

> The air in the garden smelt damp. Leaves had been raked together across the grass, piled like a soft gold mountain. Something thin and green scuttered out from the mound and disappeared behind a straggle of bushes.

This is the 'felt sense' of the setting (Gendlin, 1982: 32). The initial experience of an autumn garden has been re-captured in writing, bringing the place into focus but without overwhelming the reader (Boulter, 2007), enabling action to move amongst the visual detail.

This 'felt sense' works on places we have known, and from where we can draw on our stores of memories, experiences and senses.

In depicting the garden, there may have been a range of choices that offered potential for the above three sentences. Choose scenarios that pupils will be familiar with, and come up with a list of words that capture a typical outdoor space. Mine is a garden in a small town, but maybe concreted courtyards will work better with city-born children. Some pupils may more easily recognise a communal space, or a lavish overgrown wilderness. The main thing is to not make assumptions, but to collect the information. Identify:

1. An outside space.
2. The time of year.
3. The weather.
4. Time of day.

Then evolve a list that incorporates senses, sounds, colours and specific visual detail.

Autumn, damp and drizzly, early morning:
Grey sky   Damp   Lawn   Grass   Leaves   Mounds   Bush   Trees   Branches Gold   Brown   Rake   Wheelbarrow   Rustling   Soggy   Soft   Sodden   Red

The list can help understand the scene, and to underpin the essential detail that will enable a 'found sense' to fill in the gaps. Discuss something simple that happens in this place – a seemingly insignificant movement or action.

A bird flies   A cat creeps   A child runs   A mouse scurries

When pupils write their scene they draw from the list, from their own memories and from their imaginations. The exercise is not a 'tick box' way to incorporate particular words, but a starting point from which they can apply their 'found sense' and innate creativity.

Stephen King (2001: 204) explains how he draws from memory for his scenes in fiction, taking places he has already visited then re-envisaging them through a visualisation that he describes as 'hypnotic recall'; this enables him to access sensory memories such as smell, taste and touch, woven in with the visual detail.

Growing ideas through discussion around familiar objects can be a starting point for creating settings in fiction; the teacher suggests an object, such as a tree, adding extra detail as children imagine *their* memory of what makes a tree. New ideas around how to describe a tree in words evolve collaboratively (Corbett, 2009: 11).

This is successful when pupils recognise the object and can therefore expand something they already have associations with, but how well can even older pupils evolve an inactive volcano on a misty day if they've never actually been to one? There can again be an input of images and sounds, and an awareness of weather and time of day. Pupils can make the associations between what they do already know, and connect these with a place they may never have visited.

Patricia Highsmith (2014: np) considers that setting must have the clarity of a photograph. There should be no 'foggy spots'. Foggy spots would lose the credibility not just of the story, but also of the writer. Not every detail needs to be crammed into the writing, but should any reader ever get the author in a corner, snarling aggressively and demanding 'what else is there?', then the author should be able to recount that scene as if they've been there, even when they haven't. In fact, in good writing the reader would never even ask the question. They know the writer knows. That's why they trust them. That's why they are willing to spend their valuable time reading on.

The process of scene-building has additional challenges when asking young writers to imagine fantasy or science-fictional worlds. Prior to starting a session drawing from these genres, I provide images of strange terrains, mountain ranges, waterfalls, cratered landscapes – even total darkness – to set up a range of options. This can all follow the same patterns as with Corbett's tree (2009) or my 'garden' exercise, but offering more alien creative possibilities.

Moving on

Once images and ideas have been gathered, setting and detail can interact with character (see Chapter 8). For more advanced levels of writing, visual detail can continue to be dripped in, sometimes from the initial list but sometimes as part of a moving scene that now interacts with character and plot.

> Seb sniffed the damp air. It still held the scent of last-night's fireworks. He kicked at a mound of soggy leaves. Something small and fast scuttered out from the bottom and darted behind a straggle of bushes. Seb wanted to look more closely but Mum hammered on the kitchen window. "Seb? What are you doing? If you don't come in and get organised you'll miss the school bus."
>
> Ten minutes later, Seb was out on the street.
>
> A gang of three boys from his sister's year were messing about by the bus stop. One of them called across to Seb, "Hey Curly, cool haircut."
>
> Seb pretended he hadn't heard. His red hair always went frizzy in this sort of weather. He slowed down, scuffing more leaves. Then he stopped. "That's weird…" he muttered. Something green lay twisted up among the browns and golds. It was cracked and scaly, like a thin empty bag. Except, it had tiny clawed legs and a lizard-like head.

Mean, magical or mysterious: scenes as entities

In creating a story from setting, the scene can manifest as a character in itself. It has moods and temperaments. The terrain has a backstory. This place has needs and desires, even if these are purely environmental. Atmospheres evolve, and the setting itself interacts with the time of day and the time of year.

Think about words that describe a mountain:

Jagged   Craggy   Rugged

Consider names for the mountain:

The Misty Mountain   Melancholy Mountain   Mountain of Mystery

Choose one and consider how this mountain might look, and how it might use its terrain to get what it wants.

Anywhere environmental can be evolved in this way, from bogs and forests to rivers and oceans. Buildings can exert their own personalities too, offering up settings that impact on the narrative:

Derelict	*Empty*	*Lonely*
The barn that bled	*A house of hope*	*The Watching Tower*

Villages, schools, dystopian wastelands, forests, tower blocks and even boiler rooms can all be evocative spaces waiting to be filled with stories (Smith et al., 2015: 43–8). Create the scene and wait to see who walks in through the frame.

Joining the dots

Making scenes can be collaborative activities; the substance develops as pupils add in detail drawn from their own memories and experiences.

Using creative process, create a class setting that involves a river. Show images of rivers, and discuss where your class river is. Explore a range of options, including countryside and towns or even alien landscapes. Choose a type of river and a setting. Write a class list of things you might notice at the river, then try the following exercise.

Exercise: Setting the scene

- Imagine the river, decide in groups:
  - What time of day it is.
  - What the weather is like.
- Make a new list adding in weather and sound details.
- Visualisation: picture this river individually, in your mind – what can you see?
- Describe this river in three sentences. Try to make it vivid, so the reader can 'see' what you can see.

Wordtamer sample model

The river was wide and the water ran fast, smashing round the great grey boulders. Daylight was fading. A forest loomed up ahead and the trees stretched their gold-leafed branches up towards the sky.

- Work in groups. Read your three sentences to each other.
- Discuss each scene. How easily could the listeners 'see' the scene?
- Is there anything else you can add to make sure that what was in YOUR imagination can be passed to a reader?

We have seen how Dahl combined setting with character-viewpoint in the earlier *BFG* extract (see page 78). Following through with this chapter, pupils have created their settings, they know their characters. Chris Powling (1993: 74) discusses how difficult it might be to 'Do-A-Dahl', stating, 'if it were that simple wouldn't umpteen authors have caught up with him by now?' – but it never hurts to try. Let pupils add a touch of the 'Dahl-esque' to their own writing through pace, action and character viewpoint:

- Describe your character moving through the setting you have created. Let them see the setting as they pass through it, noticing small details that will let the reader know where they are, but without clogging up the action.
- Think first about how your character might move through the scene, and why:
  - Will they run because they are late, or being chased?
  - Will they move slowly because they are searching for something, or deep in thought?
  - Are they just ambling, content – not knowing that something bad is either up ahead, or creeping ominously behind them?
- Visualise this scene in your mind – think of it like a film:
  - How does your character look?
  - What sounds are there?
  - What are the colours?
  - What is the mood?
  - What detail might your character notice, and how much do you need in order to let the reader watch this scene with you?
- Now, write it down.

Gods of small things

Understanding setting opens up wider potential for a whole world-building exercise. This can be particularly valuable within fantasy and science-fiction scenarios, where the writer becomes God of their own imagined environment. From Tolkien, to C. S. Lewis, through to Rowling and even up to present-day computer games, the author's understanding of how their created world looks is key to how the characters behave and how the plot advances. Tied to this, the computer game, which draws much of its imagery from fantasy and science fiction, can be another lure for the reluctant writer. Potentially this is even a career choice for the future, and gives context and value. The issues around boys' writing have sometimes been provoked by an attitude that fictional writing is purposeless (Warrington et al., 2006: 152–3). Connections with writing that has scope beyond 'being a writer' can add fresh dimensions for all pupils, but may be especially valuable for those who wouldn't otherwise see the point in exploring their own imaginations. I devised a wordtamer writing activity that seems to stimulate reluctant writers, but also has value for all writing levels and abilities. The following six samples show extracts from the same creative writing activity, the former three trialled at primary level and the latter at secondary (see *Virtual Reality* activity):

Jemma was plummeting to her death! She saw a bouncy mushroom. She fell onto it she was flung miles into the dirty air.

Harvey, Peel Common Junior School

Tom's eyes opened. As he rose from the mossy floor, he looked up to the dank winding staircase. The rusty metal railing slithered up the tower for what seemed like forever.

Josh, Peel Common Junior School

Lucy woke up and looked curiously around her. She saw a bright red tree. She frowned. She thought she must be dreaming. She pinched herself as hard as she could but nothing happened. She started to explore.

The vast, desolate landscape was as scary as it was beautiful.

Casey, Peel Common Junior School

It shimmered and sparkled as she gazed in wonder, the blue light seemed to pull her towards it... She woke up with a chilled feeling. She heard water rushing – maybe there was a river. She opened her eyes and looked around. It was dark, a small tunnel of light was all she could see. There must be a way out somehow.

Bethany, Cantell School

I gasped as I was dragged into the glowing light. It felt warm and fuzzy yet uncomfortable all the same. I shut my eyes and tried to scream for help but not a sound escaped my lips. I soon after blacked out.

I hear muffled voices reach my ears. I blinked trying to get the sleep out of my eyes. Once, twice. Many adult women in odd clothing were staring at me.

Nari, Cantell School

It was nothing she had seen before. She looked in awe at this forsaken paradise. Beautiful, yet enchanting and a land with promise of mystery, adventure and sights she had never laid eyes on. Trees, sky scraping wonders that stood together in clusters. The green of the foliage, the blue of the sky and the gorgeous golds and reds danced in her eyes in a mystical blur.

Francesca, Cantell School

Ultimately, regardless of whether pupils are creating whole new worlds, or just the leaf-strewn garden in a street like theirs, being able to 'see' it in their imagination enables them to draw the reader closer, to communicate detail and to convince the reader that this place exists. Pupils are writing like writers, and drawing stories that make pictures. Everyone is a genius with a lower-case 'g' – and maybe some rare and special souls have been gifted with a capital 'G' too. We're all of us waiting for the next Roald Dahl, and the next Einstein.

References

BBC Sound Effects Library (1993) *Essential Weather Sound Effects* (CD). London: BBC

Boulter, A. (2007) *Writing Fiction*. Basingstoke and New York: Palgrave Macmillan

Clegg, A. (1964) *The Excitement of Writing*. London: Chatto and Windus

Corbett, P. (2009) *Jumpstart! Storymaking*. Abingdon: Routledge

Dahl, R. (2016) *The BFG*. London: Puffin

Fisher, R. (1996) *Active Art, Picture Pack*. Cheltenham: Nelson Thornes

Fisher, R. (2015) *Teaching Thinking* (4th edn). London: Bloomsbury

Gendlin, E. (1982) *Focusing*. London and New York: Bantam

Green, A. (2004) Creative writing: taking risks with words, in R. Fisher and M. Williams (eds) *Unlocking Creativity*. London: David Fulton

Highsmith, P. (2014) *Plotting and Writing Suspense Fiction* (Kindle edn). Sphere

Jones, R. and Wyse, D. (2004) English, in R. Jones and D. Wyse (eds), *Creativity in the Primary Curriculum*. London: David Fulton

King, S. (2001) *On Writing*. London: Hodder and Staughton

Michalko, M. (2001) *Cracking Creativity*. Berkeley, CA: Ten Speed Press

Powling, C. (1983) *Roald Dahl: A Biography*. London: Puffin

Schulze, K. (2016) *Mirage* (CD). Hannover: Mig Music

Smith, R., Heneghan, J. and Burns, C. (2015) The village of your novel, *Writing in Education* 65. www.nawe.co.uk/DB/wie-editions/articles/the-village-of-your-novel.html

Warrington, M. Younger, M. with Bearne, E. (2006) *Raising Boys' Achievement in Primary Schools*. Maidenhead: Open University Press

CHAPTER 8

CHARACTERS – THE GOOD, THE BAD AND THE UGLY

How to create characters for all genres of fictional writing

Chapter contents

Come with me, into the playground. We just need to watch for a while. How many pupils are there here? Oh, OK — two hundred and eleven. Look at them all, the same blue cardigans and jumpers. Grey skirts and trousers. It's hard to pick one from another. They look happy. It's a happy school. But no ... look over there ... that girl just took that boy's lunchbox. The boy with red curly hair. She's playing with it, throwing it to her friends, those girls in the blue tops and the grey ... well, never mind. The girl's got a pony-tail. The boy looks as though he might cry. What a thug that girl must be. What a bully.

***

Come with me, into this stranger's kitchen. Two children, clearly getting ready for school. Blue and grey uniforms. The girl has straight brown hair. The boy's hair is a dance of red curls. The girl finishes her toast then goes to the mirror, scrunching her hair back into a ponytail. The boy prances round her, pulling faces. He yanks at her pony-tail and she shouts a word she probably shouldn't know. "Bella!" A woman in a dressing gown comes down the stairs, holding a baby. The baby is crying. "I won't have that sort of language in this house."

"Seb started it."

"Stop answering back. You're grounded for the rest of the week."

"But Mum, it's Mapenzi's party. *Everyone's* going."

"I don't care. You need to learn to watch what you say." Mum heads back upstairs, murmuring sweet-something's into the baby's ear.

Bella glares at her brother. He glares back.

***

Come with me, back through time. Let's loiter around in the night before. Here's Seb, look. He's stood at the bottom of the stairs, holding a book. "Mum, will you read to me?" he calls.

Mum's voice has that echoing sound, the sound of someone in the bathroom. "I can't, sweetie. I've got to bath Daisy."

Bella comes out from the kitchen. "I'll help you bath Daisy, Mummy."

"Thank you." Mum sighs. "She's got a rash and I'm not sure..."

Bella passes Seb in the hallway. "You should learn to read by yourself, dumbo," she whispers.

Seb wanders into the front room. He opens his book but words never stay still for him. They seem to flitter about. He loves stories but it's too hard to read them on his own. He drops the book on the floor and picks up the remote for the TV.

Making a difference

The creation of convincing characters in fiction is essentially about building empathy for the reader. If the reader doesn't make a connection with the main protagonist, they won't care what happens to them, and consequently won't keep turning the page.

We can apply this need for empathy to the writer too. If the writer doesn't understand what their character is going through, or is not concerned about their outcomes, they're not going to have the drive to keep writing. Bland characters inhabit bland stories. Bland stories fade to nothing, like a weak watercolour left too long in the sun.

With inexperienced writers, very often all characters sound the same. They think the same. They talk the same. They feel the same. Fiction should be distinct, and the characters should be distinct too. Consider a brick, and a rose. A brick is hard and rectangular. It is solid and static. A brick likes to work as a team and has a clear job to do. A rose is soft, has petals and has an underlying potential to get prickly. It grows where it can. It moves with the wind.

When we take these attributes and apply a dab of anthropomorphism, we get two very unique individuals. What are the chances of them being friends? What might they like about each other? What might annoy them? Try the same approach with other opposites.

Established writers may spend weeks, months or even years letting their characters grow. They keep diaries written in their characters' voice, or write letters from the character to themselves. They might take the Stanislavski (2013) approach, substituting 'method acting' for 'method writing'. (Method acting is where someone doesn't just act the part of their character in the film or play, but they become that person in their everyday lives. The same approaches can be adapted for writing.) I have experimented with all these things, and with significant results. In a letter 'written' to me by a secondary character called Rael, I learned that he saw himself as the one in charge, not my main protagonist. Rael was manipulating Howard, who was the puppet leader of a sinister cult. This revelation caused me to change the whole direction of the plot for a young-adult novel *Forbidden* (Waite, 2004). In a different story, *Trick of the Mind*, Erin was a character in a dual-voice narrative. In early drafts she had seemed outwardly benign, until I asked her to write a journal page and let me read it. It turned out she was seeking wicked revenge on the other character, Matt – and she would stop at nothing to get back at him.

I have experienced my own stories in role; living rough in London (Waite, 2003), auditioning to be in a boy band (I didn't get the part!) (Waite, 2005), and even being locked up in prison for a night (Waite, 1999). Many of these approaches may seem beyond the scope of a standard literacy lesson, but much of this can be adapted and improvised.

It's amazing what imagination can do.

It's all about you

Some authors talk about characters evolving from 'inside yourself' with protagonists being part of the physical body as well as an intellectual construct (Hilary Mantel in *The Writing Life*, 2011). For inexperienced writers, a useful approach is to take this one step further and make the story actually about them. They step inside an existing story and navigate their way through. This can be extended to pupils developing characters that are born of their own personalities. Connections made through this sense of self enable reflective and critical thinking skills as pupils consider why 'they' have behaved this way, and even to challenge their own assumptions about what they do, and why they do it (Fisher, 2005: 54).

Take a simple but engaging narrative such as *Dilly the Dinosaur*. Dilly doesn't want to get clean, and grows increasingly smelly throughout the story (Bradman, 1986). Encourage primary-age pupils to explore their own inner-dinosaur. 'What sort of dinosaur might *you* be, what might *you* not want to do, and what might be the consequences?' The resultant writing will engage young learners because they have empathy for themselves, absorbed within their dinosaur form. Older pupils get inspired by 'zeitgeist' popular fiction, possibly because the associated hype enables connections with peers and group experiences. I have seen teenagers queuing up at school libraries, desperate for the next in the series of *Skulduggery Pleasant* (Landy, 2008) or *Twilight* (Meyer, 2007). Inner detectives, vampires, werewolves, villains or even super-heroes will all enable engaging but meaningful discussion that can impact on writing, as well as wider debates.

I take this further through an activity where pupils, in a real-time school setting, find themselves transported into the past. Pupils explore this past as themselves, and through their reactions to what happens both plots and settings are strengthened (pp. 169–174). Drama and role play are effective here too. Ian Rankin (*The Writing Life*, 2011) considers himself a role player – an actor: his view is that writing characters is not so much the act of stepping into someone else's clothes, but climbing inside their skin.

As pupils act out their naughty dinosaur persona, or tiptoe in amazement through a Stone Age landscape, they are thinking the story with their whole body (Fisher, 2015: 111). Time can be made for discussion and reflection, which in its turn will enable young writers to articulate thoughts, feelings and outcomes (Fisher, 2015: 193).

Not quite human

Humans are not the only beings who inhabit fiction. Dogs, cats, dolls, steam-trains, monsters, dragons, leaves, yellow sponges wearing strange square pants: they all have personalities that beg for development.

How might we characterise a much loved toy bear, using synonyms?

Kind   Cuddly   Gentle

What traits would we give a smelly old bin, using synonyms?

Mean   Shifty   Manipulative

What if the bear gets thrown in the bin by accident? The dynamic between these two creates a simple 'good versus bad' storyline. It's two-dimensional and predictable, but it's a starting point. As with any subject, writers need to master the simple forms before they tackle more complex scenarios.

Characters of card

The development of two-dimensional characters is very often perceived as an insult for established authors: is it not part of the skill, the talent and the craft to flesh characters out so that readers believe in them? Don't we always want characters who are so convincing that they step out of the page, even while the writer is still scribbling around the edges of their ideas? These characters can be seen to have opinions that are clearly not those of the author, and actions that force their creators to hastily adapt and amend their plots.

Isn't this what we want? Isn't this what good characterisation is?

Well yes – and no.

Two-dimensional characters – cardboard cut-outs that masquerade as living beings – arguably have a place not just in early writing, but in certain types of fiction. There is a particular role for them in fiction for younger readers.

If rounded characters are embedded with history and emotion then it would be easy to assume that the cardboard variety are shallow. They are there merely to serve or advance the plot; to make their point, and then leave. This isn't always the case but these cardboard types have clearly identifiable characteristics. They always behave in predictable ways. The story can be told without their interference and it is the plot that surprises, or twists away somewhere unexpected. It is sometimes as simple as that. In Francesca Simon's *Horrid Henry* (2004), Henry is always unfailingly horrid. His perfect brother, Peter, is permanently good.

These are basic comic strip personas who have a job to do. We don't imagine a backstory for them, nor do we worry about some dark history that warped Henry's view of life. We don't question Peter, or show concern about his scope for real happiness when his only motivations are to do well and to please others.

Much of Dahl's fictional writing draws from the duality of good versus bad. The main characters are likeable, trustworthy types pitted up against those who are selfish and self-seeking. The two aunts who control the poor orphaned boy in *James and the Giant Peach* are 'selfish and lazy and cruel' (Dahl, 2016b: 1). Miss Trunchbull in *Matilda* (Dahl, 2016c) is hideous. How about those giants in the BFG (Dahl, 2016a)? If Dahl had manipulated his readers so that they cared about the fate of the gruesome Gizzardgulper, children would have been traumatised when he and his best buddies were banished deep in the bowels of the earth. Dahl was a man of great humanitarian concerns (Treglown, 1994). His books have depths and messages despite the ease with which they can be read, but the characterisation within his writing plays out with a simplicity that suggests a yearning, rather than a reality, around human motivations.

Like Dahl, younger readers also want the safety of right and wrong. They want the good character to live happily in a castle of silver turrets, and the bad to rot in the stinking cellars beneath. This is also a way for children to explore their own moral codes.

Young people have a strong sense of what is fair, and stories can be used to tease out a sense of outrage for something, or someone, who has been wronged (Fisher, 2005: 143). Readers may delight in the downfall of the baddie, but that is because they believe selfish, cruel and wicked behaviours must be dealt with. Discussions around why someone was bad can be brought in as perceptions develop. These can be a valuable tool in discussing cultural and personal differences at a philosophical level, but essentially young readers are empowered by the journey of the kind but vulnerable cardboard hero. This hero rushes about valiantly, overcoming cardboard monsters that exude great globules of evil intent. Children are forming their own viewpoints, and working out where they sit in the moral maze. Even with a storyline such as *Horrid Henry* (Simon, 2004), where the protagonist almost never gets his come-uppance, young readers give their judgements as harshly as the thunderous smack of a ceremonial mallet. On asking Year 3 pupils their responses to a *Horrid Henry* ending where Henry got everything he wanted through devious and unpleasant means, their opinion was unanimous. Henry was naughty. He got away with it, but it wasn't right. They wouldn't want a Horrid Henry in *their* classroom.

Paper creatures

Anthropomorphism is the attribution of human traits, emotions and intentions to non-human entities, and personification relates to abstract concepts such as emotions, seasons and weather. In fiction for young readers, these create a safe distance via which terrible dramas can happen.

For instance, let me introduce you to a small brown rabbit who wears a blue jacket. The naughty rabbit has been stealing lettuces from the farmer's garden. The farmer is intent on catching him and baking him in a pie. Yum yum.

Now let me introduce you to a six-year-old boy who wears a blue jacket. This little boy has been stealing lettuces from the farmer's garden. The farmer is intent on catching him and baking him in a pie. Yum yum.

In the first scenario, we meet one of Beatrix Potter's (2002) famous anthropomorphisms: Peter Rabbit.

In the second both the characters behave in exactly the same way, but the rabbit is a little boy. It may not have been pleasant to picture the cooking of a small rabbit, but it seems more bearable than the idea of cooking and eating a small boy.

Potter was a children's writer. She knew what she was doing. In both anthropomorphism and personification, that which is uncomfortable or 'uncanny' is clothed (in Potter's case, literally) to soften the impact whilst still making the point. 'Uncanny', in this context, means not something that is unknown, but something that is strangely familiar. The uncanny (a Freudian expression) derives from the German *Das Unheimlich* and represents a scenario that is known, yet repressed (Melrose, 2012: 64). Fears, dark thoughts and violent action can all be camouflaged through anthropomorphism and personification. Prejudices can be explored from this safe distance too. Black cats and ginger cats are at war. Then a black 'teen' tomcat falls for a ginger purr-princess. The two cat families are horrified, and the relationship forbidden – until a new litter of kittens appear. Two black, two ginger – and one black and ginger. Are the warring grandparents going to be able to ostracise their new grandson based on colour (Butterworth, 2005)?

Fixed mindsets and narrow thinking can be challenged not just by what young people read, but also by what they write. As they create their own stereotypes, the ideas can be combed through, the snags and burrs found and scrutinised. What a young person writes is arguably more powerful than what they have read – the inner politics can be explored as pupils discuss each other's ideas, offering up a platform for philosophy and diversity (Fisher, 2015: 18–19).

Heroes, monsters and myths

Stories with clear heroes, goodies and baddies are a simple way to explore character with younger or less experienced writers. The differences should be as extreme as a brick and a rose.

In order to create a monster that is truly two-dimensional and as bad as can be, ask pupils to come up with a list of traits they consider unsavoury. This is best done as a shared class activity so that opinions can be steered away from uncomfortable stereotypes. For instance, many baulk at some of Dahl's description of the giants having 'small piggy eyes' or certain types of lips, despite Dahl himself having amended what was described as 'derisive stereotypes' in his initial descriptions (Treglown, 1994: 236). I still encounter this type of casual stereotyping in attitudes at both primary and secondary level and it feels important that classroom activity doesn't perpetuate these mindsets, however innocently they may be expressed. Keeping the focus on personality traits pulls the guts up from the monster's innards. What is bad is not what is visual, but what lies beneath.

Possible 'bad' traits:

Greedy   Bullying   Vicious   Mean

Descriptive ideas about how this menace might move through its world:

Skulk   Writhe   Creep   Lurk

Ideas about how this bad-being might sound:

Hiss   Slurp   Roar   Scratch

Move on to the hero, and consider the same personality trait question:

Generous   Caring   Kind

It is worth adding in here some discussion about other 'heroic' qualities.

It would be ill-advised, in a teaching context, to make our hero too meek or mild: the notion of a sweet, kind and exploited Cinderella is not helpful for the wider cultural debates on feminism (Zipes, 1997) unless those discussions are going to underpin the session (Fisher, 2015: 105–8). Instead evolve characters who will cope with adversity, even if the strengths need development through the narrative. Confidence builds as this initially vulnerable hero/heroine overcomes the most monstrous of monsters: they are on an emotional journey and will be empowered by the end of the experience (Chamberlain, 2016: 78). Sophie, in *The BFG*, is introduced in the first chapter as an orphan living under a controlling regime, which is as much backstory as Dahl reveals (Dahl, 2016a: 1–3), but she is no wimp. Having been snatched through an open window at night and flown into hostile territory by a giant, she is able to stand up for herself and confront the giant. She is offended (for instance) by the BFG's view that Turkish children are, apparently, more tasty than the English variety. She offers up her own spirited opinion on the matter (Dahl, 2016a: 18).

Heroic qualities:

Bold   Brave   Inquisitive   Protective

Think about where this story is set, what the heroic protagonist wants, and what the 'baddie' wants. It can be as complex as a rich fantasy landscape, or somewhere simple, familiar and close to home.

Set in a park.
The protagonist wants to get to a birthday party.
The monster has plans to steal the present to add to its hoard of toys and games.

Create a story where one character is essentially good, and one is very very very bad. From this, moral debate can evolve, depending on the maturity levels of the pupils and the required outcomes of the session. *Why* might the bad character have become so abhorrent? This moves the activity into a deeper level of investigation, drawing out empathy for both the good and the bad characters. No one in life just appears from nowhere. Everyone has a history. Everyone has a reason.

Rounding things up

Creating a history – a backstory – is the first step in moving from two-dimensional characters to those that are multi-layered, flawed and believable. As authors delve deep into their characters' existence, they understand the ways those characters are likely to think, the ways they are likely to behave and the reasons why they respond in these ways (Bell and Magrs, 2001: 96). History includes knowing where they live, family detail, personality traits, loves, hates, fears and friends.

Developments and dilemmas

Try using a simple information sheet for pupils to fill in about their characters. Be clear as to genre and intention. Liaising with a Year 5 teacher in advance of a school visit, I once suggested pupils evolved characters in the week before I arrived. The brief I sent was for the characters to be human, and of a similar age to the pupils I would be working with. However, the teacher went off sick and a supply teacher took over. When I arrived, the year group had clearly created their characters with energy and enthusiasm, but as they described them my heart sank. There was a scarecrow, a shape-shifting monster and a two-headed pig. My prepared workshop drew on magic realism, with characters pupils would perceive as familiar in the early scenes – the magic was to come later. The creation of strange, surreal mutations from the start gave these writers nowhere to go – other than perhaps a dive down that rabbit hole into Wonderland (Carroll, 2015).

With a basic identification and background detail, characters will begin to emerge. They will look around and check out the scene they find themselves in. Be careful. They may not always head off in the direction the writer meant them to go in. (See Wordtamer Create a Character sample model on p. 97 and template sheet on p. 183).

'Out of my way, I've got something to say'

Backstory impacts on the frontstory too. As characters emerge, they talk to their authors. They tell them what matters, and how they are feeling.

Exercise: Freewriting

(The Create a Character example offers a good starting point for this.)

Each pupil chooses a character (human or otherwise) and gives that character a name, and a physical description.

Tell me what you love?

Pupils write for up to 5 minutes from their character's first person point of view (POV). Their character explains one thing they love, and why.

Tell me what you hate?

Pupils write for up to 5 minutes from their character's first person point of view. Their character explains what they hate, and why.

(cont. in next box)

In my own experience, freewriting enhances this process. Freewriting essentially means writing without interruption. There is no concern for grammar, spelling or punctuation. There is no need to stop and worry whether what is being written is right or wrong. It can't possibly be wrong. It is merely an outpouring of ideas.

Pupils may not easily be able to read back what they have written, and teachers may struggle even more, but within the context of the activity the character has been awoken and the pupil's sense of their existence is heightened. By developing characters through this stream-of-conciousness approach pupils are combining language skills with the deeper levels of sensory, emotional and creative responses. As young writers become immersed in their ideas, the intuitive feelings take over: characters emerge from the shadows of the subconscious and, unchallenged, they grow in both confidence and control (Newbery, in Cremin and Myhill, 2012: 168).

For younger writers, or for those who may find the act of writing by hand physically difficult, freewriting can be adapted to comprise a multi-sensory approach. This can include drawings, doodles, simple single notes, mimes, improvised drama and verbal reactions to questions.

Exercise: Freewriting (cont.)

Create a 'bin of good things' and a 'bin of bad things'.

Pupils write down their character's biggest loves and worst hates onto separate slips of paper – this can be a single word, or just one sentence.

They put them in the bins.

Other pupils, or the teacher, play a game of raffles, pulling out random 'loves' and 'hates' from each bin (generally about three or four from each).

The class discuss how these might work in terms of story.

Pupils write a short third person story using their original character, and plots that have evolved as they've considered scenarios that evolved from their character's loves and hates.

A bit of an act

Drama is one approach that enables pupils to wriggle comfortably inside a different skin. Role play has been seen to have value for imaginative responses when young people act out and then write from the perspective of characters in existing texts (Cremin et al., 2015: 81). The effects can be even more potent if pupils work with their own original characters and ideas. When pupils 'become' their characters the sense of engagement is enhanced. This is someone they really care about. This is someone they understand. Acting the part of a character is a whole-body activity. Pupils experience the world through their character's eyes, learning not just who they are, but how they move, think and feel.

Discussion of character in role also helps root ideas more deeply. Pupils can meet each other's characters through hot-seating (taking turns to interrogate each other about the character's background) or sharing information, and all of this seemingly light-hearted play is actually another form of note-taking and planning: an active expression of 'dabbling'. It underpins the character before he/she steps into the narrative and the real writing evolves.

When pupils are writing from the perspective of characters developed through role play, the writing output often appears 'seamless' (Cremin and Myhill, 2012: 150). When they work within a state of Flow (Czikszentmihalyi, 2002), the voice that emerges is confident and assured, pouring out thoughts and feelings that are multi-layered, energised – and unique.

The following activity can be approached in one of two ways. I have a suitcase that acts as a dressing-up box. It contains scarves, hats, ties, waistcoats, gloves, etc. I get each pupil to pick an item and wear it. The simple act of draping a scarf round the shoulders, or putting on a bow-tie can be transformative. Pupils will 'become' someone else and through this metamorphosis they can improvise and evolve scenes for stories.

An alternative slant incorporates drama and improvisation evolving from a previously written character development (as with the Create a Character sample). If selecting the latter, it works well for pupils to make and wear badges or sticky labels denoting their character's name.

Regardless of which of the above is selected, pupils individually come up with a brief backstory and a secret for their character but – shhh – it's secret. They tell *no one*.

Exercise: Secret stories

Ensure writing paper and pens etc. are out on tables so that pupils can move between role play and writing without coming out of character.

Create a whole-class scenario – this could be a busy town; a funfair; a party.

Drama
Pupils move around the classroom or hall, 'meeting and greeting' characters with their peers. They are allowed to tell those they meet anything about their backstory *except* their secret.

From time to time the teacher calls out an action or activity, and the pupil must freeze, in role, in the way their character would respond.

Writing
Pupils write a short, fictitious but dramatic scene involving this character.

Drama
Pupils act out an element of their scene and freeze, in role, when the teacher tells them to do so. They try to think like their character. What will they be feeling? What will they be thinking?

Writing
Pupils identify the current emotion the character is feeling, and continue writing, working in ways to reveal the secret.

Feedback by reading in groups or to the whole class just one favourite section of what has been written.

Who am I?

In defining the body as a shadow, John P. Conger (1991: 84–5) discusses how clothes, image and material goods mask deeper anxieties and needs. There is scope to extend the development of characters through looking beyond the external in more depth, particularly as young writers gain advanced awareness of social behaviours and identities. This in turn offers potential for deeper philosophical debates around what is projected and what is hidden.

The development of more complex characters and their varying motivations may be a step too far for some writers at the younger end of the spectrum, but more mature pupils will gain new insights through these multi-layered, psychological explorations. Gifted and talented pupils with an aptitude for writing should also welcome the chance to delve deeper into the motivations of their creations, and almost all levels will benefit from the discussions such approaches ignite. Characters in fiction, as much as in real life, can be good and bad simultaneously. Many repressed feelings are primitive and negative (Whitmont, 1990: 15). A charity worker may harbour a burning anger. The sporting hero may be deeply prejudiced. When their 'shadow self' is revealed, do we love them or despise them? They invoke powerful stories but whose side is the reader going to be on? Is it right that the author creates empathy for the darker side? The flip side of this is the character who does something terrible, but for good reason. The moral debate around this has significant value in itself, and understanding what makes individuals 'tick' has merit in the wider context of young people's social and community awareness.

A simple but effective exercise draws from props and discussion. Helen Bromley (2002) created storyboxes using artefacts that suggest pirates, Egyptians or perhaps a world war evacuee, and I use a similar technique for character development.

Exercise

Prepare a suitcase, or large bag, packing it with six items that belong to one single unnamed fictitious person. Mix items of clothing with items of interest. For instance a hat, a pair of shoes, a magazine, a food wrapper, an old letter or birthday greeting, a ticket. Attach a label to the suitcase or bag, but leave it blank.

Create a scenario for the class to discuss. The baggage has been left behind somewhere. No one knows whose it is. Did they just forget it? Did they have to leave in a hurry?

Discuss the items in the baggage in groups, or as a whole class, and evolve the character who owned it.

Consider the importance of names. Choose a class-agreed name that seems to connect to the items: Anna or Annabella? Jack or Julian? Hand out labels for pupils to work in groups, pairs, or even individually. Fill in the name of the character on the blank label.

Pupils write a first person monologue from this character's perspective. Who are they? Where are they going? What is going to happen to them?

The way I see it

This chapter has been about character, but it has also been mostly about writing through a single point of view (POV). In fiction, the stories are stronger if the author stays with a specific mindset. By exploring the world of a distinct protagonist, both writer and reader can connect with one identifiable individual.

Secondary characters have immense value too, but if readers are asked to align themselves with too many opposing needs and demands, the narrative becomes diluted. Other skills, such as implication and dialogue, can help to give the second character a voice. For younger and inexperienced writers the single viewpoint narrative works best in terms of reading and writing. The BFG is an amazing character, but Dahl (2016a) only lets us see him through Sophie's eyes.

Morpurgo (2007) never deviates from showing us the world from the horse's perspective. Stories can be told in first or third person, but the POV remains the same.

Secondary-level writers can explore alternative options, such as dual or multiple voice narratives, often told through separate chapters. I have written young-adult novels where all the key players have a voice. For instance, in the *Next Big Thing* (Waite, 2005) I told the story from the POV of the main character, his father, his music manager, his girlfriend, a jealous 'love-rival' and even a journalist. The challenge here (for me as the writer) was to evolve unique voices for *each* character by developing motivation through backstory. My aim was to elicit reader empathy for each individual, giving a multi-layered experience for the reader.

A less common alternative to these approaches is the narrated story where the author is telling the story in a God-like, omniscient way. They view the characters and their behaviour as if they are looking down from above. This may seem simple but in fact to do it well is both subtle and complex. When this omniscient style is handled by an inexperienced writer, the author often becomes too present in the text and can be imposing and didactic (Bell and Magrs, 2001: 166). The very best example of this that I have seen, in a publication for school-age readers, is Lemony Snicket (Handler, 2012) in *A Series of Unfortunate Events*. Here, Handler has created a character who is also the narrator in that God-like sense. Handler's invention creates a very different form of narrative style; it would need its own chapter, possibly a whole book, to explore what makes Lemony Snicket the success that it is.

In fact, character development as a subject deserves a whole book to itself. Or at least, that's what my characters are telling me.

> Come with me, into the playground. Look over there ... that girl just took that boy's lunchbox. The boy with red curly hair. She's playing with it, throwing it to her friends. The girl's got a pony-tail. The boy looks as though he might cry. Something bad must have happened between them. Maybe even something sad. Let's take them aside and talk to both of them. I bet they've both got a story to tell.

Wordtamer sample model: create a character

The model below can be adapted for a whole-class lesson, or recreated as a photocopiable handout for pupils to work on basic character development. The sample outlines my own evolvement of Seb who, with his sister Bella, appeared at the beginning of this chapter.

Name and age (of character):

Seb Williams 11

Description (what do you think they look like?):

Skinny. Green eyes. Red curly hair

What sort of character are they most of the time? (Choose two or three)

Moody   Grumpy   Friendly   Kind

Anxious   Shy   Confident   Mean   Happy   Sad

What sort of home do they live in, and who do they live with?

Small house in a town with Mum and two sisters

> Write down one thing they love:
>
>   *lizards*
>
> Write down one thing they hate:
>
>   *Literacy Lessons*

References

Bell, J. and Magrs, P., eds (2001) *The Creative Writing Coursebook*. London: Macmillan

Bradman, T. (1986) *Dilly the Dinosaur*. London: Piccadilly Press

Bromley, H. (2002) *Fifty Exciting Ideas for Storyboxes*. Cambridge: Lawrence Education

Butterworth, N. (2005) *The Whisperer*. London: Harper Collins

Carroll, L. (2015) *Alice in Wonderland*. London: Macmillan Children's Books

Chamberlain, C. (2016) *Inspiring Writing in Primary Schools*. London: Sage

Cremin, T., Reedy, D., Bearne, E. and Dombey, B. (2015) *Teaching English Creatively* (2nd edn). Abingdon: Routledge

Conger, J. P. (1990) The body as shadow, in C. Zweig and J Abrams (eds) *Meeting the Shadow*. New York: Jeremy P. Tarcher

Cremin, T. and Myhill, D. (2012) *Writing Voices*. Abingdon: Routledge

Czikszentmihalyi, M. (2002) *Flow*. London: Rider – Random House

Dahl, R. (2016a) *The BFG*. London: Penguin

Dahl, R. (2016b) *James and the Giant Peach*. London: Puffin

Dahl, R. (2016c) *Matilda*. London: Puffin

Fisher, R. (2005) *Teaching Children to Think* (2nd edn). Cheltenham: Nelson Thornes

Fisher, R. (2015) *Teaching Thinking* (4th edn). London: Bloomsbury

Handler, D. (2012) *A Series of Unfortunate Events: The Bad Beginning*. London: Egmont

Landy, D. (2008) *Skulduggery Pleasant: Playing with Fire*. London: Harper Collins

Melrose, M. (2012) *Monsters Under the Bed*. Abingdon: Routledge

Meyer, S. (2007) *New Moon*. London: Atom

Morpurgo, M. (2007) *War Horse*. London: Egmont

Potter, B. (2002) *The Tale of Peter Rabbit*. New York: Warne

Simon, F. (2004) *Horrid Henry's Big Bad Book*. London: Orion

Stanislavski, C. (2013) *Building a Character* (5th edn). London and New York: Bloomsbury

Treglown, J. (1994) *Roald Dahl: A Biography*. New York: Farrar, Straus and Giroux

The Writing Life: Authors Speak (2011) Author interviews with Sarah O'Reilly (CD ROM). London: British Library Board.

Waite, J. (1999) *Eclipse*. London: Scholastic

Waite, J. (2003) *Trick of the Mind*. Oxford: Oxford University Press

Waite, J. (2004) *Forbidden*. Oxford: Oxford University Press

Waite, J. (2005) *The Next Big Thing*. Oxford: Oxford University Press

Whitmont, E. C. (1990) The evolution of the shadow, in C. Zweig and J. Abrams (eds) *Meeting the Shadow*. New York: Jeremy P. Tarcher

Zipes, J. (1997) *Happily Ever After: Fairytales, Children and the Culture Industry*. New York and London: Routledge

CHAPTER 9

PLOT – WHAT'S THE POINT?

Plotting stories through graphs, timelines and mindmaps

Chapter contents

Imagine standing outside a house, by the front door. The door is shut and you are looking away from the house. A street runs past the garden gate, and you can see this street stretch to another, older gate that leads into a field. At the far end the ground dips and you know at the bottom of the dip there is a river fringed by trees. The trees get thicker. You can't see everything from where you stand, but you've been told a path runs through the wood. Beyond this is Fire Mountain, which you can just see the tip of, rising hazily in the distance. It was once a volcano. A fire-breathing mountain. Why, as you gaze at it, do you feel its lure pull at you, like some deadly magnet? You know you should turn back to the safety of the house, but something has stirred in you. Something has called you. You need to find out what wants you, and why. A lizard scutters by, heading down the street towards the field. It moves quickly, almost urgently. You feel compelled to follow. You walk through the gate, and begin your journey.

The journey begins

A plot, quite simply, is a journey. It's a journey through the story.

In school, young children are generally taught that a story must have a beginning, middle and end. This is a viable starting point for struggling or inexperienced writers. The character starts their journey, moves to a point where something happens, then heads off happily towards their final destination.

However, in 'real' storytelling it's not always that simple. Plot is not static or rigid. It shifts and resists, sometimes moving steadily forward but sometimes tilting or even changing direction, like a ship on a wild sea.

Plot, in its wild sea environment, can seem almost impossible to teach (Newbery, in Cremin and Myhill, 2012), but there are approaches within plotting, and methodologies to explore, which draw from the complexities yet adapt the process for a less storm-battered creative session.

Just because

One reason why the 'beginning, middle and end' model can be so limiting is that plot is not about actuality: it is about cause and effect.

Consider 'actuality': a girl shows a boy her dragon puppet → the boy throws the puppet into a forbidden field → the girl climbs the fence and is bitten by ants in the process → she gets her puppet back.

Add in cause and effect: a girl shows a boy her dragon puppet *because* she wants the boy to like her, even though he never takes much notice of her. She hopes he'll be impressed by her puppet → the girl has loads of toys and the boy has very few. *Because* the boy is jealous of the girl, he throws the puppet into a forbidden field that is full of dangerous snakes and lizards → the puppet was once owned by a much loved grandparent. *Because* the puppet symbolises so much and she knows she'll be in huge trouble if it gets lost, the girl climbs the fence to get it → she gets the puppet back, but *because* she climbed the fence she is bitten by giant red soldier ants that inhabit the fence → *because* she was bitten by giant red soldier ants the boy is horrified by the dangers he has exposed her to and knows he'll be in big trouble. He runs away. → *Because* the boy runs away, etc, etc.

Because…

Because…

Because…

Early introductions to the charting of plots through narratives can draw from the analysis of fiction by established authors. Pupils in school are more likely to be asked to write short stories rather than longer narratives with chapters, so a simple dissection of published short stories arguably has the most value, particularly compilations by established authors such as Susan Cooper et al. (2011), collections by a single author such as Joan Aiken (2007) or Maggie Pearson (2013). At secondary level some possibilities are Butler (2013) or Tony Bradman's (2009, 2011) collections (see reference list for all titles). The story choices should be linear, so that pupils can clearly identify beginnings, middles and ends. Discussion around the impact of cause and effect can be built in at these initial stages.

More competent writers can scrutinise chapters in longer works, particularly those taken from familiar and well-loved texts (Cremin et al., 2015: 56–7). Chapters are, in essence, short stories in their own right. They have beginnings, middles and ends. The shape of their journey can be followed in a microcosm of dramas and cliffhangers.

Beyond this, complete novels can be unravelled, with pupils considering the (possible) intentions and methodologies of their favourite author. How might Dahl (2016) have plotted *The BFG* within a five-point story arc (Corbett, 2009: 54)? Can a class collaboratively dissect *Private Peaceful* (Morpurgo, 2003)? What is the core plot and how does it journey through the narrative from the very beginning to the end? It can help to make a timeline running from the first chapter to the end. I sometimes describe it as a piece of string that is threaded all through the novel. There are markers on the string that identify key moments in the plot. Examining stories in this way is constructive in encouraging pupils to move from thinking like readers to thinking like writers (Chamberlain, 2016: 43, 126), and can broaden out into the discussion of themes, characters and settings (Cremin et al., 2015: 56).

All the above options can be interpreted as a linear story mountain (Corbett, 2009: 59) or broken down in graph form. This simplification of process is valuable in the early stages of understanding plots that already exist, but as a springboard to precede the development of original fiction it can result in writing that is 'stiff, and [stories] that try too hard' (King, 2000: 196).

What gets lost in too much planning is the voice of the imagination. Writers should work with 'zest, gusto, love and fun'. They need to be excited about their ideas; feverish with enthusiasms (Bradbury, 1996: 4).

The approaches for embedding imagination with plot in a classroom setting begs some combination of the more formulaic approaches used through the analyses of existing texts, married with King's organic explorations and woven through with Bradbury's explosive energies.

Getting started

In my own writing I generally start by pre-writing, exploring ideas around themes and subjects, with perhaps some sense of the mood of the ending, but not troubling myself with the detail. However, once some sort of clarity begins to emerge, I take a step back to plot. Without any idea of the journey of the story I would be likely to get lost, wander around in circles or simply never reach my destination.

Linda Newbery (Cremin and Myhill, 2012: 169) considers that the teaching of plot in a classroom scenario can inhibit creativity, and 'doom' good writing. This is a valid observation and I agree with the sentiment, but I also believe there are ways to inject magic into plotting so that it becomes exciting, organic and effective.

In teaching 'story-journeys' to young writers, I have evolved a technique drawn from the notion of there being seven basic plots (Booker, 2005). A simple quest narrative follows a predictable path, but still offers scope for imaginative and innovative detail.

1. The character starts in a relatively comfortable place. They are chosen for a task – this is sometimes referred to as a 'call to arms'.
2. Life will be difficult if they don't rise to the challenge, albeit reluctantly.
3. They set off across hostile terrain where they encounter wild weather, monsters and archetypal menaces.
4. They overcome each challenge, but only just. The next thing waiting is worse.
5. They survive everything, but still the greatest challenge awaits them.
6. A high drama ensues, but they overcome all. Everything is achieved.

A stripped-down starting point would be to draw a straight line, then write the six plot points. Add in basic detail. Who is the character? Where is this initial comfortable place? At this stage the process can seem dry and pupils may lack engagement, so elements of drama can raise motivation through kinaesthetic applications.

Kinaesthetic techniques, using practical 'hands-on' activities that involve the whole person, have demonstrated raised achievement in schools, particularly for reluctant learners (Warrington and Younger, 2006: 166–83). Even in the most basic plotting of stories, some elements of 'whole person' experiences (Fisher, 2015: 111) can stimulate reluctant writers. For instance, the six plot points can be physically walked along, and talked through. Try chalking a line in the playground, or in the hall, marking the place where each new action, twist or change comes. What happens here? Is it more exciting than the event that took place at the previous mark? Can the next key moment be more exciting still?

A timeline is also an effective aid in helping pupils to feel the scope of their story, to understand where the highs and lows might need to be and to consider what could be left out. If the character is spending three days in a murky swamp, the reader will probably get glugged inside their own soggy depths if the author insists on writing down every detail. Conversely, if the character experiences the swamp and then the next action doesn't happen for three days, could events be closed up? How quickly could we move our character though this timeline without compromising on plausibility, drama or descriptive detail?

This stage now expands out, as pupils create storymaps that chart the six points through mindmapping techniques.

Mindmaps and motives

Mindmapping (Buzan and Buzan, 2003) uses a combination of colour, symbols, pictures and words. It also offers scope for collaborative discussion and planning. Collaboration is considered key to individual creativity. In recognising that learning partners or groups of learners can support and foster new possibilities for stories, young writers not only gain confidence and validation for their own ideas, but also learn how to give and receive feedback: to be part of a creative team (Fisher, 2005: 6–20). The process of combining colour, words and images is perhaps even a metaphor for freeing the mind from school-size lined sheets and the familiar pen or pencil. The brain, on some level, thinks 'Oh, this is different' – and when the brain is in 'different' mode exciting things happen. The process achieves logical clarity whilst at the same time expanding ideas organically and deepening the concept.

A mindmap draws on a search-and-find premise. A central image or key word marks the starting point. This central point then branches out. Each new branch has a new pivotal focus, and these form their own branches (Buzan and Buzan, 2003: 136). Multiple ideas can, and should, be evolved from the same initial image or key word. Some of these will scurry off on journeys of their own, while others curl round and make new connections with each other. A successful mindmap is a busy place, and it can elicit ideas with extraordinary speed. I once plotted a series of four novels in less than an hour with this approach (Waite, 2017).

What lies beneath

In a typical plotting workshop, after establishing the task and discussing the six-point quest narrative, I put pupils into groups. Each group shares a big sheet of paper, and individuals have different colour felt-pens. I find it useful to provide images that can inspire the development of a main character. Pupils create a character (see character p. 97 and template p. 183). The character, and the task, form the central point and the drawing of the mindmap establishes both the setting and the journey of the story. As pupils chart the hostile terrain collaboratively, they draw branches that explore the potential within each encounter and further consider how 'cause and effect' will move their character to the next place.

They then write a descriptive scene from *one* of the encounters, and this works particularly well if each member of the group takes responsibility for a different point on their mindmap.

The plot has evolved from a single character so the scenes can be joined together. The pupils have, effectively, produced a quest narrative told in chapters, but with each chapter captured as if it were a short story.

World-building

Building a world can take years – a lifetime. Tolkein (2005) arguably took nearly forty years to create Middle-Earth – most literacy writing sessions will have a maximum of an afternoon! True world-building means understanding terrain, geography, history and politics. For experienced writers who are embarking on some great voyage through a fantasy or sci-fi trilogy, this pre-planning can be a vital element that gives visual detail, character motivation and triggers plot ideas, but trying to delve too deeply in a short time undermines the value or relevance of the experience.

However, some key elements can be evolved by drawing physical maps (as opposed to the mindmaps in the previous activity). The identification of terrain, key landmarks and points where the most action will take place can have immense value within an emerging piece of writing.

Pupils can draw maps in groups, plotting the journey the protagonist will make through their landscape, considering various elements, dangers and additional characters. This can then be evolved into individual writing and later compared. The whole group will have started with the same premise based on their map. Hearing how peers evolved these group backgrounds is inclusive and develops confidence: everyone has had a different approach. Every idea has had value. The following three samples came from a story planning, world-building exercise where pupils (in groups of four) drew a map and worked out setting and plot points together. In the consequent independent writing samples pupils have used descriptive language to paint the landscape because they could 'see' it themselves, but they are also using this landscape to identify plot-points as they move the main character (Lucy) through the journey of their first draft interpretations.

[A] rushing river of mystreys flowed by ... In the distance a lush tree of magic stood firm. Vibrent orange flowers bursted to life as she takes a couple of steps. Lucy looked in the rivr to see her face. Suddenly, a bright golden ball of light shines in her eyes, she reaches in and grabs it. Suddenly her hand starts to shake.

Lacey, Peel Common

Lucy was apon a very high hill as she heard a sparkle noise she looked behind her and trees of magic stood their. Lucy smelled a burning or cooking smell As she walked towards the smell it began to fade like it was some sort of trap. She wouldent give up... The next thing that happened was she came across the rivers of mysteries as she went up to it She had a picchure of her going on to a adventure a great adventure... Then she walks towards darkness...

Angel-May, Peel Common

Laying on the green bright grass Lucy listens to the rushing water. She gets up looking at a glistening river of water. Lucy dipps her hand into the water and grabs a flowing green paternd ston. The grass faces the stone. She wispers wow and wonders into the forest. She touches a birch tree. The tree moves back SNAP! the wood turns to arms. Lucy throws the bright green stone at the tree. The grass covers the tree. The tree shreaks.

Ethan, Peel Common

Back to front

An advanced approach for more confident young writers might be to work backwards. Terry Pratchett (Marcus, 2006: 164), on being questioned about whether he always knew from the start how a book would end, replied 'No, but I do know that it is going to end, and that is a vitally important thing.' We can subvert Pratchett's response. What if we know where the story ends, but don't know how it starts?

Exercise

As a class, discuss the following separate endings.

1. Seb stared at Fire Mountain for one last time. It was hard to believe he'd been to the burning centre of it. Even harder to carry the secrets of what had happened. But it was over now. Seb turned away, and walked back along the edge of the river, across the field, to home.

2. The wolf cub disappeared into the swirling mist. "He's gone," said Tola. "He's gone from us." Kabir nodded. "But he's back where he should be. We did what we needed to do."

3. Ethan smiled as a small yellow bird settled on the roof of the crumbling house. "Welcome home," he whispered. "Welcome home."

4. A small brown duck swam by. It was splashing happily. Far below, in the darkest depths of the murky water, something stirred.

Working in groups, choose one ending, or write a new original one, and discuss ideas in the light of what the story *might* be about, using mindmap techniques that consider cause and effect.

Discuss the emerging storyline, then chart the 'cause and effect' plot points, working backwards.

Working independently, write the beginning of the story.

The mindmap approach can be applied in the same way as the earlier example, but this time pupils work backwards, moving the story through the six points to find the beginning.

The use of mindmaps draws from simple storylines pupils already recognise, but enables their more subconscious responses to come into play. Although a mindmap is drawn on a two-dimensional sheet of paper, the infinite chains of branching patterns embody a multi-dimensional reality that draws from personal associations, rather than a replication of the thoughts of others (Buzan and Buzan, 2003). Because the associations are unique to each pupil, each young writer now has something to say that is partly drawn from collaboration and group discussion, but also means something to them individually. This ownership of original ideas enhances motivation.

End of the road

If the story is a journey, then the plot could be described as footprints in the mud that mark the route (Bradbury, 1996). Yet, however deep these tracks, the story only comes alive when the wind screams through the trees. The characters slip and slither. The mud they squelch through seeks to suck them down. The beginning may lead us through the middle to the end, but the end may open up a whole new beginning. Plot, whichever form it takes, is simply a device to help us know where we are going.

References

Aiken, J. (2007) *A Necklace of Raindrops*. New York: Dell Yearling

Booker, C. (2005) *The Seven Basic Plots*. London: Continuum

Bradbury, R. (1996) *Zen in the Art of Writing*. Santa Barbara, CA: Joshua Odell

Bradman, T. (2009) *My Kind of School*. London: A&C Black

Bradman, T. (2011) *Inner City*. London: A&C Black

Butler, C. (2013) *Twisted Winter*. London: A&C Black

Buzan, T. and Buzan, T. (2003) *The Mind Map Book*. London: BBC Worldwide

Chamberlain, L. (2016) *Inspiring Writing in Primary Schools*. London: Sage

Cooper, S., Delaney, J., Doherty, B., Gavin, J., Haig, M., Jarvis, R., et al. (2011) *Haunted*. London: Andersen Press

Corbett, P. (2009) *Jumpstart! Storymaking*. Abingdon: Routledge

Cremin, T. and Myhill, D. (2012) *Writing Voices*. Abingdon: Routledge

Cremin, T., Reedy, D., Bearne, E. and Dombey, B. (2015) *Teaching English Creatively* (2nd edn) . Abingdon: Routledge

Dahl, R. (2016) *The BFG*. London: Puffin

Fisher, R. (2005) *Teaching Children to Think* (2nd edn) . Cheltenham: Nelson Thornes

Fisher, R. (2015) *Teaching Thinking* (4th edn) . London: Bloomsbury Academic

King, S. (2001) *On Writing*. London: Hodder and Staughton

Marcus, L. S., comp. and ed. (2006) *The Wand in the Word: Conversations with Writers of Fantasy*. Cambridge, MA: Candlewick Press

Morpurgo, M. (2003) *Private Peaceful*. London: Harper Collins

Pearson, M. (2013) *The House of Cats and Other Tales from Europe*. London: A&C Black

Tolkein, J. R. R. (2005) *Lord of the Rings*. London: Harper Collins

Waite, J. (2017) *Chelsea's Story: The Street*. London: Bloomsbury

Waite, J. (2017) *Kai's Story: The Street*. London: Bloomsbury

Waite, J. (2017) *Lena's Story: The Street*. London: Bloomsbury

Waite, J. (2017) *Sanjay's Story: The Street*. London: Bloomsbury

Warrington, M. and Younger, M. (2006) *Raising Boys' Achievement in Primary Schools*. Maidenhead: Open University Press

CHAPTER 10

TALKING OF GOOD DIALOGUE

Writing fictional dialogue that is effective and convincing

Chapter contents

Ghostly whisperings

I once had a conversation with a spiritualist who told me that when people begin to talk about ghosts, the ghosts in the room edge closer, as if they are intrigued. As if they are listening.

I have a similar experience when characters in written fiction first speak. I get the sense that the character has somehow been woken up. They move nearer, hungry to reveal themselves through conversations. Real people need their voices to be validated; their opinions heard. Fictional characters need this too. Through what characters say, and how they say it, the reader's connection with them is strengthened.

Spaced out

Added to this sense of life 'magicked' onto the character, dialogue offers a physical appearance in terms of space on the page. Space on the page, achieved primarily through the correct layout of dialogue, allows the story itself some element of elbow room. Another place to breathe.

Many stories for children and young adults are deliberately written with extensive dialogue for this specific reason. Great lumps of prose can be daunting, and a reluctant reader in particular is likely to flick through the early pages and put the book down if there is no physical space around the words.

The correct layout of dialogue works on the same premise as the laying out of paragraphs. Each paragraph is a topic in its own right, and the beginning of each paragraph signals that a new element or turn in the subject is being addressed. It is not usual for a paragraph to be made up of a single sentence, but this is where dialogue differs. Each character's spoken sentence – or even single words – should be treated as a new paragraph (Strunk and White, 2000: 16). This is done to aid the reader and to make clear who is speaking. When dialogue is laid out correctly it is not always necessary to inform the reader who is actually speaking, as it will be implicit in what is being said.

This all sounds simple, but it can get tricky, especially for young writers trying to learn the rules.

"Excuse me," a pupil tugged at the author's sleeve. "I'm not sure how to lay out dialogue properly."

The author smiled at the girl. "That's easy. You need a new line every time a different character speaks."

"Even if it's only one word?"

"Yes."

The girl thought for a moment, then said, "What about when the same character is saying lots of things without being interrupted." She looked out through the window, as if searching for a better way to explain what she meant.

The sky had darkened. A storm was brewing.

The girl turned back to the author. "For instance, what if the character is angry and storming about the room, throwing things all around and ranting?" The girl paused for breath. "He might shout, then stop, then shout again." The girl frowned. "If the second character isn't saying anything, does all the extra shouting stay in a single paragraph?"

The author smiled again, "Yes, normally. But sometimes the second character might react, even if they don't speak. The reaction then needs to be treated as a new a paragraph. Otherwise the reader might not be clear who the action belongs to, or it just might get lost in all those sentences. I would imagine if the first character is ranting, the second character might be quite worried. They may adopt body postures or actions to convey this concern. That, in itself, is a sort of unspoken dialogue. Is that making sense?"

The girl nodded, then went back to her desk.

Looking through the window, the author saw the storm clouds had rolled away. The sun was out.

Making it real

Dialogue in fiction does not exist in a void. It is integral to both character and plot. It could be argued that it is an impossible task to create viable dialogue until character, at least, has been established.

This is because *who* a character is determines how they are likely to react to a situation; how they will behave when they talk about it, and what they will actually say.

Plot also directs dialogue in a fundamental, albeit different way. Any eavesdropper of random conversations will know that much real-life dialogue is littered with aimless banter. There are remarks about the weather, holiday chat, questions about how well someone slept last night – none of them leading to some final great showdown of events.

Real-life dialogue is full of awkward pauses, weak phrases and pointless repetition (McKee, 1998: 388). That does not mean that dialogue in a story cannot be peppered with its own flaws and pauses, but these are the flaws and pauses relevant to the character and to where the story is headed. The writer's skill enables a sense of spontaneity, and the conversation feels natural, but this is because the crafting process has weeded out anything superfluous whilst retaining what is necessary to maintain this illusion (McKee, 1998: 144). Dialogue in particular is a construct that pulls the narrative through towards the plot.

I find that my characters remain fairly consistent throughout the drafting process, but the plot alters as the ideas evolve. Whenever the plot heads off somewhere new, almost every line of dialogue in the previous draft has to change so that everything 'said' still connects with the plot. If this is happening I know that the dialogue is focused, relevant and effective throughout.

Playing tag

Dialogue is often combined with what is known as a 'dialogue tag'. Tags are small phrases that come before, after or in between the dialogue itself – words such as 'said', 'asked', 'replied'. They are generally invisible to the reader, and if the characterisation and writing itself are strong enough, there is no need to go overboard with additional verbs, or indeed use any verbs at all, and nothing will be lost. At a more advanced level, dialogue is sometimes not tagged at all and acts like a game of verbal ping-pong: the reader switches attention from one character to the other as the conversation passes between them. This, however, is more difficult to achieve with inexperienced writers, or in shorter pieces where there has been less time to build in character trait motivations. Most teachers would expect to see tagging to support the dialogue in pupils' writing.

Adverbs support and advance a dialogue tag. They are sometimes known as *ly* words: quickly, nervously, cautiously, sleepily, angrily and so on. For established writers these 'ly' words are annoying, buzzy little things that contaminate the page like flies at a summer picnic. Flick them away. Get out the insect spray. In schools, they are as welcome as butterflies. Teachers can assess how well the pupil has engaged with their own writing, and young writers can extend language choices by making the character's mood and tone of voice explicit.

Compare the examples below:

Invisible dialogue tags:
   "I just saw a wolf," <u>said Kabir</u>.
   "Molly, where are you?" called Ethan.

Adverbs that support dialogue tags:
   "I just saw a wolf," Kabir said <u>excitedly</u>.
   "Molly, where are you?" Ethan called anxiously.

In the second example, we now know that Kabir is not scared or shocked or traumatised in any way.

Ethan, however, can be seen to be concerned and anxious and both these adverbs enhance the spoken information. For young writers who may not have developed the skills around characterisation, or who are not going to write very much, the adverb earns its place in the food chain of linguistic devices.

The reason for the rush for the insect spray by established authors is because 'ly' is deemed to be the result of lazy or sloppy writing. With excited<u>ly</u> and anxious<u>ly</u> writhing around in their final death-throes, the author has to think more deeply, and work harder, to convey the same information. Very often, this work is done well in advance of the dialogue in question. Kabir's character has been developed and introduced right from the start. Readers know his motivation. He's on a quest – a hunt for a rare silver wolf cub. Perhaps a whole species' survival is at stake. Readers know this too, and they are as excited as Kabir is by the appearance of a wolf. Ethan has been built as someone who is supposed to be responsible for a younger girl. If he goes back to the hotel without her, he's going to be in *mega* trouble.

Making it flow — what don't you know?

When characters in stories speak they are, in some sense, working for the author. The role is for them to reveal identity, advance plot, establish backstory or mood, and sometimes foreshadow the future (Burroway, 2003: 92). An exchange of dialogue in fiction, particularly at more advanced levels, is a complex activity and established authors are generally skilled at making this exchange feel authentic, whilst at the same time sending out a multitude of messages. For less experienced or younger authors there are minefields to navigate through, and certainly at primary level there is little expectation that pupils will connect with either the complexities or subtleties of these elements. There are, however, simple devices that are within the scope of early writers, or anyone who finds they sometimes stumble through dialogue scenes. The first device is, quite simply, to use contractions within speech.

Contrast

>   *"I do not want to go into that cave. I do not think it is safe."*

with

>   *"I don't want to go into that cave. I don't think it's safe."*

The former is stilted and unnatural and not the way most people would speak. The only time (in fiction) that it works is if the character themselves has been identified as someone who always talks in a formal and stilted way, perhaps because they are not at ease with the language, or because they are cast in the role of someone who either doesn't 'fit' well – a bit of an outsider – or someone who is given to using legal or 'correct' phrases as an aspect of a personality trait.

It feels important to give some space here for those pupils who wrestle with literacy skills. Research demonstrates that those who struggle with words read slowly, and so any sense of 'flow' in dialogue is lost on them. This group must always have the speech tagged (he said, she said) as contractions are very hard for them to work out. The advice I have received, when working with specialists, is to avoid contractions with 'have'; for example, 'could've', 'would've' (although 'I've' is acceptable). 'We're' is often interpreted as 'were'; 'she'll' becomes shell; 'we'll' becomes 'well' (Reid, pers. Comm.). Consequently, when commissioned for writing projects pitched for less-able readers, I have learnt to apply these same approaches and keep the focus away from contractions in dialogue.

The second device relates to exposition and backstory. Inexperienced writers, perhaps in the belief that dialogue in fiction has a job to do, interpret this as a green light to plonk backstory and information into a spoken exchange.

The Land of the Lost

Compare

>   Ethan's bike skidded as he braked and stopped. "Look at this sign, Molly. I think it's a warning. This place is dangerous. Look at all the rocks that have come down from the mountain. Your mum would be furious if we went any further. Or at least, she'd be cross with me. She's always cross with me, because she's not my real mum and she just wishes she didn't have to look after me while we are here on holiday in Greece. My dad should have come with us but he couldn't because he's working."
>
>   Molly braked beside him. "My mum won't find out. She's having a sleep back at the hotel. That's how we got to come out here without her stopping us. Being pregnant makes her tired all the time. Stop being such a wimp. That lake down there looks awesome. We could swim for a bit. Cool down."

with

> Ethan's bike skidded as he braked and stopped. "Look at this sign, Molly. I think it's a warning. This place is dangerous." He didn't like the look of the scattered stones and rocks that were strewn across the track. "Anyway, your mum would be furious if she knew we were here. Well, with me, anyway…"
>
> Molly braked beside him. "Mum won't find out. I bet she's still asleep when we get back to the hotel. Stop being such a wimp. That lake down there looks awesome. We could swim for a bit. Cool down."

The first example is clouded with explanation – things the characters would already know about each other and their situation and would therefore be unlikely to say.

The second example says as much as it needs to with regards establishing character, motivation and setting – the rest the reader can infer, or the author can 'feed in' later in the narrative.

Making magic: writing dialogue that sparkles

The introduction of body language is a more advanced technique that enables authors to be explicit about the way something is said, and also to enhance character and situation. The term 'body language' is important in itself as it implies an unspoken conversation that can either affirm what is being said, or can work in conflict with it.

Body language connected to dialogue

> "I just saw a wolf," Kabir said, hopping from one foot to the other.

> 'Molly? Where are you?" Ethan stood in the shadows, his arms hugging his chest as he scanned the empty buildings. "Molly? Please."

These examples do a better job of connecting the reader with both character and action. The reader has not been *told* what the character did but instead they have been invited to watch the delivery of the sentence, and learn more about the mood and personality in the process.

This leads us to the land of 'show not tell'. Telling, in terms of writing fiction, has been regarded as another buzzing, irritating insect that should be wiped out at all costs. This frenzy to exterminate yet another writerly device has evolved for similar reasons as the attack on the luckless 'ly'. Telling a story is easier to do than *showing* it. Writing that is all 'telling' is flat, monotonous and sometimes feels like a synopsis. It has an arm's length quality; the reader is not invited into the narrative but instead has to stand back and be told. 'Just listen, or else!'

Compare the following two samples. The second example is longer, and beyond the scope of early or inexperienced writers, but we can see all the places where 'showing' has sparkled its magic on the former 'told' version, and we also learn more about Kabir and Tola, and their relationship with each other.

Compare

A way with wolves

> Kabir saw a wolf. It was grey and it had green eyes. It was standing amongst a clump of trees and it was watching Kabir. He ran to tell his friend, Tola. Tola was outside the hut.

They went up the mountain to the place where Kabir had seen the wolf. The wolf was gone but Tola found its tracks and they led to a cave.

with

A way with wolves

The wolf was standing amongst a clump of trees. Its green eyes glowed like jewels. Kabir stared, his heart thudding. The wolf sniffed the air but it didn't move. "Awesome," whispered Kabir. He ran down the mountain to the hut.

Tola looked up from sorting berries. "Are you OK?"

"I just saw a wolf," Kabir said, hopping from one foot to the other.

Tola got up slowly. "Are you sure?" She followed Kabir back up the mountain track.

"It was by these trees here," Kabir panted, pointing to where the grass had been crushed. "It was watching me. It can't have gone too far away."

Tola pulled a face, walking in small circles and staring at the boggy ground. "Hey, look … wolf tracks," she said softly. "It's gone down there, towards the caves."

The following exercise is a way to demonstrate dialogue, character and action. For lower school groups I make magic wands out of sticks, cardboard and glitter to give the activity that extra sparkle.

Exercise: Enhancing dialogue skills

A Way with Wolves, a scene where two characters encounter their first wolf.

Discuss the differences between the following two options, drawing out how much more energised the second version feels.

> Kabir felt pleased that Tola was coming on the wolf hunt with him and he told her it would be amazing.

Reworked into action and dialogue, this sparkles back with:

> Kabir punched the air and grinned at Tola. "You're coming on the wolf hunt with me. That's amazing," he said.

Analyses

<u>Kabir punched the air and grinned at Tola</u>: This part of the 'sparkle' example gives action and captures emotion through behaviour and body language.

<u>"You're coming on the wolf hunt with me. That's amazing," he said</u>: The dialogue explains what is happening and reinforces the character's mood.

Read this synopsis to the class

Kabir saw a wolf in the woods. Kabir went back to get his friend, Tola. She agreed to go with Kabir to find the wolf. When they returned the wolf was gone. Tola felt nervous as she told Kabir that the marks in the mud looked like wolf tracks. Kabir was excited and he told her they should follow them. Tola grew more anxious as she realised that the wolf tracks led to a nearby cave. Kabir bravely told Tola to wait while he went to the cave to find the wolf. Tola watched Kabir go and she warned him that wolves could be dangerous. She didn't want Kabir to be alone in the wolf's cave so she said she would go there with him.

Notice that the synopsis has a flat, matter of fact style. It is just an overview from which a story can be brought to life.

Divide the class into six groups

Each group is given *one* sentence. The task is to use character and dialogue to 'wave the wand' and magic life into the sentence. As showing is a more advanced process than telling, groups may find they need to produce more than one sentence to convey sufficient detail.

Pupils should convert the sentences provided into more interesting, impactful interpretations by discussing the following two questions:

- What is the emotion given off by the character in the sentence? Use body language and/or tone of voice to depict this. (Pupils can explore relevant descriptions that capture the character's mood.)
- What might the character actually say, based on the information provided? Put this into dialogue. (Pupils can explore variations that connect the information with character mood.)

Pupils can discuss and agree on a final version. They only need to respond to *their* group's sentence and should not carry on the story.

1. Tola felt nervous as she told Kabir that the marks in the mud looked like wolf tracks.

2. Kabir was excited when Tola showed him some wolf tracks in the mud and he told her they should follow them.

3. Tola felt anxious as she told Kabir that the wolf tracks she had just shown him led to a nearby cave.

4. Kabir felt brave as he told Tola she should wait for him while he followed wolf tracks to a nearby cave.

5. Tola was worried as she watched Kabir follow wolf tracks to a cave and she warned him that wolves could be dangerous.

6. Tola was worried because her friend Kabir planned to be alone in a wolf's cave so she said she would go there with him.

When all groups have sparkled magic on their sentence, they read out the enhanced versions to the class. There may need to be some editing as the exercise may have produced some repetitions, but overall the combination of all six will be a piece of writing that demonstrates the difference between flat overviews of stories and writing brought alive by actions, emotions and dialogue.

Exercise: A sprinkle of setting

This activity can follow on from the previous one, linking the dialogue with scenery and so giving a sense of place. The whole class discusses where the story is taking place and, once agreed, they can suggest descriptive phrases to enhance the writing further.

The example below is a top group Year 6 response to the six previous 'dialogue' sentences. The additional highlighted setting details are my teacher modelling responses, drawn from the pupils' suggestions. The piece was then edited to remove repeated phrases, and to achieve a better flow.

A Way with Wolves: class response

Tola felt a shiver run through her. Her heart beat fast as she pointed to the ground. "These marks in the mud must be wolf tracks," she said.

Kabir's eyes widened as Tola pointed to paw prints in the mud, then he grinned. "Well spotted. This is awesome. We need to follow these tracks," he said.

Tola stepped back, her voice shaking. "The tracks go to that cave just over there," she whispered.

They both looked towards the side of the mountain. Huge grey rocks lay like sleeping giants. The nearest had cracks down one side, and they could see the yawning black mouth of a cave underneath.

Kabir made himself stand tall, his chin jutting bravely. "Wait here. I should do this on my own," he said. "I'm going to that cave to find the wolf."

"Be careful," Tola called, her heart thundering as she watched Kabir head off down the steep, slippery slope towards the gaping mouth of a cave. "Wolves can be dangerous."

Tola watched Kabir for a moment, then scrambled down the slope after him. "I can't let you go into a cave and face wolves on your own. Who would help you if you got attacked?" she said.

Extended independent writing

Pupils can continue the story of what happens inside the cave, using dialogue, action and 'show not tell' techniques.

The truth of the matter

'Show not tell' can also reveal character though action and dialogue in order to manipulate the intention of what is being said. This is a more advanced skill, but it can be a powerful device. The reader gains insight into not what is obvious, but where the truths lie (Boulter, 2007: 158–9).

In real life, we are constantly assessing others not purely through what they say, but through all the subtle facial expressions and body postures that they present subconsciously. Although it is possible to adopt a physical stance that aims to deceive, the reader senses the deceit. In real life, someone might say, 'I don't know how, but I *knew* she was lying.' A writer can use body language and behaviour to challenge the reader to pick up the same unspoken signals.

Compare the following two examples:

"I'm not scared of ghosts and vampires and stuff." Ethan shrugged and kicked a stone across the dusty ground.

"I'm not scared of ghosts and vampires and stuff." Ethan shrugged, but he walked more slowly, keeping closer to Molly.

Both use actions as a way to 'show' but this time the first sample suggests certainty; the second teases out the possibility that Ethan may not be feeling as confident as his words suggest.

Acting it out

This engagement with 'show not tell' techniques opens up potential for drama and role play within literacy. Extended drama sessions have been shown to engage pupils with characters in books, and expand the flow of ideas prior to writing them down. Through improvisation pupils can communicate imaginative scenarios incorporating both thinking and actions, which they are then able to reproduce effectively through writing (Cremin et al., 2015: 81).

Pie Corbett (2009) also advocates the benefits of drama related to both reading and writing; outlining how pupils can re-enact existing published stories, which in turn trigger additional fictional possibilities.

Corbett's approach can be evolved to encompass pupils' original writing too. This supports learning theories that recognise that not all learners absorb information in the same way, and not all learners can respond equally to the same teaching styles (Mindham, 2004: 134–5). Motivation is enhanced through constructivist recognition: the learner constructs their own knowledge through a combination of their prior ideas linked with the taught input (Porter, 2004: 52). Pupils' internal responses are valued. They are no longer merely acting out the work of others, but have the gratification of seeing their own material given life and meaning.

An extended drama session is not necessary: in terms of writing an original story it may even be counter-productive because if the whole story gets 'told' to the satisfaction of the storyteller, this negates the need to communicate it in written form. It is already a 'job done'. For this reason I often focus on short interruptions to the writing, using drama to connect with drafts for stories already in progress, and where characters, settings and plots have already been 'dabbled' in (Chamberlain, 2016).

Pupils first make notes about a scene where two of their characters are talking. What is the thrust of the conversation? What are the moods and reactions of the characters? What types of things might the character need to say?

Working in pairs, each pair improvises this short scene through role play. They reflect on impressions around mood, motivation and content, and consider this in context with the writing. They then re-draft, being mindful of ways to incorporate body language and tone of voice, replicating the 'character's' role-play experience now as part of their work of fiction.

The application of drama as a tool for enhancing skills in dialogue has a secondary benefit in that pupils develop an ear for the patterns and rhythms of everyday speech. In writing, sentences need to 'sound right'. Language is a physical entity and relationships between words can be marked by both the sounds and the silences (Le Guin, 2015: 1). Sentence lengths and patterns in dialogue encapsulate what is *heard* within the story, beyond the plot, pace and exposition (Cremin and Myhill, 2012: 75).

With this need for rhythm in mind, once pupils have written their dialogue scene they should be encouraged to read it back to themselves out loud. Their focus should centre on how much they captured the scene they acted out. Does it 'sound right'? Have they written in hesitations? Have they integrated body language? Has the pace and mood of the scene been conveyed? I do this myself – muttering at my computer, adopting body postures or gesticulating wildly with my hands. I grimace, I frown, or laugh out loud. I think. I feel. Then I write. So far there has been no screech of sirens in the street outside, and no men in white coats rushing in through the door. And if they ever did, I would just tell them I'm a writer. They'd probably just apologise profusely and leave.

Being creative gives permission for behaviours that may appear crazy. Give permission for learners to experience 'crazed'. The most interesting results linger in the more unusual places. Stories can start with dialogue, they can finish with dialogue. At any point in a work of fiction, speech deepens and enhances the quality of the writing. Good dialogue helps stories to be heard (see Wordtamer 'Dialogue' activity below, in three stages).

Exercise

Stage one

Land of the Lost

Two children cycling through the mountains whilst on holiday in Greece come across a lake. The path from the lake will lead them to a village that has been abandoned for over fifty years. Stories will evolve from developing backstory – why was the village abandoned and what secrets might it hold?

The activity

Put pupils in groups, then divide the class into two – half the class are 'Ethan' and the other half 'Molly'. There is also a narrator.

Hand out character traits, one to each group:

  Shy Confident Bossy Lazy Kind Selfish Cowardly

Pupils brainstorm the character trait and act out, within their groups, how the character will need to behave to denote that they are 'lazy' or 'bossy' etc. Take a sample 'Molly and Ethan' plus a narrator from each group and let them act out the scene where Ethan and

Molly arrive at the lake. Pupils can improvise as much as they want, but must not deviate from the main thrust of the scene.

Pupils watching should decide which trait they believe each character has, based on the body language and language choices.

Stage two

What the characters do and say (script): Ethan and Molly are riding down a mountain path that leads to a lake.

> Ethan: "Look at this sign, Molly. D'you think it's a warning about falling rocks?"
> Narrator: Ethan's bike skids as he brakes and stops.
> Molly: "I don't know. I can't read it. It's all in Greek."
> Narrator: Molly braked beside him. Beneath them, water shimmered in the dip between the mountains. A yellow bird skimmed the surface, then flew away into the distance.
> Molly: "Perhaps the sign says swimming in that lake is forbidden."
> Ethan: "It may do. There might be all sorts of dangerous currents and stuff."
> Molly: "Are you scared?"

Stage three

All pupils continue the story by writing the next scene where Ethan and Molly first see, and enter, the abandoned village. Pupils should select *one* main character, and the other as secondary. Pupils depict this village through the reactions of the two characters, utilising dialogue, body language, tone, mood and setting. Pupils read out their scene to each other, and amend based on how the piece sounds when they read it aloud.

References

Boulter, A. (2007) *Writing Fiction*. Basingstoke and New York: Palgrave Macmillan

Burroway, J. (2003) *Imaginative Writing: The Elements of Craft*. New York: Longman

Chamberlain, L. (2016) *Inspiring Writing in Primary Schools*. London: Sage

Corbett, P. (2009) *Jumpstart! Storymaking*. Abingdon: Routledge

Cremin, T. and Myhill, D. (2012) *Writing Voices*. Abingdon: Routledge

Cremin, T., Reedy, D., Bearne, E. and Dombey, B. (2015) *Teaching English Creatively* (2nd edn). Abingdon: Routledge

Le Guin, U. K. (2015) *Steering the Craft*. New York: Houghton Mifflin Harcourt

McKee, R. (1998) *Story*. London: Methuen

Mindham, C. (2004) Thinking across the curriculum, in R. Jones and D. Wyse (eds) *Creativity in the Primary Curriculum*. Abingdon and New York: David Fulton

Porter, J. (2004) Science, in R. Jones and D. Wyse (eds) *Creativity in the Primary Curriculum*. Abingdon and New York: David Fulton

Strunk, W., Jr and White, E. B. (2000) *The Elements of Style*. Upper Saddle River, NJ: Pearson Education

CHAPTER 11

CAPTURING THE MOOD

Evolving suspenseful, tense and dramatic scenes in fiction

The lizard moved quickly, darting through the scatter of rust red leaves in the gutter. Seb hurried after it.

"Hey Seb, where are you going?" Bella called. "Mum will go mad if you miss the school bus. It's due any minute."

"I won't miss it. I'll be back in a minute." Seb was desperate to catch the lizard. He'd never seen such a vivid green one before. It had spikes of flame red along its back, like a baby dragon. He followed it down the street towards the gate that led into the bottom field.

"Seb, come back!" Bella's voice was insistent now. "You can't go that way. It's dangerous."

Seb knew the field was forbidden. Children had gone missing. Something bad kept happening there. But this lizard was special. If he could grab it before it ran under the gate, he could race back up the street and still make the bus. There was time. Just.

Conflict

Most pupils are familiar with the 'hook in' – that first line or paragraph that is going to grip the reader from the start. However, this can result in first lines that are constructs – lines without legs, or roots, or any other phrase that connects to a lack of underpinning.

The hook should not be an empty threat. If the opening scene quivers with the promise of dangers, drama and dastardly deeds, then what come next has to deliver on that promise. The menace creeps ever closer, enticing the reader along with it. The hook not only catches the beginning, it is the barb that scratches open the conflict.

Without conflict, there really is no story, and conflict is rooted in character. Some level of connection with character is essential. The reader needs to be convinced that something momentous is going to happen, but also to care about who it is going to happen to. Suspense comes from the tension building towards that scenario: when it hits, the pay-off for the reader is release, but only for so long as it takes to reach the next dramatic scenario… and the next… and the next.

Behind the suspense there needs to be a backdrop of atmosphere: atmosphere relevant to both setting and genre. Atmosphere is not *always* about dark dangers and not all young writers want scary places in their minds. Not all adults do either. I once had a student in adult education, an elderly lady, who wrote me a lovely descriptive scene of a summer garden. "Great," I said. "But … something needs to happen. Can't there be a body in the corner or something? Even a dead bird would do it." She seemed to physically shiver. "I don't want that," she told me. "I grew up during the war, and I've had enough bad things in my life. I just want to write about beautiful things."

I have remembered the lesson she taught me, and often applied it to my school workshops, particularly when working with pupils I don't know. It feels important to give young writers the option, and Sweetie-Land, with its marshmallow clouds and lollipop trees, needs atmosphere too.

Golden sunlight, pastel rainbows, bubbling streams and all things sparkly have their place, but when we talk about conflict, suspense and cliffhangers this generally relates to scenarios that depict some nameless dread. So, for the purpose of this chapter, I am drawn back to the dark.

It's urgent

Writing with atmosphere can start with weather, sound and setting. Trees moan in the wind. The wild sea smashes against rocks. Suspenseful language is inherent in both, and young writers can discuss how language plays out suspense for Michael Morpurgo (2007) in the following scene from *War Horse* (this paragraph does not lead to the climax itself, but serves to tighten tension and lead the reader through to a developing, even more horrible, horror):

> [A] great grey lumbering monster that belched out smoke from behind as it rocked down the hillside towards me. I hesitated only for a few moments before blind terror tore me at last from Topthorn's side and sent me bolting down the hill towards the river. I crashed into the river without even knowing whether I should find my feet or not and was halfway up the wooded hill on the other side before I dared stop and turn to see if it was still chasing me. I should never have looked.
>
> (Morpurgo, 2007: 119)

Aside from the introduction of a monster (actually a tank as seen from a horse's point of view), Morpurgo's language choices support a sense of dread, rising to terror that leads to an attempt to escape. A useful exercise is to get pupils to highlight those words that support the tension.

Great   lumbering   monster   belched   rocked   hesitated   blind terror   tore   bolting crashed   dared   chasing

A simple identification of key 'suspense' words in a passage such as Morpurgo's works well in a literacy lesson and this can develop into a collaborative activity around synonyms – great for thesaurus practice too! I've collected a list of my own that have a direct link with previous passage:

Gigantic   lurching   beast (dragon)   choked   paused   raw fear   ripped   hurtled smashed   risked   rushing

From this, the activity can move to either a whole-class 'Talk for Writing' (Corbett, 2011) rewrite using the new words, or more confident pupils may work independently. Shuffling myself into this more confident group, I have reworked my synonyms into a passage that has different subjects and themes, but that follows the Morpurgo style:

Dragons can happen
[T]he gigantic beast lurched forward. Seb gasped as a raw fear flooded through him. The dragon paused, but not for long. Rising on its hind legs it ripped at the tops of the trees, hurtling branches into the air like matchsticks. Seb choked on his fear. Could he risk running? But suddenly, there was no time to think. The dragon rushed towards him, smashing through the bushes until it was towering over him. Seb backed away three paces, then ran.

An imprint of urgency has been achieved, but for me there is no strong sense of achievement. It feels like learning the strokes for swimming without ever getting in the water. I used the language well enough, but I didn't *feel* it, and without the emotion any independent continuation of this work could be inconsistent. I'd always need to emulate another author. The equivalent could be likened to swimming with arm bands. They're great, and they stop me drowning in the local pool, but what happens when I go out in the sea and the armbands snag on a spiky sea anemone? Pouff! They've burst. And a wild wave is coming – it would have been so much better to have learnt to swim without them.

That's not to say that the basics can't be learnt from the deconstruction of familiar texts, but good suspense writing needs acknowledgement that it's not just about playing with effects.

A warning to all

Morpurgo (2003) uses omens in his First World War novel *Private Peaceful*. Birds (for instance) encapsulate elements of the countryside where the story begins, but the crows in these early scenes are not creatures of delight, soaring majestically above the trees. They are primitive, savage, foregrounding all the horrors to come.

With portents, the screeching owl sends a warning. A message is scratched across a tree trunk. There may be something broken, or abandoned.

The creaky floorboard approach

Even at the most basic levels, the acknowledgement needs to be that suspense grows when the reader cares about the character and is fearful about what might happen to them.

This fear, as with the Morpurgo example, can be evoked through the language choices around the character's emotion:

Anxious   Worried   Desperate   Scared

These can also be depicted through emotion and body language. Hearts can hammer, fingernails can dig into palms, characters can hunch up, creep or freeze at sudden sounds.

There needs to be some sort of conflict, and the suspense scene is very often where the character is being watched or chased. Tension mounts if there is a race against time. There are only seconds before the bridge collapses. The tides are turning. When the clock strikes thirteen, the monsters awaken.

Shadowy figures, footsteps, eerie silences, cobwebs, mists and distant howlings can all be part of the extending ideas process. *Ethan felt something brush his shoulder. The floorboards creaked as he crept on.*

Ellipses go down a storm in suspenseful writing. A storm on a dark night, of course. One with advancing thunder and sudden cracks of lightning. Oh, and add in a dash of flash lightning that reveals that shadowy figure in the corner…

The long and the short of it

Variation of sentence lengths can build suspense: longer sentences draw out tension, and shorter ones deliver impact. Through examples, pupils can be shown that pace slows down at crucial moments, demonstrating how tension is achieved. A simple line-graph may help as a visual aid, plotting the journey and rise as suspense heightens, followed by the punch of short sentences as the action kicks in (Newbery, in Cremin and Myhill, 2012: 169).

Land of the lost
The house with the pillars was taller than all the others, as if it had been built on three or more floors. A window shutter banged softly. A rhythmic thud thud thud of sound. Like a hearbeat.

Ethan wondered how long it had banged like that for. How many years?

There were stone steps leading up between the pillars, and a tangle of trees draped a welcome shade across them. Ethan decided it would be safe to wait for Molly there, by the rotted doorway. The roof of the house was long gone, and apart from the flaked paint on the pillars the building looked fairly stable. Sitting sideways along the top step, he twisted round and peered in through the doorway. He could make out a crumbling stairway. A rotting piano. A scatter of yellow feathers, as if a bird had died somewhere near. And then he saw it. Or at least, to begin with, he didn't see it. Not clearly. There was just a shadow on the stairs and it was swaying.

Something was watching him. Something not human. Ethan felt his throat close over. His heart seemed to stammer. Thud thud thud.

Whatever it was, was watching him.

In the above extract the tension builds (first paragraph) then it lets go, then it builds again. Mastering the long and the short of sentences brings light and shade to the writing overall. Writing that hurtles at a constant gallop is exhausting. The poor horse will drop down dead before it reaches the end of the chapter.

Contrast a sunny day, blissful with ice creams and sandcastles, with the slow approach of a shark in the sea. The metaphorical shadow produced by the suggestion of the shark has a more powerful effect because it darkens this day of delights. Young writers can learn 'the rules' and analyse published works and each other's writing, reading aloud to pick up the points where the pace quickens, or slows. As they do this they begin to appreciate the 'musicality' of language.

Musicality means exploring the beats and rhythms in a piece of writing, and this is particularly relevant to evolving suspense and atmosphere, where the writer is manipulating the reader through tension and release. Beyond the meaning of the words themselves, it is the sounds and the patterns not just of the whole piece, but of each individual sentence, that keep the story moving (Le Guin, 2015: 23). In the development of suspense, young writers can hear where the more drawn out sentence needs to come, and at which point they should zoom in for the kill. They compose the symphony of their own ideas.

Feel the fear

So far I have been suggesting methods to enhance developing suspense from 'outside in', using familiar crafting techniques to achieve results. I now want to explore ways to write from 'inside out'. These approaches are the least often applied, but – for writers – they have the potential to produce the most powerful results. This is where the armbands come off.

The monsters that lurk in children's imaginations are just as powerful as those that haunt the adult mind. Traditional children's stories reflect these fears, which can range through falling, fighting, being eaten, being lost, fear of darkness and being chased by wild and unpredictable forces (Melrose, 2012: 62). Adults might rush to protect young people from the shadows in their own minds, but to truly explore and develop suspenseful, atmospheric writing writers need space to feel and to think (Fisher, 2015).

Effective talk in the classroom, through focused and guided discussion, can initially gather prior knowledge around what 'fear' means. Pupils will have (almost always) watched horror films, or read scary stories, and have their own banks of individual memories too. I once asked a group of Year 2 pupils what things worried them, and one of the main responses was fear of being lost – particularly being separated from a parent. I built a picturebook story around this called *Nanuark: A Bear in the Wilderness* (Waite, 1999) that drew directly from this identified fear.

Young people will have been chased through nightmares. They will have seen the dressing gown on the door slowly morph into a sinister stranger. 'Things' live under the bed and lurk in cupboards or attics. We don't need to just draw from the outside to create suspense in writing. Pupils will have memory-cellars full of their own fears, and when we draw on feeling, we have the most dramatic writing of all. Suspense happens not just with the language, structure or style, but with what happens in the spaces in between. This 'felt sense' (Gendlin, 1982: 32–40) gives the background of foreboding that isn't stated, but implied.

The aim is not to dredge up (or introduce) dark places in young writers' minds, but to channel *collaborative* primitive and felt knowledge at a level where it can be productive. As emotions connected to empathy and sensation are drawn out through thinking, sharing and free-writing, these can be followed by drafting skills that bring the external tools – the language, the ellipses, the metaphors. These now lay over what has been felt, and not simply dropped into what has been taught and applied. This approach is an affective, and effective, technique, with links to experiential education that connects with emotion and experience-based learning (Lindblade, 2011: 171).

Suspense writer Patricia Highsmith (2014), reflecting on what it is that makes her writing successful, concludes that there is no secret. It's about individuality and the ability to express differences through 'the opening of the spirit', which is 'a new kind of freedom, an organised freedom'. However, this isn't mystical, dreamy or 'hippy-dippy'. There is no great formula: the most suspenseful writing is about drawing from the self.

Time to write

The following exercise offers a basic 'creaky floorboard' format for developing suspense writing from the outside in. The second exercise evolves beyond this and has suitability for more-able young writers, or for teachers who want to experiment with 'inside out' approaches to creating suspense. With both lessons I begin by playing a Hitchcock (Golden Stars, 2015) screenplay soundtrack and talk about how film uses music to underpin action and suspense. In writing, the implied drama and tension is evoked through word – and therein lays the challenge. I also use a derelict house in the story scenario as this is easily recognisable as somewhere with creepy potential, but this can be replaced by any setting or building.

Exercise: Feel the fear (and write it anyway)

Provide paper and pens to write on and with, and LED tealights.

Discuss with pupils what has scared them in the past. What scares them now?

Consider typical suspense scenarios: Old houses, castles, woods, caves.

Now consider the opposite – beautiful places where surely only good things happen – sweetie-land, fairyland, a magical grotto, a palace of flowers.

Discuss portents – harbingers of doom.

Create a whole-class character – someone we would like to know. Someone we believe readers will care about.

Pull down the blinds, dim the lights, turn on LED tealights.

Guided writing

1. Place the character in one of the beautiful places. They are enchanted. Delighted to be there. Describe how happy they are, and how wonderful this place is…
2. … there is something bad amongst all this beauty. The character doesn't know it yet, but they are moving towards it. Describe the character wandering through this place of delights, and use portents appropriate to the setting.
3. This might be sounds, actions, or physical beings. A strange bird flutters up out of nowhere. There is the mournful howl of a distant wolf. A bottle is broken. A flower lays crushed on the floor.

Independent writing

Build the scene where the character heads towards the danger…

Feedback ideas

Pupils share independent writing by reading in pairs, groups or to whole class.

The case of the creaky floorboard

Underpin the session with whole-class discussion around favourite 'scary bits' in films and in books. Collect individual words and ideas. Whole class builds a group story from the script.

Props

LED tealights, music CD (try *The Master of Suspense Alfred Hitchcock* (2015) or for something with a more surreal edge *Mirage* (Schulze 2016)).

Script

> Here is a house, a derelict house (point to blank whiteboard). But I can't yet see it. What does it look like?

Pupils suggest descriptions of house. Derelict house evolves.

> There's someone in the house. Someone we would like to know. Someone we know readers will care about. But I haven't met them yet. Who is it?

Pupils suggest a character. Character evolves. (Doesn't have to be human – could be a dog or cat, for instance).

> There's something else in the house, but not in the same room. Something bad. Something dangerous. But I haven't met them yet either. Who is it?

> Pupils suggest a character. Character evolves. (Doesn't have to be human – could be an animal, a monster, a ghost etc.)

> Our first character is moving round the house. We know it's derelict. We know they are inside. But what room are they in, and what is it like?

Pupils describe the room.

> Suddenly there is a sound. A creaking. It comes from somewhere in the house …
> our character is drawn towards that sound.

Pull down the blinds, dim the lights, hand out tealights.

Independent writing

Remind pupils of the character and the room they are in. Remind pupils of the sort of language that creates tension. Write a scene where the character is moving through the house towards some hidden danger. Pupils can choose 'their' danger from the list of suggestions on the whiteboard. Feedback writing through peer share, or individual pupils reading to the whole class.

Extension activity

This incorporates individual memories with character development, visualisation, setting, freewriting, drama and revisions.

Expand the discussion into things that have scared *them* in the past. What scares them now?

Develop a character, either as a group or individually.

Underpin the initial visualisation by explaining they are going to listen to music, and to just allow the music to let them think and feel.

Dim the lights and hand out tealights. Explain pupils will sit in silence – no writing, no talking, while listening to the music.

Play music while pupils listen (2–5 minutes depending on group's concentration span).

Soften the music, but keep it playing.

Pupils write down three words, or quick sentences, that capture thoughts and feelings that were evoked by listening to the music.

Raise the music level again and listen in silence again. This time think about the type of place that comes to mind. Is it somewhere calm, or scary? Beautiful or dangerous? Maybe both.

Soften the music, but keep it playing.

Pupils write down three words, or quick sentences, that capture places that were evoked by listening to the music.

Raise the music level again and listen to it once more. This time pupils think about their character being placed at one of the settings, and consider something suspenseful or even dangerous that their character might encounter.

Soften the music but keep it playing. Write a 5 minute stream of conciousness about their character in this tense scenario.

- Turn the lights back on, and feedback the writing to each other.

- Beyond this, introduce popular texts and shared reading ideas.

- Revisit their own freewriting draft.

- Act out the scene they wrote in mime, working in pairs. What mood or atmosphere is being evoked?

- Discuss language manipulation.

- Read their scene aloud to each other, looking for the 'musicality'.

- Amend and redraft.

The suspense is killing

Sweetie-Land can, after all, be a tsunami of troubled waters. Who is that creeping towards the lollipop people – or worse still, is it the lollipop people we should be most afraid of?

Suspense is often held at the end of a chapter, or if it's a series, even a whole book, by a cliffhanger. A cliffhanger is essentially a fictional writing devise where the ending is unresolved; the scene ends abruptly and the reader does not know what happened.

The term 'cliffhanger' originally came from a novel by Thomas Hardy, *A Pair of Blue Eyes* (1995). Two characters, Elfride and Henry, are sat on the top of a cliff. Henry's hat blows away and when he tries to retrieve it, he slips over the cliff. Elfride rushes to help, but makes things worse. With Henry suspended, his hands gripping at tufts of grass, Elfride runs away. She may have gone for help, but Henry doesn't know this for sure, and they are miles from anywhere.

The writing of a suspense story involves putting the main character into a scene of extreme danger, whilst provoking reader sympathy, anxiety and fear. The writer can best manipulate the reader if they themselves feel the pull of that danger, the rush of sympathy for their character and bucket loads of anxiety. In a similar fashion, I can only persuade my own readers from within these pages if I understand how to write suspense myself. Will my efforts be enough? As I hang over the edges of my own metaphorical cliff, I listen for voices of assent. I think I can hear them, but they are distant. I'm not sure they will reach me in time. The wind screeches around me. Small stones loosen and scatter in a sudden rush, clattering into the chasm below. My arms ache with the effort of holding on.

References

Corbett, P. (2011) *Talk for Writing*. Maidenhead: Open University Press

Cremin, T. and Myhill, D. (2012) *Writing Voices*. Abingdon: Routledge

Fisher, R. (2015) *Teaching Thinking* (4th edn). London: Bloomsbury

Gendlin, E. (1982) *Focusing*. London and New York: Bantam

Golden Stars (2015) *The Master of Suspense Alfred Hitchcock* (CD). EU Original Soundtrack Recordings

Hardy, T. (1995; orig. pub. 1873) *A Pair of Blue Eyes*. London: Wordsworth

Highsmith, P (2014) *Plotting and Writing Suspense Fiction* (Kindle edn). Sphere

Le Guin, U. K. (2015) *Steering the Craft*. New York: Houghton Mifflin Harcourt

Lindblade, T. (2011) Fritz Perls: Gestalt therapy and experiental education, in T. E. Smith and C. E. Knapp (eds) *Sourcebook of Experiential Education.* New York and Abingdon: Routledge

Melrose, A. (2012) *Monsters Under the Bed.* Abingdon: Routledge

Morpurgo, M. (2003) *Private Peaceful.* London: Harper Collins

Morpurgo, M. (2007) *War Horse.* London: Egmont

Schulze, K. (2016) *Mirage* (CD). Hannover: Mig Music

Waite, J. (1999) *Nanuark: A Bear in the Wilderness.* London: Magi

PART III

SHOWTIME

WORDTAMER creative writing activities

In my 'author in schools' role I very often need to create interactive creative writing sessions that have the scope to last for as little as 50 minutes. Sometimes I get a full morning with a class or year group. Sometimes I get a whole day.

The ideal scenario would emulate a typical lesson plan, embedding the subject and themes at the start, and ensuring adequate feedback at the end.

For this reason the following ten 'acts' all offer original creative scenarios that can be adapted and evolved from 40 minute activities to sessions that run for longer periods, or extend across different days.

The templates offer a mix of approaches that stimulate writing ideas, and these can be woven in with all the character, setting, plot, dialogue and suspense techniques outlined throughout the former part of this book.

Each Showtime act has elements that are immersive, interactive and collaborative.

Each Showtime act has some element of silent reflection, visualisation and independent writing. When visualisation is specifically stated refer to Chapter 6, where there is a template script that can be tailored to work with the activity.

The aim is to motivate young writers through engaging sessions, and consequently many of the activities do not require stories to start at the beginning and move through to the end.

Early 'dabblings' are the beginnings. Endings can be evolved and enhanced beyond the sessions. The key function is to inspire young writers to produce narratives that excite them, born from sessions where they have felt engaged and encouraged.

Many of the Showtime acts evolve ideas through 'chunks' of writing. The pupils write in scenes but when these are linked together the reader doesn't see the joins. The benefit here is that each scene is the focus of intense detail – there is no rush to get to the end because the pupil doesn't yet know when the end is going to come – the following three paragraphs were part of a guided writing exercise using the 'Past Times' Showtime act. It is clear where the 'chunks' start and finish in each one, yet the stories still flow. Also, these are only the beginning of the exercise but they could still be assessed as complete short stories in terms of beginnings, middles and ends:

I am sat underneath the frosty dark tree. The sky is a winter grey couler. I can hear other children play on the otherside of the playground. It is cold and my jacket is not thick enough to protect my body from the cold air.

Then I notice a small stone. I have never seen anything like it. I picked it up, it felt hard on the edge, and then everything else felt smooth. It was very cold.

Then I became dizzy. I was no longer in the playground but going through a huge vortex. I could see myself go through time, 2005, 1980, 1960, I couldn't count how many ages I was going through I could hear screams and laughter, was this the end?

Tia, Siskin School

I was sat down in the asty all alone with all my friends on holiday or ill. It was raining hard, flooding the place. Hail hit my head as people slowly walking like slow motion.

I moved into a bush by the year 4 door. A light was flickering in front of me but what was it? It was an ice cold Arrow-shaped flint from thousands of years ago. But surely it wasn't.

Just at that time I knew something was wrong. My sight was swirling and spinning then darkness arrived. I awoke on solid rock ground in ragid clothes. Where am I? Am I dead? Times changed.

Maska, Siskin School

I sat under a cold, damp tree. It was heavily snowing but it was a bright blue sky. I was slouching and rubbing myself to make myself warm. It was a long, wet, lonely break.

As I looked around, I saw a stone in the corner of my eye. As I picked it up it stood out compared to all the others. I held it in my hand and it heated up and It had a strange orange glow to it. What was I to do?

It was like travelling through a black whole. I heard screams and laughter and they sounded like family. It gave me a sicky feeling. I got closer and closer to daylight but it wouldn't end. I thought the world was coming to an end!...

Ruby, Siskin School

For drafting and editing purposes, pupils can work on random chapters, or just enhance a single paragraph. In the same way that there is no order to the teaching of craft skills, there is no need to always start a story at the beginning and finish at the end. Writing the middle might be the scene that a pupil finds most gripping. An idea might be too big for a short story scenario – pupils can learn a lot from writing a dramatic chapter, or even just a scene from a scene, and many authors work in these non-linear ways too.

All these pieces of writing have value. Even a paragraph has a beginning, middle and an end. Any section within a bigger idea will still contain scope for character development, reader empathy, settings, atmosphere and dialogue. The full plot may not be revealed in this section but the story will still be on a coherent journey.

Each Showtime act includes suggestions for feedback focus – what to look for and comment on beyond the activity, and redrafts and edits can be applied at this stage. Teachers will have their own agendas to build in as well.

For more experienced writers, there is also scope to extend skills through rearranging the linear telling of the story. As pupils redraft, could the end come first as a hook in? Could the story switch between past and present? Writing can be cut up and re-positioned, with new connections made to bring in an added value to the assessing of continuity, structure and style.

In my own writing workshops in schools I use notebooks for gathering ideas and freewriting, and pupils generally have a separate sheet or book for the point when they are ready to move from explorations of ideas to more polished drafts. I find it invaluable to have everything prepared out on tables so there are no distractions once the session starts. Pupils should have something to write with, pencil sharpeners and erasers. Notebooks and writing books/flipchart paper and coloured pens should be handed out. If dictionaries or thesaurus material are being allowed, have these easily available too. Pupils – particularly reluctant writers – seem to have an almost superhuman ability to fix their attention to any distraction. The overall aim is to keep the session focused. Unnecessary 'fussing' impacts not only on individual learners, but also on the whole-class experience. That doesn't mean a Showtime act should feel formal and ultra-organised: creativity incites a fantastic buzz but this is better achieved beneath a veneer of control. Kinaesthetic, interactive and playful approaches are not random or casual, despite how they may look to an outsider. Lack of preparation around essential props and prompts cuts into the flow of the session.

Each Showtime act includes author-model suggestions at key points, but teachers will see increased benefits if they create and model their own original work (see Chapter 5).

The Showtime acts offer a range of genres that pre-suppose the teacher will have some awareness of, and that pupils will have had grounding in prior to the activity.

Each Showtime act also suggests additional literacy and topic activities that support and enhance the subjects and themes.

Beyond all this, anything can happen.

Anything at all.

WORDTAMER SHOWTIME PROGRAMME

These ten sessions can all be adapted for a range of levels, ages and abilities. They move through initial basic storytelling and writing skills to more in-depth activities that enable pupils to experiment with narrative voice and style. More advanced sessions also engage pupils with moral and ethical issues that can open discussion alongside their creative outputs.

ACT ONE: LEGEND OF THE FADING SUN
Fantasy myths and legends quest

A simple quest narrative developing a hero, a fantasy setting, a villain and a resolution. Ideas will evolve through staged scenarios and involve typical fantasy creatures from mythology. The hero is in a race against time to stop the sun going out. The sun is controlled by the fire-dragon, and this beast is missing. The writing ideas will be achieved through discussion, 'dabblings', notes and then chunks of drafts that will be punctuated by new possibilities. The final scene can be written independently and then joined onto the previous chunks to achieve a complete short story.

The set up involves ownership of a friendly griffin but this could be adapted to work for other creatures that fly such as unicorns, dragons, chimeras or other flying hybrid beasts.

Learning and curriculum values

Creative writing skills: explore ideas, character development (heroes and villains), empathy, motivation and voice, plot development, setting development, descriptive and suspense writing, story writing, writing dialogue.

Literacy skills: genre awareness (fantasy), myths and legends, reading, reading aloud, note taking, shared writing, independent writing.

Extended topic potential: myths, legends, strange beasts and 'other worlds', science (the sun), volcanoes, terrains and how creatures evolve.

Cross-curricular skills: drama, role play.

Life skills: Discussion, collaboration, purposeful talk, thinking, visualisation, listening, telling the time, time awareness.

Outcome: pupils will create characters and settings relevant to the fantasy genre. They will develop descriptive settings and scenarios through varied 'writerly' activities, to evolve a fast-paced quest narrative with a dramatic ending.

Props, prompts and materials

- Fire-dragon factsheet (photocopiable resource on p. 137)
- Rolled scroll (photocopiable resource on p. 139)
- Cloak for teacher or pupil helper who will deliver the scroll (optional) – this can be as simple as a silky piece of fabric or scarf
- Images of fantasy world terrains as triggers for discussion
- Learning resource clock face (optional)
- LED tealight candles
- Writing paper
- Notebooks
- Pens, erasers, sharpeners, etc.

FIRE-DRAGON

FACTSHEET

There is only one true fire-dragon left in the land.

The fire-dragon's natural home is inside a volcano.

The light from the dragon's glow keeps the sun alive.

The dragon is weakened by water.

Activity: Legend of the Fading Sun

Teacher: Model a pre-conceived fantasy world inhabited by strange mythical or hybrid creatures. There are mountains and deserts. It is best to be specific about what lives in each area in order to control the direction of the plot, and naming the place may also help. The fantasy world needs to include tribes of human-type beings. There is also a fire-dragon who lives in a volcano at the furthest edge of the land.

> ### Wordtamer sample model: Legend-Land
>
> Mostly mountains, with stretches of desert in between. The mountains are inhabited by herds of unicorn. There is a mountain-dwelling ogre, and sylphs live in the wooded areas. The desert is populated by multi-headed snakes and poisonous lizards.
>
> There are humans-types here too. Known as the Smallings these are beings slight of stature and with pointed ears. They live in tribal communities at the feet of the mountains. Smallings have trained griffins to help them travel across the terrains.

Teacher: Create a class fire-dragon with whole-class ideas – a beast that everyone can visualise.

Pupils: Create individual 'Smalling' hero and griffin characters.

> ### Wordtamer sample model
>
> Rana, an eight-year-old Smalling child. He has dark hair and brown eyes. He is kind, but can be bossy at times.

> ### Wordtamer sample model
>
> Destiny, a green griffin with a curved yellow beak. He is restless and gets bored easily.

Pupils: Share brief details of hero with a partner. Move to the other side of the room and share brief details of griffin with a different partner.

> ### Wordtamer sample model: Rana and Destiny on an ordinary summer's day – *time 2.00 pm*
>
> Rana and his griffin, Destiny, were lazing in shade at the edge of the village. The afternoon sun burned brightly. The paths that wound between the village huts were rich with colourful flowers.
>
> "Those flowers look tasty," said Destiny, picking at one with his curved yellow beak.
>
> "Don't you dare eat them," Rana said. "We'd both be in trouble."
>
> "But I'm borrrrrrred," sang Destiny softy. He flapped his emerald green wings restlessly. "Can't we DO something?"
>
> Rana sighed. "It's too hot to rush about. Let's just relax and enjoy the sunshine."

Pupils: Imagine your *own* hero and griffin enjoying the sunshine on an ordinary day. Nothing much is happening in this fantasy land. Write dialogue (as above) that captures this scene to establish where they are sat (see Chapters 7 and 10).

Teacher: Ask for a helper or wear a cloak: cloaked figure delivers a rolled scroll to one of the pupils *or* have the message on the class screen.

WARNING

THE FIRE-DRAGON IS MISSING

A long-ago legend warns that if the fire-dragon is not found by midnight, the sun will never rise again.

This land may be DOOMED.

Teacher: This is the 'call to arms' (see Chapter 9). The character is a hero. The griffin is a feisty mythical creature. They will want to find the fire-dragon and, indeed, save the whole land.

But what is this land that they are going to have to venture into like?

Mythical Mountains

Teacher: The sun is shining but its light isn't strong. Will the fire-dragon be found in time? First, the hero and their griffin have to cross the Mythical Mountains. What is it like to fly on a griffin? *Set off time: 3.00 pm.*

Pupils: Role play flying over the mountains on a griffin. How will it feel? What might the hero see if they look down (see Chapter 7)?

Wordtamer sample model

"We have to go and help," said Rana, folding the scroll and putting it in his pocket.

Destiny was already spreading his green wings. "Hurry up, climb on," he said.

Soon, Rana and Destiny were soaring across the mountains. A soft wind whirled round them. It seemed to be whispering, "Turn back, turn back." They flew for a long time. The mountains grew more rugged, and more desolate. Down below, Rana saw a herd of unicorns stretch their wings. "Uh-oh." Destiny half turned his beaked-head. "The unicorns are restless. There must be ogres nearby." Rana gripped the feathers on Destiny's neck. His fingers ached with the effort of holding on. "Keep going," he called back. "Hurry." Destiny flew faster, surfing the breezes that swept through the cavernous valleys.

High in the sky, Rana could see the sun already had an ominous dark shadow drifting over it. They were running out of time.

Pupils: Write the scene where the characters fly over the mountains.

The Desert of Dread

Teacher: Next, they have to cross the Desert of Dread. What dangers might lurk there? How can these be described (see Chapter 11)? There are distinct shadows across the sun. *Time: 4.00 pm.*

Pupils: Visualise flying over the Desert of Dread (see Chapter 6). What will it look like from above? What will the hero be feeling? What might happen that is frightening, or dangerous?

Pupils: Independent writing – write this imagined scene.

Wordtamer sample model

As they flew on, Rana and Destiny left the mountains behind. Soon they were soaring across the Desert of Dread. They flew for a long time. The desert seemed to stretch on forever; a burned and barren place.

A great sand storm swirled up around them. "I can't see," cried Rana. He longed to wipe the stinging sand from his eyes, but he was scared of loosening his hold on Destiny. The storm buffeted the griffin. Rana gripped his feathers even more tightly but they seemed to be spiralling down... down... down...

"Please try to keep going," Rana squealed. His streaming eyes could make out three-headed snakes slithering across the sand. If they landed here the snakes would squeeze the breath out of them.

The darkest dangers

Teacher: The hero and the griffin manage to fly over the Desert of Dread and reach the volcano, but they can't see the fire-dragon. Instead they are met by someone, or something, who wants to stop them finding the fire-dragon. This is 'The Villain' (see Chapter 8). Discuss ideas around who, or what, this might be. What are their motivations? There are more shadows darkening the sun. There is almost no time left at all. *Time: 5.00 pm.*

Pupils: Make notes and 'dabble', discuss ideas.

Pupils: Visualise scene.

Pupils: Write a scene describing the hero and their griffin battling 'The Villain', and winning – just.

Teacher: The hero and their griffin search for the fire-dragon. It is almost dark now, and they can't see easily. They remember that the fire-dragon is weakened by water. Where might it be, and what might they do? Can they save it in time, or is it already too late? *Time: 6.00 pm.*

Pupils: Make notes and 'dabble'. What happens next?

Pupils: *Go it alone* – continue the story. There are six hours left – this *should* be plenty of time. But first the pair have to find the fire-dragon, and it may not be easy to catch, or rescue. Build in suspense and action. Think of how *your* characters might behave. What other dangers might be lurking? Describe the new setting. Build towards the scene when they find the fire-dragon. Where will it be found? Can they restore it to the volcano by midnight – or are they truly all doomed (see Chapter 11)?

Teacher: Feedback based on characterisation, suspense and setting. Do the characters behave consistently? Has the writer achieved reader empathy towards the hero? How well conceived is this setting and how has language been used to achieve this? What techniques has the writer used to create drama and suspense?

Non-fiction exercise

Design and write a brochure to attract holidaymakers/tourists to visit this fictitious land. Think about the terrain, possible accommodation and places of interest. Also consider the journey – will they buy tickets for the 'Griffin-shuttle' for instance?

ACT TWO: OUR HEAD TEACHER'S BRAIN IS MISSING
Who dunnit

This is a who dunnit, and through a mix of group work, discussion, visualisation and independent writing the pupils explore character motivation within a science fictional premise. They additionally combine crime fiction scenarios with ideas evolved from familiar settings. (The setting can also be the pupils' own school, run forward into the future by about twenty years.)

Learning and curriculum values

Creative writing skills: Explore ideas, character development, empathy, motivation and voice, plot development, setting development (from a familiar setting), descriptive writing, story writing.

Literacy skills: Genre awareness (science fiction and crime), reading, reading aloud, note taking, shared writing, independent writing.

Extended topic potential: Mind versus brain, the future and technology, crimes and investigations.

Cross-curricular skills: Mindmapping, experiential learning (using locations within the school to trigger ideas).

Life skills: Discussion, collaboration, purposeful talk, thinking, seeing (like an artist and like a crime investigator), visualisation, listening.

Outcome: Pupils will discuss ideas around character motivation and plot. They will work independently to produce a piece of fiction with a slightly off-beat and humorous edge. Pupils will explore the connection of characters to plots, and advance the development of scenes that build atmosphere.

Props, prompt and materials

- Image of brain plus initial premise (photocopiable resource on p. 145)
- Story-starter (p. 146)
- Printed 'suspect' cards (photocopiable resource on p. 148), or class can create their own.

The ones here are chosen deliberately to reflect ethnicity and diversity, so names could be replaced by those relevant to the area where the school is situated.)

- LED tealight candles
- Flipchart paper
- Marker pens (ideally for all pupils)
- Writing paper
- Notebooks
- Pens, erasers, sharpeners etc.

It is the year
2037

Technology has moved a long way. There is space travel. There are robotic tools. The brains of the most brilliant can be removed from the body and wired up so that they can keep on thinking their brilliant thoughts beyond death. Many schools have head teachers who have brains instead of bodies.

(name of school) ...., in the future, is one of those. Mr Wunder, the old head teacher, no longer exists – but his brain does, and it is his brain that continues to run the school.

Activity: Our Head Teacher's Brain is Missing

Teacher: Read out the initial premise (see previous page).

How might the head teacher's brain be preserved? In jelly? In a glass case? In a special box? What will it look like? Will it move at all? Will it make any sounds? What special 'thing' might a head teacher's brilliant brain be able to do?

Decide where in the school the brain will be situated. Ideally pupils go there with notebooks and discuss where the brain will be positioned.

Teacher: Read the beginning of the story to the whole class.

One morning, when Abal Mitri arrived at school, she found the automatic doors were locked. She couldn't get in. She couldn't even *see* in. "It's dark inside," said Abal, who had been a pupil there since she was four years old. It was boring coming to the same school every day. Some days she wished her life could be more exciting. "I wonder what's happened?" she said.

"It seems horribly quiet," said the new boy, Janko Bajek. Janko had moved from a different part of the country and didn't like the school very much. His last school had been a zillion times more modern. He missed his best friend, Alfie, too.

"Now then children..." Miss Pringle clapped her hands as she walked towards them. "Don't just stand around gawping. Get inside." Miss Pringle had worked at the school all her life (well, since she'd been a grown-up) and she didn't like it when things went wrong.

"We can't get inside," said Janko. "The doors won't open."

"Won't open? That's ridiculous," grumped Mr Crotchet, the caretaker, putting down the supersonic air-spade he had been using to dig over the school flowerbeds. He gave a tug at the door but it wouldn't budge. "It was working fine last night. I'll go and get my laser-tools."

Mr Brite appeared. "I'll sort this," he said. He was a trainee teacher and he had only just started working at the school. He was hoping to get a good report for his new teaching methods, and he didn't want to waste time standing about in the playground. He took his 'Galaxy-Glow' mobile phone from out of his pocket and Googled *school doors won't open*. "Oh, diddly-squat," said Mr Brite. "It's come up with a hundred million solutions. It will take me weeks to read through them all."

Magic, the school cat, came prowling by. She arched her back and rubbed it against the pillar at the side of the door. "Meow," she said loudly, and then, when no one took any notice, she meowed again.

"Poor thing, she's hungry," said Miss Pringle. "She needs her bowl of milk." Miss Pringle knew how Magic felt. She felt the same way. She was missing her morning cup of tea.

Just then, Mr Crotchet came shuffling back. "Found this lad ducking beneath the barrier zones," he said, pushing Toby Hanley towards the two teachers. "He's lucky he didn't scratch the new fluorescent posts, or I'd be programming my robotic spanner to tweak his ears."

"That's not fair," Toby frowned. "I was late and I thought I would get here quicker if I ducked the barriers."

Miss Pringle sighed. "Well, at least for once you were trying to get in, and not out," she said.

Other children arrived. They pushed and jostled. "We want to be inside," they grumbled. "It's cold out here."

Suddenly there was a shriek and a shout. Nellie Norris, the smallest and youngest girl in the school, came running along the path that led to the back of the building. "I've just peered into the window of the [insert name of room chosen for the brain to have been kept]. The glass has

been broken." Nellie hopped from one foot to the other. She liked being able to announce such IMPORTANT news. "The head teacher's brain has gone."
Dum Dum Dum ...

Teacher: Discuss what impact the next twenty years might have on technology within a school. What will school dinners be like? What will uniforms be like? How might learning be different? Pupils should use this type of detail to establish the futuristic elements in their writing, and teachers can then give feedback on how effective this is, as well as on the plausibility of the emerging story ideas.

Put pupils in groups of four (ish). Each group has a card with brief details about a suspect.

Pupils: Discuss character motivation (see Chapter 8) – imagine this character is the guilty one – why might they have stolen the brain? Mindmap ideas (see Chapter 9).

Toby Hanley

Toby is always getting into trouble.

He was ducking the barrier to get to school because he was late. Again. The head teacher's brain had warned him that if he did one more thing wrong, he would be expelled.

Miss Pringle

She has worked at the school for many, many years. She doesn't like new ideas. She is very strict.

She longs for the 'good old days' when teachers were teachers and head teachers' heads were firmly on their shoulders.

Mr Crotchet

He is the school caretaker. He takes pride in keeping the school running smoothly. He is often grumpy because the children make his school untidy. He used to be great friends with Mr Wunder when he was alive.

Mr Brite

He is a trainee teacher.

He wants to get a good report. He likes having new ideas, and sees himself as a genius. He hopes he will one day be celebrated as someone who has discovered new and dynamic ways of teaching.

Abal Mitri

She has been a pupil at the school since she was four. She is often bored, and she likes lots of attention. She longs for something different to happen.

She was the first one to realise the door was locked.

Janko Bajek

He is new.

He is not keen on his new school as it is too old fashioned.

He misses his friend, Alfie, from his last school. He wishes something would happen to make his parents realise they should go back to their last home.

Nellie Norris

She is the youngest child in the school. She is very clever. She had gone off on her own to investigate what happened.

She hates being the youngest, and the smallest. No one ever takes her seriously and she often feels left out.

Teacher: revisit the whole class discussion about character motivation for the crime, detail about the room the brain was stolen from, and time of night it probably happened.

Wordtamer sample model

(This character and their motivations have been created for the purposes of the modelled sample, in order not to 'infect' creative ideas around the other suspects.)

Mrs Magoro

She is the school cook.
She hates cooking.
She once dreamed of being a space scientist.

Motivation: Mrs Magoro is upset because she had wanted to give the pupils nutri-pills for lunch, rather than messy old-fashioned food. The head teacher's brain had refused. Mrs Magoro is going to be stuck making macaroni cheese and apple flapjacks *forever*. But – perhaps she can swap a sheep's brain for the headmaster's brain, and put in her idea about nutri-pills again. The sheep's brain is unlikely to respond intelligently – and she can do whatever she likes!

Teacher: Whole-class discussion on writing a scene from a single character viewpoint. Also consider how the character will behave and react based on the information already supplied (see Chapter 8). Include setting and time of day (see Chapter 7). Consider what the brain will do at the point when it is stolen. Will it try to resist (see Chapter 11)?

Wordtamer sample model

Mrs Magoro crept towards the school hall. She had a parcel under her arms. It was a squidgy, lumpy sort of parcel, and it was disgustingly damp. Her flat shoes squeaked slightly, and she stopped as a dark shadow pounced out from beneath the gym equipment. "YOWWWWL!" It was Magic, the grey school cat. "Shhh," Mrs Magoro put her fingers to her lips. She knew Mr Wunder's brain could sense sound and movement. It could probably even hear her heartbeat. She stood still for a moment. The brain still seemed to be making its usual soft gurgles. She crept on, entering the hall. The green light from the brain's jar pulsed softly, and a soft glow shone around the edges like a halo.

Mrs Magoro moved nearer. She wondered if it was asleep. She'd never really thought about what the brain did for all those long hours when the school was closed.

Would it set off an alarm when she touched it? Could it even attack her? Mrs Magoro knew she would have to move fast. Her plan was to swap the silly sheep's brain with the pulsing, buzzing, brilliant brain of the head teacher. She stretched one arm forward. Something seemed to buzz, and bleep. Suddenly ...

Teacher: Consider pupils' characters and their own scenarios. They will write a creative piece from their group's perspective, based on the character that groups have been given, and drawing from the discussions and ideas that have evolved. (For a shorter version of this wordtamer *Showtime* act leave out the character development and motivation elements and work with the Mrs Magoro character and wordtamer sample model to develop what happens next.)

Pupils: Visualise suspect creeping towards the brain (see Chapter 6). Think about how the suspect will move. Will they have anything with them? Remember it is night-time. What sounds might there be in the empty school? How will the brain look? Think about colours and movement.

Pupils: Independent writing – describe the scene as the suspect creeps towards the brain.

Pupils: Shared reading – read scenes to each other. Don't tell each other what is going to happen next – not yet…

Teacher: Discuss cliffhangers (see Chapter 11).

Pupils: *Go it alone* – what happens next? Bring the scene to a resolution, or to a cliffhanger.

Teacher: Feedback based on character motivation and plausibility. Do the characters behave consistently? Are they recognisable from the initial information supplied? Do they have a viable reason that supports their having committed the crime? Which techniques has the writer used to create an air of mystery? How well has the writer utilised the 'real' places in the school and integrated them as settings within the fiction (see Chapter 7)?

Non-fiction exercise: report writing

This resource can be used as a role-play interview: pupils work in pairs, one in role as reporting officer and one in role as a witness drawn from the photocopiable character cards available on p. 148. The reporting officer writes in a concise, clear and impersonal style which can be compared with the more creative language used in the fictional narratives.

Official Police Report

Notes from the Reporting Officer:

Describe the nature of the incident

Who alerted the police to the incident?

Where did the incident occur?

Based on the available evidence, what time did the incident occur?

Were there any witnesses?

Who is the main suspect?

What is the evidence against them?

What does the main suspect say in their defence?

ACT THREE: SEA WORLD
Thriller/adventure set under the sea

A visual focus to writing using imagery, group work and discussion. Pupils develop scenes of descriptive writing that are backdrops to characters and story ideas. Pupils will evolve under-the-sea settings inspired by sounds and images, collaborate on characters who might inhabit this world, then apply freewriting techniques to explore story ideas.

Learning and curriculum values

Creative writing skills: Explore ideas, character development, empathy, motivation and voice, setting development, visual writing, descriptive writing, suspense writing, cliffhangers, story development.

Literacy skills: Genre awareness (fantasy), reading, reading aloud, note taking, shared writing, independent writing.

Extended topic potential: Oceans, sea life, famous shipwrecks.

Cross-curricular skills: Mindmapping, awareness of life forms under the sea.

Life skills: Discussion, collaboration, purposeful talk, thinking, visualisation, listening.

Outcome: Pupils will produce the beginning of a potentially longer piece of fiction developed from discussion and engagement with images; they will learn how to use visual description as a backdrop to story, to develop characters appropriate to the setting and write a story that emerges organically from these combinations.

Props, prompts and materials

- Selection of 'undersea' prompt images (could be shown on screen)

- Ambient underwater sounds (www.youtube.com/watch?v=UjQxhOXco_k)
- Selection of 'undersea' prompt nouns: fish, weed, coral, rocks, caves, sea snakes, sea horse, shells, star-fish, anemone, etc.
- Selection of 'undersea' prompt adjectives: glittering, shimmering, murky, wild, calm, lapping, roaring, eerie, silent, bubbling, etc.
- LED tealight candles
- Flipchart-size sheets of paper
- Marker pens (ideally for all pupils)
- Writing paper
- Notebooks
- Pens, erasers, sharpeners, etc.

Activity: Sea World

Teacher: The initial aim is to create an underwater mood, drawing imagery from sound, images and visual thinking (see Chapter 7). The ambient music can play very softly in the background, the volume raised when pupils are visualising early ideas in silence (see Chapter 6). However, once the story ideas begin to take effect, it is best to fade the sounds out. This is because these more generic sounds won't be suggestive of action, drama and suspense (see Chapter 11).

Arrange pupils in groups of four to six: one flipchart sheet of paper per table.

Pupils: Collaborate on ideas, producing a mindmap (see Chapter 9) of what it is like under the sea. Don't start stories. Just discuss and write down all suggestions.

Teacher: Show images, and suggest additional possibilities with noun and adjective prompts. What else might there be under the sea? Shipwrecks, sharks, jellyfish and other sea creatures.

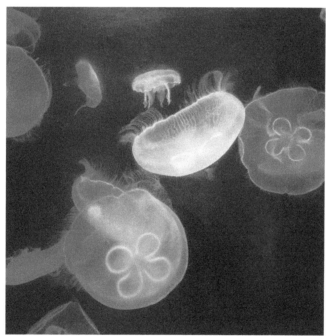

Consider additional detail using metaphors and similes:

Eerie squid with snaking, twisting tentacles.
Starfish glittering like underwater treasure.

Pupils: Visualisation – create an 'under the sea' scene (see Chapter 6).

Pupils: Make notes and 'dabble'. Write independently; create a descriptive setting story-starter.

Wordtamer sample model

The water glowed turquoise blue. Seaweed swayed across the rippling sand. Deep down amongst the rocks a squid snaked its tentacles. A glitter of glowing starfish shuffled sideways to escape its reach.

Teacher: Turn the mindmap sheet over: each group is to create a 'mer-child' – either a boy or girl.

Whole class discuss traits of mer-child as opposed to a human child. Also consider names appropriate to underwater characters: Rocky, Tyne, Pearl, Coral, Shelly, Sandy, Marina, Brook, Bay, Caspian, Aqua, Hydra, Jordan, Nerio, Lily.

> ## Wordtamer sample model
>
> Dark green curly hair. His 'fish' body is a greenish blue and the fin at the end glimmers as he swims. He enjoys swimming, and exploring old wrecks with his friends. He is friendly and confident but is sometimes a bit lazy at sea-school.
>
> His name is Jordan.

Pupils: Work in groups. Create a 'mer-character' using the mindmap technique (see Chapter 9). What do they look like? What do they enjoy doing? What is their personality like? What are they called? Where might they live (see Chapter 8)?

Pupils: Each group shares their mer-child with the whole class.

Pupils: Returning to the description at the beginning of the story, visualise this mer-child entering the scene. Where are they going? What else might they swim past?

Teacher: Use visualisation techniques to enable ideas to grow.

Pupils: Write independently. Describe a detailed, visual scene that adds on to the original beginning.

> ## Wordtamer sample model
>
> The water was turquoise blue. Seaweed swayed across the rippling sand and deep down among the rocks a squid snaked its long tentacles. A glitter of glowing starfish shuffled sideways to escape its reach. **Jordan saw the starfish move as he swam by, and smiled to himself. He loved the way they shone like treasure, but he didn't stop to collect one. Instead, he swam on past the empty sand-palace towards the coral forest.**

Teacher: In all the best stories, lovely or vivid description isn't enough. Something needs to happen. Will it be something dangerous, or wonderful? Consider the character and the ways they might behave, and consider what dramatic event might happen next. Discuss cliffhangers.

Teacher: Use visualisation techniques to enable ideas to grow.

Pupils: Write independently; bring drama and action into the story, adding on from the previous scene.

Wordtamer sample model

The water was turquoise blue. Seaweed swayed across the rippling sand. Deep down among the rocks a squid snaked its long tentacles. A glitter of glowing starfish shuffled sideways to escape its reach. Jordan saw the starfish move as he swam by, and smiled to himself. He loved the way they shone like treasure, but he didn't stop to collect one. Instead, he swam on past the empty sand-palace towards the coral forest. **He saw the shadow of the wreck before he saw the wreck itself. It darkened the seabed, as if it were sucking away all the light. Jordan felt cold as he swam towards it. He could see strange shapes drifting across the deck, and wondered if they were the spirits of the doomed humans. As he reached the rotted hull, he put his hand out to pull himself up, but something rushed at him. Something huge and white. Its jagged teeth were bared, and its dark, evil eye gleamed like a black diamond through the quivering shadows.**

Pupils: *Go it alone* – carry on the story, keeping the detail going, and stopping to 'see under the sea' through visual thinking. End on a cliffhanger (see Chapter 11).

Teacher: Feedback based on characterisation and setting. How well has the setting informed the writing? How has imagery been utilised? Does this feel like a place under the sea? Are scenes easy to 'see' because of the descriptive language used? Do the characters behave consistently and has the under-water theme been established throughout?

Non-fiction exercise

As a class, create a school for mer-children using ideas drawn from an under-sea setting.

Decide a list of school rules.

Create a lunchtime menu.

Write a list of ideas for book titles for the school library.

Plan the mer-child school summer fete, create rides and activities and then write a letter on a shell to the 'mer-parents' outlining the event.

ACT FOUR: VIRTUAL REALITY

Science fiction/fantasy virtual reality computer game development

Pupils work as a creative team developing a game for a new virtual reality (VR) computer company.

Learning and curriculum values

Creative writing skills: Explore ideas, character development, setting development, descriptive writing, plotting, story maps, story writing.

Literacy skills: Genre awareness (magic realism and fantasy or science fiction), reading, reading aloud, note taking, shared writing, independent writing.

Extended topic potential: Gaming and computer industry, maps and geology – emerging landscapes and properties of rocks, fauna and flora.

Cross-curricular skills: Marketing, business, media, writing advertising copy, mindmapping.

Life skills: Discussion, collaboration, purposeful talk, thinking, visualisation, listening, team work, public speaking.

Outcome: Pupils will produce a plausible commercial idea developed from group work and maps. The output will be a potential VR computer game in either the fantasy or science fiction genre. Pupils will gain confidence in plotting ideas and writing vivid scenes that can be re-interpreted by an illustrator. Pupils will present a pitch in a professional format.

Props, prompts and materials

- Fictitious advert from computer VR gaming company (photocopiable resource on p. 160 or design own and have on screen)
- Character (hero) pictures, passport size
- Fantasy or science fiction world prompts: images on screen or printed out
- Story-starter sheets (photocopiable resource on p. 163)
- LED tealight candles

- Business tie/hat/false moustaches etc. to role play GamePlan representative (optional)
- Flipchart-size paper
- Marker pens (ideally for all pupils)
- Notebooks
- Writing paper
- Pens, erasers, sharpeners, etc.

Activity: Virtual Reality

Teacher: Begin the session by introducing the advert, or have someone in role as the GamePlan representative.

At **GamePlan**, it's our mission to support computer game developers and to encourage storytelling as part of our new VR games expansion programme.

In the past, computer games have been more about action than stories – we want to change all that. We want to develop games with young authors who can write strong plots and exciting scenes in a believable way.

We are looking for ORIGINAL stories in the fantasy or science fiction genre that can be adapted into dynamic VR computer games. Do you have a strong central character for a story? Can you write scenes that are vivid and dynamic for our artists and animators to work with?

Can YOU be part of the future of storytelling?

Work in teams, develop stories, then persuade us that yours is

BRILLIANT

Fantastic

Teacher: Discuss a typical quest narrative story structure (see Chapter 9): in quest novels, the hero generally overcomes great danger, but after escaping one dilemma is faced with another, often worse than the last. In computer games the player makes choices for their hero, with different outcomes depending on the direction they take. Each team will work with a shared hero (see Chapter 8), and each individual within that team will develop their own area of a team-built virtual world.

Provide passport-size head and shoulder shot photographs of young people the same age as the teams taking part in this activity. (Mine are generally taken from Flickr images, selecting a mix of gender and being mindful of ethnic values within the area the school is situated in.) These photographs can either be printed and cut out, or just shown on screen for teams to choose their favourites. To scale down even further, just one boy image and one girl image – or even just one single image – could be chosen and shown on a screen.

Stress that this character is the same age as the pupils in the room, and in the same year at school. They live somewhere fairly typical: a very ordinary house in a very ordinary street and a very ordinary place.

Pupils (in teams): Study the chosen character image closely to look for clues around personality. Name the character, then identify the sort of house they live in. Discuss what sort of person this character might be (see Chapter 8). Teams introduce their characters to the whole class. *If only using one character, their development could be achieved by engaging a whole-class activity.*

Teacher: Hand out story-starter sheets. Groups fill sheet in (see story-starter sample model below).

Pupils: Complete story-starter sheet by filling in name and gender gaps.

Wordtamer sample model

Please put your character's name, and either 'girl' or 'boy', 'he' or 'she', 'him' or 'her'. Also put in where they live. All these things just need to go in the spaces provided.

VIRTUAL REALITY

Brook was a fourteen-year-old girl.

She lived in a small modern house with white walls.

Brook had a very ordinary family, and liked very ordinary things.

She went to a very ordinary school, and had very ordinary friends.

One day Brook was messing about on her computer. It was a *very* ordinary afternoon.

UNTIL ...

Brook heard a strange sound. It was a whispery, whooshing and shooshing sort of sound.

Brook saw a whirl of silvery blue light coming out of the screen. It shimmered and sparkled and as she gazed in wonder, the blue light seemed to pull her towards it.

For the purpose of this activity I have worked with fantasy imagery but these can easily be reconceived as those appropriate to science fiction.

Please put your character's name, and either 'girl' or 'boy', 'he' or 'she', 'him' or 'her'. Also put in where they live. All these things just need to go in the dotted spaces provided.

Virtual Reality

.... was a .... -year-old ....

.... lived in a ....,
had a very ordinary family, and liked very ordinary things. ....
went to a very ordinary school, and had very ordinary friends.

One day .... was messing about on .... computer. It
was a *very* ordinary afternoon.

UNTIL

.... heard a strange sound. It was a whispery, whooshing and
shooshing sort of sound. Looking up .... saw a whirl of silvery
blue light coming out of the screen. It shimmered and sparkled and as
.... gazed in wonder, the blue light seemed to pull ....
towards it.

Teacher: Establish the difference between fantasy and science fiction and decide prior to the session which will appeal most to the group. (Fantasy is generally magical and not grounded in reality whereas science fiction – however fantastic – could actually happen).

Teacher: Discuss with whole class the concept of a portal. The blue light has been a portal that has pulled the character through into a VR computer game scenario. The character is the central hero in the game.

Teacher: Show fantasy world images on screen, or give each team a print-out of different fantasy worlds to respond to (see Chapter 7).

Pupils: Draw a rough image of the world onto the *centre* of the flipchart sheet, quite small – no bigger than 5cm square, so that there is still plenty of space around the outside of the image. Team members position themselves so that each member takes responsibility for one area of the flipchart sheet, and has room and space to work. This sheet will now evolve into a visual map of this imagined world.

Teacher: Discuss the types of additional terrains that might be typical in a fantasy world: mountains, rivers, waterfalls, caves, bridges, castles, etc.

Pupils: Each team member selects a terrain and draws it on the map, in visual detail, on their portion of the sheet.

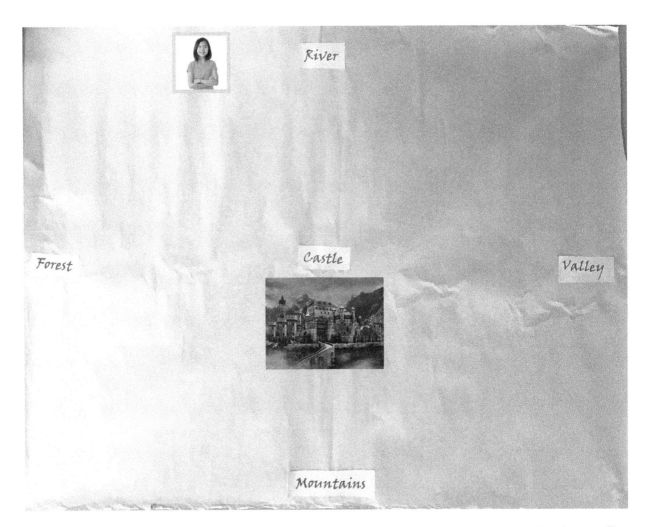

Pupils: Each team member considers more exotic or dramatic names for their places. For example: Melancholy Mountains, Waterfall of Dreams, Burning Bridge, Fearsome Forest.

Teacher: The character has been pulled through the portal to a VR fantasy world – the world evolving on the map. Allow pupils to move away from their teams and sit somewhere private in the room. They may sit on the floor, or turn chairs to the wall. The aim here is to separate the team development and enable independent creative thinking to be woven into the activity.

Pupils: Visualise the team character experiencing individual terrains for the first time (see Chapters 6, 7 and 11). For instance, the pupil who took responsibility for drawing and developing Melancholy Mountains visualises the character waking up there. The pupil who developed the Waterfall of Dreams will visualise the same character waking there, etc.

Pupils: Return to desks. Make notes and 'dabble' – write a paragraph in the notebook that focuses on 'their' portion of the map, showing the character waking up inside the computer game world.

Wordtamer sample model: Waking up on Melancholy Mountain

Brook heard a moaning sound. She looked around. She was lying on a narrow path. She was high up, halfway up a mountain. Far below she could make out a circle of rocks, but that was a long way away. The dark clouds that swirled around the mountain kept blocking her view. She stood up slowly. There seemed to be a noise coming from somewhere nearby. It was a shuddering, moaning sound. She realised the ground was wet. There was water everywhere. The moaning noise grew worse. It seemed to be that something was in great pain. Suddenly she realised what the sound was. The mountain itself was crying.

Teacher: Discuss the needs of a designer, illustrator and animator that will enable them to interpret the scene visually. What detail could pupils add to make sure the various professionals understand what needs to be included in the scene?

Pupils: Redraft, rework to enhance visual quality, setting, sounds and suspense.

Pupils: Feedback visualised, redrafted written scenes to team. All read to each other. How will that look in a VR game? Is there any extra detail that might add to, or improve, the scene?

Pupils: Decide on a mission for the hero. What objects might the hero collect to help them achieve this mission? What rewards will they get for different scenarios? What other creatures or characters live in these areas? What are their needs and motivations? Will there be dialogue (see Chapter 10)?

Teacher: The Last Battle: discuss story structure. In a typical quest scenario there is often a major obstacle, worse than anything the hero has encountered thus far, that needs to be overcome right at the end.

Pupils: How might this dramatic final encounter occur? How will the other scenes and characters that have evolved on the map play their part in the overall story, and how does it connect to the overall mission?

Pupils: In teams draw in roads and paths, etc. that link the various locations, and build more detail, identifying where (and how) this Last Battle will take place.

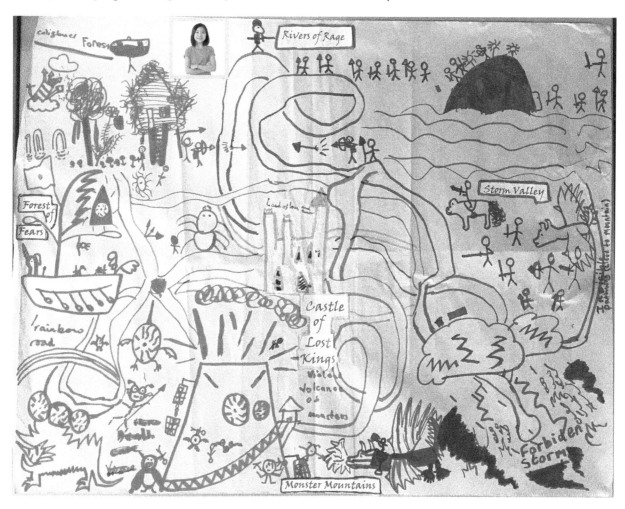

Teacher: Discuss existing computer and VR games, and their dramatic titles:

Doom   Half Life   Enemy Unknown

Pupils: Teams discuss ideas and give their VR fantasy world a title.

Pupils: Teams write a blurb for the game that captures the place, and the different challenges the hero will have to overcome.

Pupils: Write up their favourite paragraph from visualisation notes.

Pupils: Prepare a pitch for the GamePlan representative outlining the title, the main character and the mission. Pupils can use their map to show the journey through the game.

Teacher: In role as GamePlan representative, listen to the ideas.

Pupils: Read favourite scenes from the written 'character waking' part of the session.

Teacher: Feedback based on branding – the connection of the title to the game. Does the game itself seem creative and viable? How original are the ideas? How visual is the 'favourite scene' and would it be possible for a games designer and illustrator to recreate artwork from the descriptions?

Non-fiction exercise

Look at popular brands such as:

- Nike
- Apple
- Amazon

How do they reflect the product? Design a logo for your VR computer game.

ACT FIVE: PAST TIMES
Historical, time slip

The session draws on three elements that make it unique. The setting is the school site. The character is the pupil, telling the story in first person as they experience it first-hand. The activity uses authentic local area history, and also brings that period to life. The writing takes place in distinct scenes, which, when joined together, complete a seamless flow of story. (For the purposes of this activity I have selected the Mesolithic period, which would have common value regardless of where the school is based, but the material is easily adaptable.)

Learning and curriculum values

Creative writing skills: Explore ideas, setting development, descriptive writing, story writing.

Literacy skills: Genre awareness (magic realism, historical fiction, science fiction) reading, reading aloud, shared reading, note taking, independent writing, poetry.

Extended topic potential: History, clothes and costumes, geology – how land forms, eras through time, development of civilisation, evolution of species, potential futures.

Cross-curricular skills: Awareness of local history, research, handling artefacts, drama, role play.

Life skills: Discussion, purposeful talk, thinking, visualisation, community connections.

Outcome: Pupils will produce a sustained piece of independent creative fictional writing told as a first person narrative; they will learn how to meld reality with fiction. They will experience setting through visualisation and emotion through drama and role play. They will evolve an appreciation of their local area and its history and connect fact and personal experiences with fictional outputs.

Props, prompts and materials

- Historical artefacts or images (I purchased a set of Mesolithic tools very cheaply from eBay but a screen image or printed images would be fine; although pupils do like to handle physical objects and they seem to connect in more imaginative ways if these are available)

- Poem script, can be read with whole class, particularly for younger writers (optional – photocopiable resource on p. 171)
- A mock-up newspaper or internet article, citing the area where the school is situated
- LED tealights candles
- Writing paper
- Notebooks
- Pens, erasers, sharpeners, etc.

Once, Long Ago

Once, long ago,
Before [insert school name] existed.
Before [insert town] even existed
This place, right here, was a land of ice and snow.

Slowly, over thousands of years, the sun melted the snow.
Trees and grasses, flowers and bushes, all began to grow.

NEXT CAME THE CREATURES.
Some crept, some swam.
Some went leaping, others ran…

… and then came …
HUMANS
They made tools from flint and stone.
They hunted, and built homes.
But it was *thousands* of years ago.
There's so much we don't know.
Now they're all just dust and bone.
We can't ring them up to ask.
And nothing's been invented
That sends texts to the past.

But would you time slip if you could?
Do YOU think you really would?

Activity: Past Times

Teacher: Read poem script if desired.

Teacher: Put pupils in pairs.

Teacher: Commence the session with a guided visualisation (see Chapter 6). The visualisation will be balanced with brief periods of freewriting and brief periods of shared reading. Pupils should stay silent as they visualise and write so as not to break the train of thought. The reading section should be controlled, with 'share' partners and clarity over what needs to be read and discussed. Pupils don't offer feedback; they just read the section they wrote to each other.

   Script – Imagine yourself sitting somewhere in the playground. It's an ordinary day. Decide what season it is. What time of day is it? Is it hot or cold? What are you wearing?

Pupils: Write the scene from their imagination. Write at least three sentences. Do not discuss it. Read to 'share' partner. Do not discuss what is read.

Teacher: Introduce local newspaper article or something similar. Other devices might be an 'internet download' or something 'found' by someone working in the school grounds.

Wordtamer sample model

Evening News 1960

Following excavation work preparing the ground for new houses in the Gosport area around HMS Sultan, a collection of stone tools and axe heads have been unearthed. These suggest there was a Mesolithic settlement located in the area.

Teacher: Introduce artefacts or images. Group the pupils and share out artefacts.
   Artefacts: touch them, hold them, sniff them etc.
   Images: discuss the visual detail.

Pupils: Return to visualisation scenario.

Teacher: *Script* – take your mind back to the scene where you were sitting in the playground. This time, as you look around, you notice a strange stone lying near to you. You pick it up. Something unusual starts to happen to the stone. Does it glow? Does it tingle in your hand? Maybe it seems to whisper something to you.

Pupils: Write the scene from imagination. Write at least three sentences. Do not discuss it. Read to 'share' partner. Do not discuss what is read.

Pupils: Return to visualisation scenario.

Teacher: *Script* – the stone is going to give you the power of time-travel. You will travel back to the past; to the time when (*refer to artefacts*) were being used. What might it be like to travel back in time through thousands of years?

Class discuss ideas around how time-travel might feel.

Pupils: Make notes and 'dabble', then write a description following on from when the stone was found, a paragraph that captures a sense of someone moving backwards through time. Stop writing when the character has arrived somewhere, but don't say where they are.

Read to 'share' partner.

Teacher: If possible, clear a space in the classroom for a role-play activity. The role play is not essential, but it offers an inclusive kinaesthetic experience. There will still need to be areas to write.

Script – You have arrived in this long ago land of forests and rivers, right here where your school is built now. Fantastic isn't it? What might you see?

Teacher: Ensure pupils all understand they are in the same place (and not gone off track to somewhere of their choosing). There might be animals grazing. There could be some sort of settlement in the distance. Maybe there are swamps. A lake. Keep to possibilities that sound plausible based on the era.

Script – We are getting to the main action part of the story. In this long ago land you will be involved in something important, dramatic – maybe even dangerous (see Chapter 11).

Pupils: Choose from (*these are options for a megalithic session but can be adapted depending on the point pupils have time travelled to*):

1. Save an injured or hunted animal.
2. Be captured by someone, or something.
3. Make friends with one of the long ago children.

Pupils: Role play in mime the moment when the character (who is also the pupil) first becomes aware they are somewhere different. Look around. Investigate.

Teacher: *Script* – there is someone, or something watching. Think about the story choice you have made. You are seeing this animal, child, or 'thing' for the first time. What will you do? Will you reach out to whatever it is, or will whatever it is reach out to you? Will you be afraid and shrink away? Think about how you feel, and what action you will take. Remember the landscape you are in. There may be bushes, swamps and difficult terrain.

Pupils: Role play this moment – *just* this moment.

Pupils: Return to tables and write this scene bringing in as much drama and description as possible. This may involve dialogue and interaction with setting, other creatures or characters (see Chapter 10).

Teacher: Discuss the different ideas and developments. Consider what might happen next. Discuss cliffhangers (see Chapter 11).

Pupils: *Go it alone* – use this scene to finish a chapter as a cliffhanger, or complete a short story where they (as the character) either travel back to the present day, or stay in this past time forever.

Teacher: Feedback based on a sense of the past – how has the sense of era been achieved and is the detail consistent throughout? What techniques has the writer used to create drama and suspense? Does dialogue reflect the era being re-created?

Non-fiction exercise

Research the local area for key events that have happened in the vicinity. Write a non-fictional report to demonstrate a local find relating to some aspect of this event. This could happen as the result of building work, excavation work or something washed up on a riverbed or seashore. Depending on the chosen era, it may also be something written – the fragment of a letter or page from a diary, for instance. Investigate the differences between then, and now. How might a contemporary character experience this period in time?

ACT SIX: ONCE THERE WAS AN EGG
Fantasy dragon adventure

This fantasy genre session uses props, images and a story-starter to develop and inspire ideas. It moves through a whole-class writing scenario, with a focus on a slow build with intense description and detail at each stage. Pupils build their story one scene at a time whilst responding directly to images that inform characterisation. (The impact on each group having their own dragon is significant in terms of engagement with the activity. One dragon per pupil has even greater impact. However, if preparation time is an issue, images can be shown on screen, and baby dragons can be chosen this way instead.)

Learning and curriculum values

Creative writing skills: Explore ideas, character development, empathy and motivation, plot development, setting development, descriptive writing, suspense writing, world-building, story writing.

Literacy skills: Genre awareness (fantasy), reading, reading aloud, note taking, shared writing, independent writing.

Extended topic potential: Eggs, art, design (of eggs and dragons), colour, maps, terrains and landscapes, weather.

Life skills: Discussion, collaboration, purposeful talk, thinking, visualisation, listening.

Outcome: Pupils will produce a sustained piece of intense creative fictional writing achieved through a mixture of discussion and short bursts of writing activity. They will evolve empathy and motivation for fantasy characters and connect these with an appropriate setting. They will learn to look at detail, colour and shape and consider how this might impact on their descriptive writing. They will plot ideas independently and write a short scene or sequence that continues on from an initial whole group story-starter.

They will build this scene towards a moment of drama or suspense.

Prompts, props and materials

- Box of dragon homemade cards, approx 5cm square, at least one per group

- Collection of decorative eggs or large decorative 'fantasy'-type egg or image of decorative 'fantasy'-type egg
- Music – I use Max Richter *Sleep* (2015) but anything gentle and ambient will work
- LED tealight candles
- Notebooks
- Writing paper
- Pens, erasers, sharpeners etc.

Activity: Once There Was an Egg

Teacher: Put pupils in groups. Hand out eggs – one per group – or introduce single egg or egg image. Discuss colours and other detail. Write down any significant observations in notebook (or on whiteboard if using one egg for whole class).

Hand out LED tealight candles. Read story-starter (below).

Wordtamer story-starter

Once there was an egg. The egg lay hidden for a very long time. It lay hidden through changing seasons. It lay hidden through the ice-cold days of winter. It lay hidden through the burning heat of summer. It survived storms and blizzards. It survived floods and fires.

Then, one day, something changed. The egg began to _____

Teacher: Whole-class discussion. Build on from the story-starter. Each pupil's egg (or the class egg) is beginning to crack open. Nothing is hatching out yet, but the egg is clearly in a state of change. Discuss ways the egg might be beginning to change. Consider colour, sound and movement. What sound does an egg make when it's cracking? What special things might happen to a magical egg when it's cracking? It is important that the focus stays on the egg and the way it is changing – there will be a tendency with some pupils to want to describe whatever is hatching out, so stress that we don't need to know this at this stage.

Wordtamer sample model

Once there was an egg. The egg lay hidden for a very long time. It lay hidden through changing seasons. It lay hidden through the ice-cold days of winter. It lay hidden through the burning heat of summer. It survived storms and blizzards. It survived floods and fires. Then, one day, something changed. The egg began to **glow. The colours changed. The egg made small fizzing sounds. It seemed to be cracking.**

Teacher: Play music softly in background.

Pupils: Visualise the egg in this state of change (see Chapter 6).

Pupils: Describe (in two or three sentences) the scene where the egg begins to crack, continuing on from the story-starter as in the sample above. Stay with the detail of the scene. Do not move on (yet) to the stage where any creature emerges.

Pupils: Share writing and ideas either in pairs or groups. Listeners try to 'see' what the writer has written. Is there enough description? Could the writer have used sound, or colour, or other detail?

Teacher: Hand out dragons.

Pupils: Observe the dragon detail carefully. Make notes and 'dabble' – jot down anything particular about colour, or size. Consider the character: Boy or girl? Cute or scary? Timid or brave? Gentle or angry? Think of the connections between how the dragon looks and what sort of personality it might have. Make notes that capture both character details and visual description.

Teacher: This dragon will hatch from the egg.

Wordtamer sample model

Notice how the description of the actual dragon impacts on the writing as it develops (see Chapter 8):

Wordtamer sample model

Once there was an egg. The egg lay hidden for a very long time. It lay hidden through changing seasons. It lay hidden through the ice-cold days of winter. It lay hidden through the burning heat of summer. It survived storms and blizzards. It survived floods and fires. Then, one day, something changed. The egg began to glow. The colours changed. The egg made small fizzing sounds. It was cracking open. **Sparks glittered all around it. A thin green claw pushed its way through a splinter-thin gap. Then came a long arm, and a scaly green snout. Suddenly, with a whizz and a fizz, the egg smattered into a hundred pieces. A tiny green and gold dragon stood, looking around.**

Pupils: Write the moment when your dragon hatches, up to the point where it is looking around. Describe the detail of the baby dragon emerging, but don't yet describe what it sees.

Teacher: Class discussion (see Chapter 7). What sort of places do dragons tend to live? Think of fantasy lands and fantasy descriptions. Mountains? Ice? Water? Lakes? Discuss more descriptive and atmospheric detail. Jagged mountains? Shimmering ice? Rippling lakes? Orange water, the colour of fire?

Pupils: Visualisation (see Chapter 6). Imagine the dragon as it looks around. What can it see? How might it feel (see Chapter 11)?

Pupils: Make notes and 'dabble'. What setting has the dragon been born into?

Wordtamer sample model

The dragon looked round at towering, snow-topped mountains. He was beside a lake, but the water was frozen over. He peered into the iced skin of the water. There were creatures inside the lake, but they were very still. They had claws and wings, and the dragon felt sad as he looked at them. He shivered. His dappled green wings opened slowly, as if the movement hurt. A bright red tongue of fire flickered between his tiny, sharp teeth.

Pupils: Add on the next stage of the story. Describe what the dragon can see as it looks around (see Chapter 7).

Teacher: Discuss plot ideas (see Chapter 9). What might happen next? What might the story be?

Pupils: Make notes and 'dabble'. Plot ideas in notebooks through mediums such as writing, story graphs, and mindmaps to build in drama and suspense (see Chapter 9 and Chapter 11).

Pupils: Give dragons a name, and think about how they might learn their own name.

Pupils: Visualise a favourite scene from the plotted journey of ideas.

Wordtamer sample model

The dragon flew across the frozen land. He grew tired, and settled amongst some rocks to sleep. "Be careful," said a bored voice. "Your claws are scratchy."

The dragon looked and saw a small stone staring up at him. He moved out of the way. "Sorry."

"Who are you, anyway?" said the stone.

The dragon remembered the egg, the iced creatures and the frozen world. "I'm not sure. Everything seems new and strange." As he spoke, small red flames escaped from his mouth.

"You breathe fire," said the stone. He didn't sound bored any more. He started rolling around excitedly. "I'll call you Flamer. Perhaps you have come to save us by melting this terrible world."

"I don't think so," said Flamer. "My flames are very small. There won't be enough fire to make a difference."

The stone creature looked sad, then said, "Would you fly me somewhere?"

Flamer was tired, but he wanted to help his only friend. "Yes," he said.

"Then carry me in your scratchy claws. I know somewhere we can go to help us melt all this ice."

Flamer was about to ask if he could have a sleep first, but suddenly he heard a sound. Looking round, he saw an army of terrible beasts coming nearer. There were hundreds of them. Their bodies were jagged and sharp. Their eyes gleamed out a vicious blue. The beasts crackled and groaned as they marched nearer.

"We'd better go," whispered the stone. "The Ice-Ones have felt the warmth of your fire from miles away. They have come to destroy you."

Flamer lifted the stone in his claws. He tried to fly, but the stone was heavy. The dragon's wings were not powerful yet. The nearest Ice-One reached out its long, icicle arm...

Pupils: *Go it alone* – write the favourite plot scene or sequence with as much detail as possible, ending on either a cliffhanger, or as a completion to the story (see Chapter 11).

Pupils: Share writing in pairs or groups. Listeners try to 'see' what the writer has written. Is there enough description? Could the writer have used sound, or colour, or other detail?

Teacher: Feedback based on characterisation, suspense, setting and plot. Does the dragon character behave consistently? Can the reader feel empathy for the character, and how has this been achieved? How well conceived is this setting and how has language been used to achieve this? What techniques has the writer used to create drama and suspense? Is the plot viable or are there ways it could be developed?

Poetry exercise: A collage of words

Materials: Scrap paper, scissors, glue, blank A3 egg image sheets A4 or A3 (photocopiable resource on p. 180).

Hatching a poem: Pupils select their favourite sentence from any scene they have written in this previous exercise. They rewrite it on a piece of scrap paper, mark the paper so they know it is theirs and fold it up. All the sentences are collected in. Then pupils are given a new sentence that was not their own.

Pupils work in groups, with an egg image sheet per group (A4 or A3 depending on group size).

Using each other's sentences, pupils choose words or phrases they like and re-arrange them into a coherent rhyming or non-rhyming poem. When they are satisfied with the arrangement, they glue them onto the egg. This interactive activity enables every pupil's creative work to be recognised in a new format.

ACT SEVEN: THINKING HATS
Contemporary moral storytelling

A creative session that sets a moral story in a contemporary, familiar setting. Pupils will discuss the values associated with 'right' and 'wrong', developing characters and stories that are underpinned by motivation and point of view. They will write monologues and story beginnings from a third person perspective.

Learning and curriculum values

Creative writing skills: Explore ideas, character development, empathy, motivation and voice, focus on point of view, development of additional characters, plot development, setting development, first person, third person, story writing.

Literacy skills: Reading, reading aloud, note taking, independent writing.

Extended topic potential: Morality, cause and effect (of behaviour), belief systems.

Cross-curricular skills: Debate around moral viewpoints, debate around communities, drama, role play.

Life skills: Discussion, collaboration, purposeful talk, thinking, visualisation, listening, moral viewpoint.

Outcome: Pupils will produce both a first person monologue and the beginning of a story from a different character's third person perspective. They will write a short piece of suspenseful fiction that will lead into the discussion of moral standpoints. They will gain increased awareness of others' views related to what is right and what is wrong.

Props, prompts and materials

- Selection of hats
- Character sheets (photocopiable resource on p. 183)
- Pre-prepared sealed envelopes containing 'Wrong Deeds' and 'When, Where and What' questions

- Flipchart-size sheets of paper
- Marker pens (ideally for all pupils)
- Writing paper
- Notebooks
- Pens, erasers, sharpeners, etc.

Activity: Thinking Hats

Teacher: The initial aim is to create a convincing well-rounded character who is then faced with a moral dilemma. Discuss what it means to make a mistake, or to do something wrong. What experiences do pupils have? Have they ever done something wrong, but for the right reasons?

What might the 'right reasons' be? (See Chapter 8.)

Arrange pupils in groups of four to six: one flipchart sheet of paper per table.

Give each table a hat and a character sheet. Who might wear this hat?

Create a Character

Name and age (of character)

_____

Description (what do you think they look like?)

_____

What sort of character are they most of the time? (Choose two or three).

>   _Moody_   _Grumpy_   _Friendly_   _Kind_

>   _Anxious_   _Shy_   _Confident_   _Mean_   _Happy_   _Sad_

What sort of home do they live in, and who do they live with?

_____

Write down one thing they love:

_____

Write down one thing they hate:

_____

Pupils: Collaborate on ideas, and evolve a group character's details onto the character sheet.

Teacher: Hand out prepared Wrong Deeds options in sealed envelopes (one in each envelope) along with a *When, Where, What?* set of questions:

Wrong Deeds

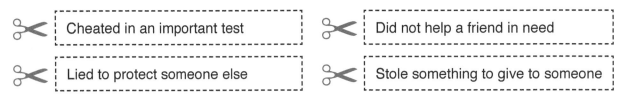

✂ ┊ Cheated in an important test ┊   ✂ ┊ Did not help a friend in need ┊

✂ ┊ Lied to protect someone else ┊   ✂ ┊ Stole something to give to someone ┊

> ## Wordtamer *When, Where, What?*
>
> When in your character's life did this happen? It could be recent, or some time ago.
> Where was your character at the time when it happened?
> What have the consequences been for your character?

Pupils: Take an envelope and open it, share the 'wrong deed' within the group but *not* with the whole class. Answer the *When, Where, What?* questions through mindmap techniques on flip chart sheets (see Chapter 9).

Teacher: Whole-class discussion: what is a monologue? (First person speech discussing their thoughts out loud.)

Pupils: Independent writing – write a monologue where the character talks to the reader about what they did, and why.

> ## Wordtamer sample model
>
> Jack (aged 62): I still feel guilty about what I did to Sobia Bashir, even after all these years. She was supposed to be in the school performance playing her flute, but I stole it from her. I was only seven and my cousin Dan told me it played a magic tune that made things get better. Grandma Harriet was very old and I thought I could play it for her and she would get young and live forever. Only when I played it to Grandma Harriet she said it was a terrible racket and wouldn't listen. Cousin Dan laughed at me and said it was lucky she was partly deaf. I cried and wanted to take the flute and sneak it back to school the next day, but Dan snatched it off me. He sold it at the market. I could never tell anyone about it because Dan was old enough to get into BIG trouble for what he did. Our family had enough troubles as it was. So I've kept it a secret, but I feel sad about it. Sobia's family were as poor as ours. If she had learnt to play really well she might have got famous and had a better life. I never knew what happened to her. Perhaps she did get famous but I don't think so. I mean, I've never heard of her since she left school. Famous people get heard of, especially round here.

Pupils: Pair up with someone from a different group. Read monologues to each other.

Discuss what the character did. Does the listener have empathy for the character? Is there any way for the character to put things right?

Pupils: Make notes and 'dabble'. Consider the person who was 'wronged'. Think about them at the time the incident happened. What were they doing? How might they have reacted?

Pupils: Role play this character: Tell the monologue listener how this character feels about what happened.

Teacher: Whole-class discussion. Consider tension and suspense in fiction within an 'everyday' setting (see Chapter 11).

Wordtamer sample model

Sabia polished her flute for one last time. The silver body reflected the lights in the school hall. Little stars seemed to twinkle across it.

"That looks magical," said little Jack Harris.

Sabia smiled but she didn't answer. She had to go back to the classroom and get her bags. It was the end of the school day and Mum would be waiting for her. They would be in a rush tonight. Tonight was Sobia's big performance. All of her family were coming to see her play the flute. Uncle Ali said she was a genius. She might even get famous one day.

She packed the flute safely in its case, stashed it behind the stage where no one would see it, and hurried back to the classroom.

"Whoa, watch where you're going." Dan Harris, Jack's cousin, was on his way to collect Jack from school. Sabia didn't like Dan much. He was always messing about and causing trouble. He scared her a bit.

Later that evening, Sabia arrived back at the school with her family. The hall was packed with mums and dads and friends and relatives.

"Have you got your flute ready?" smiled Mr Evans, the music teacher.

"I stashed it behind the stage," said Sabia, smiling back.

Mr Evans frowned. He shook his head. "There's nothing backstage. I've been tidying up round there."

Sabia looked all round the school hall. Her flute must have been moved somewhere. But even as she looked, her heart was sinking. She felt sick. Her hands shook. Someone had taken it. Someone had stolen her beautiful twinkling flute.

Pupils: *Go it alone* – begin a story in third person from the POV of the character who was wronged, at the time when it happened. Think about the place, and the time of day, when this story will be set.

Teacher: Feedback based on characterisation. How 'real' does the character feel? How much empathy can be felt for this character? Is there a sense of setting? How well does the beginning build tension and suspense? What techniques has the writer used to achieve this, and what might be improved or developed?

Non-fiction exercise

The Moral Debate – where do ideas of what is right and what is wrong come from? Can something ever be right for one group of people, but wrong for another?

Act Eight: When the World Went Wrong
Dystopian science fiction

This is a dystopian science fiction, evolved through a mix of group work, discussion, visualisation and independent writing. Pupils consider the impact of a devastating (or comic) event affecting Planet Earth. They evolve ideas through imagery, props and interactive material including cactus plants and rocks.

Learning and curriculum values

Creative writing skills: Explore ideas, character development, empathy, motivation and voice, plot development, setting development, descriptive writing, suspense writing, story writing.

Literacy skills: Genre awareness (science fiction, dystopia and utopia), reading, reading aloud, note taking, shared writing, independent writing.

Extended topic potential: Meteorites, geology, rocks and minerals (their properties), growing plants, weather and world/natural events, science, technology and architecture (new foods, structures and infrastructures for a new world).

Cross-curricular skills: Environment and impact, human behaviour, plants and habitats, geology.

Life skills: Discussion, collaboration, purposeful talk, thinking, seeing, visualisation, listening.

Outcome: Pupils will develop characters and discuss ideas around dystopian scenarios. They will connect actual objects and items (plants and rocks) and use these imaginatively to advance and enhance their ideas. They will work independently to produce a suspenseful short story or scene.

Props, prompts and materials

- Selection of potted cacti plants
- Selection of large rocks or interesting stones
- Screen images (meteorite or similar)

- Character sheets (photocopiable resource on p. 183)
- Envelopes
- Slips of blank paper
- Music CD: *Mirage*, Klaus Schulze (2016) or *Oxygen 3*, Jean Michel Jarre (2016) (optional)
- LED tealight candles
- Flipchart-size sheets of paper
- Marker pens (ideally for all pupils)
- Writing paper
- Notebooks
- Pens, erasers, sharpeners, etc.

Activity: When the World Went Wrong

Teacher: Discuss science fictional dystopia and utopia. A utopia is a world where everything is almost too wonderful; a dystopia (in this context) is a world evolved from a devastating event or overly controlled futuristic scenario. This session has a focus on dystopia, but it could be adapted to work equally well with a utopia.

Pupils: Create individual characters using 'character sheet' information. Evolve a character who is fictitious but recognisable – someone the same age and from a similar area as the pupils (see Chapter 8).

Wordtamer sample model: create a character

Name and age (of character):
Sophie Baxter aged 11

Description (what do you think they look like?):
Thin brown hair, green eyes, freckles

What sort of character are they most of the time? (Choose two or three).
    Moody   Grumpy   <u>Friendly</u>   <u>Kind</u>
    Anxious   <u>Shy</u>   Confident   Mean   Happy   Sad

What sort of home do they live in, and who do they live with?
Lives with Dad in small house on modern housing estate

Write down one thing they love:
Her spaniel dog Baxter

Write down one thing they hate:
Homework

Teacher: Play music quietly in background throughout session (optional).

Pupils: Visualise character on an ordinary day, in a place familiar to them. It might be school, their bedroom, the local park etc. (see Chapter 6). Picture all the detail in this place.

Pupils: Make notes and 'dabble'. Write the scene just visualised (see Chapter 7). Use dialogue if other characters have been introduced to the scene (see Chapter 10).

Wordtamer sample model

Sophie sat on her bed. It was hot outside. She could hear birds singing. She bet all her friends were out enjoying this weird March heatwave, but Dad had insisted she stayed in until her homework was done. He was out shopping but she knew he'd check up on her later. "Rocky planets on the solar system?" she asked Baxter. "Know anything about that?" Baxter wagged his stubby gold tail, and Sophie scratched his ears. "Me neither, and my laptop's broken so I can't Google anything. The screen keeps flashing." She stretched out on the bed, chewing the end of her pencil. Outside, she could hear the shouts of her friends in the park that ran along the back of her garden. She wished the planet answer would magically write itself across the ceiling, but no matter how hard she stared, there was nothing on her ceiling. Nothing except cobwebs and a splatter of brown stains where a fizzy drink bottle had exploded a long time ago.

Teacher: Whole class discuss potential scene of doom and devastation. What would happen if a meteorite hit Earth? Show screen image.

Would there be floods? Droughts? Fires? Storms? Darkness? Civil chaos?

Show screen images.

If a meteorite seems too unsettling for the class being worked with, gentler or more comic alternatives can be considered. An invasion of soft, feathery things? An advancing giant banana?

Teacher: Put pupils in groups of four(ish). Hand out pens and big sheets of paper.

Pupils: Draw or write an environmental catastrophe onto flipchart sheets of paper. Consider the impact this will have on the area.

Teacher: Imagine the meteorite has carried with it strange plant life or seeds from other planets. Hand round cacti – ideally one per group. (If physical cacti plants are not available, screen images can be shown.)

Pupils: What would happen if these plants were toxic? Intelligent? Or maybe they contain powers for good, or evil? Discuss and add ideas to sheets.

Teacher: Imagine the meteorite has scattered strange rock or stone formations.

Hand round rocks and stones, ideally one per group. (If interesting rocks and stones are too difficult to source then screen images can be shown.)

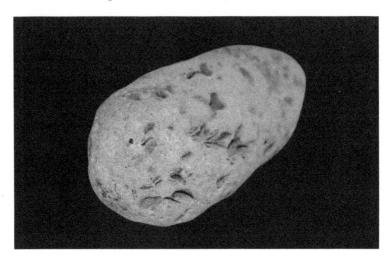

Pupils: Consider the dangers these rocks and stones might bring. They might leak toxic fumes. They might burn to the touch. They might contain strange alien powers. Discuss and add ideas to sheets.

Teacher: Write up the strongest idea from each group on the board.

Hand out envelopes and blank strips of paper.

Pupils (independent work): Choose favourite idea from the board. Without discussing or sharing the choice, write it down on the strip of paper, then seal it in the envelope.

Wordtamer sample model

Favourite dystopian idea

Every day is an endless night. Strange glowing crystals have rained down onto everything. These hypnotise humans so people don't know who they are any more.

Pupils: Write title 'When the World Went Wrong' onto writing paper.

Pupils: Visualise characters in the moment that the major event strikes.

Teacher: Guide the visualisation with a specific script: Take your mind back to the scene you pictured in the very first visualisation activity. Your character is in exactly the same place – nothing has changed, but now the crisis is coming. The meteorite is blasting towards earth. At the moment of impact, what changes might your character feel, or see, or hear? Maybe the earth shakes? Maybe everything goes dark, or very bright? Do fires break out? Do buildings fall? Is it loud, or dramatic, or very subtle? Think about the chosen secret idea you have in your envelope, and connect this with your visualisation. Is your character scared, or excited? How are they feeling (see Chapter 11)?

> ## Wordtamer sample model
>
> Baxter started whining. Sophie wondered if there might be a storm coming. "Don't be a wimp." She grinned at the puppy and stroked his silky ears. "Storms can't hurt you."
>
> Baxter whimpered. He hunched his back in the way that he always did when something scared him.
>
> It was growing very dark outside. Weirdly dark. Sophie realised that even the birds had stopped singing.
>
> Suddenly there was a smack of sound. The ceiling seemed to crack and split. "This doesn't look good," Sophie said. She jumped up from the bed and grabbed Baxter. "We've got to get out of here."

Pupils: Write your scene onto paper, after the title.

Pupils: Visualise the next scene; the aftermath of what has just happened.

Teacher: Continue guided visualisation. Is the character trapped somewhere? Do they step outside? Do they try to run, or are they in some sort of trance? Picture what they do as they try to make sense of what has just happened. What are they seeing? What can they hear? How are they feeling?

> ## Wordtamer sample model
>
> Sophie ran out into the garden. She could feel Baxter pressed tight against her, whimpering. "You're rubbish in a crisis," she murmured, but she felt like whimpering too. Her heart seemed to tremble in her chest. The sky was as black as night, but there were no stars. No moon. As Sophie looked around she saw something glowing at the far end of the garden. She made her way towards it.

Pupils: Continue on from the previous writing. Include visual detail associated with the setting (see Chapter 7).

Pupils: Things will get worse before they get better. Continue writing and escalate the drama and the tension. Keep the dystopian setting evident, but bring in more action, or a new crisis that has connections with the chosen sealed idea.

Pupils: *Go it alone* – continue to completion of either a proposed chapter or an ending to a short story.

Teacher: Pupils will now share ideas and work in their groups again.

Pupils (group work): Each member of the group reads out the most recent scene. The others in the group try to identify which dystopian scenario is sealed inside the envelope. Pupils can reveal the chosen idea once they have read their extract.

Teacher: Feedback based around the dystopian setting. Is it clear what has happened? Have the scenes been built with detail? How imaginative has the pupil been with strange and terrible possibilities? Does the character seem believable and do they behave appropriately given what is taking place? How 'real' does the character feel? How much empathy can be felt for this character? How well does the whole piece build tension and suspense? What techniques has the writer used to achieve this, and what might be improved or developed?

Non-fiction exercise: weird and wonderful plants

Google search or library search, or teacher selects a mix of books and internet sites, photocopied pages etc. to gather a range of information from. Working in groups, each group researches one plant from the list: Bat Plant, Corpse Flower, Naked Man Orchid, Voodoo Lily, Snap Dragon Seed Pods, The Shy Plant, Venus Fly Trap, The Dancing Plant, The Bottle Tree, The Dragon Blood Tree.

Gather as much information as possible and present these to the class.

The truth is sometimes stranger than fiction.

ACT NINE: 'A' IS FOR ALIEN
Magic realism, science fiction

An advanced creative session with a focus on stories drawn from science facts and a familiar classroom setting. Pupils will consider other worlds, character viewpoints and the impact of endings.

Learning and curriculum values

Creative writing skills: Explore ideas, character development, empathy, motivation and voice, focus on point of view, development of backstory and world-building, development of additional characters, plot development, setting development, descriptive writing, experiment with endings, story writing.

Literacy skills: Genre awareness (science fiction and magic realism), reading, reading aloud, prepare a synopsis, note taking, independent writing.

Extended topic potential: Planets, solar system, alien life-forms, space travel, technology, science.

Cross-curricular skills: Awareness of planets, solar system, the universe, environmental issues, debate around newcomers to a class, debate around whole groups of new people aiming to settle in one area, drama, role play.

Life skills: Discussion, collaboration, purposeful talk, thinking, visualisation, listening, moral viewpoint.

Outcome: Pupils will produce a complete short story marrying together science fictional facts with everyday classroom scenarios. They will develop strong and believable alien characters, and create alien worlds. They will also create human characters. The voice of both characters will be present in the storytelling, but the story itself will be told from a single viewpoint. Pupils discuss and explore valid environmental issues, and increase awareness of their own surroundings as seen from an alien perspective.

Props, prompts and materials

- PowerPoint or screen shot of Gliese 581g or other world that has been shown scientifically to potentially sustain life, compared with Earth.

- Music: *Solaris*, Cliff Martinez (2014)
- Writing paper
- Notebooks
- Pens, erasers, sharpeners, etc.

Activity: 'A' is for Alien

Teacher: Class discussion. What are the chances of life being discovered on another planet? What about human life forms? What would these types of beings need?

Introduce image of Gliese 581g next to Earth on screen. Which one is Earth? What are the similarities? What might the differences be? Explain the 'Goldilocks' effect in terms of other planets – these are planets where the conditions for life are considered neither too hot nor too cold – 'just right' for life as we understand it to emerge.

Create a class 'planet' based on what is discussed. The planet should be considered as more advanced, technologically, than our own. This is both 'backstory' and 'world-building' that can be used to develop plot and character reaction/behaviour in the storytelling. It will also enable genre details to evolve and be embedded in the writing.

Play music.

Pupils: Make notes and 'dabble'. Sketch ideas. Create individual aliens – something or someone who is very similar to a human in looks, but who is of superior intelligence and for whom there should be other marked differences in appearance and physical attributes.

Wordtamer sample model

Skinny, green eyes like a cat. Moves fast. Good at jumping.

Pupils: Write up a longer description as a paragraph, from the notes and sketches.

Wordtamer sample model

The alien's slanted green eyes stared out of its thin, mottled face. There were cracks in its skin and something about its expression suggested a depth of intelligence. It moved quickly; lightly, like a cat. It had long claws instead of fingers and the top of its head seemed to be more fur than hair.

Teacher: Whole class discuss additional powers within a science-fiction context: telepathy, invisibility, flight, teleportation, X-ray vision, etc.

Pupils: Make notes and 'dabble'. Add superpower to their alien's list of attributes – consider something that is drawn from their physical appearance or amend the appearance to give plausibility to the superpower.

Wordtamer sample model

(Earlier descriptions referred to staring eyes and unusual intelligence, so the eyes and mind have been given a superpower.)

Its species has evolved highly sensitised insights – the ability to 'sense, see and interpret' information beyond simply looking.

Teacher: Script – this alien's planet is doomed – but as we know, there is one planet that is 'just right' for the alien to be able to exist on.

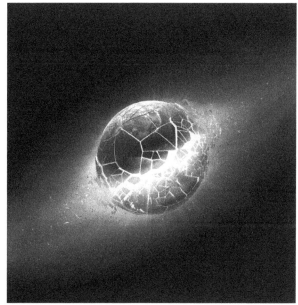

EARTH!

Teacher: Whole-class scenario: the alien has arrived on Earth, with others of its kind. They are all trying to appear as 'human' as possible and the real humans are not yet aware that aliens have arrived in their midst. This is the alien's first day at an ordinary school.

    Consider how it might look in a normal classroom whilst it is trying to remain incognito.

    What might other pupils think about it? How might they behave towards it?

    Consider the hook in to the story. How might it begin (see Chapter 11)?

Teacher: Suggest ordinary items that might be in the classroom – a pen, a map of the world, a book (see Chapter 7).

Pupils: Take notebook and move around classroom in 'alien' role – try to see items through an alien's eyes. Make notes about what the alien is seeing and feeling.

Pupils: Make notes and 'dabble' – what sort of story might evolve from this alien in the classroom? Write a synopsis that summarises both character(s), premise and plot. Within this synopsis consider a human character who will interact with this alien. Identify who this character is and how they might react to the alien.

> ### Wordtamer sample model
>
> The alien tries to befriend another child, Kirsten. Kirsten's best friend, Matt, feels jealous. He doesn't trust the alien, who the teacher says is called Norman Smith. The alien looks weird, and Matt is determined to find out who, or what, this new pupil really is.

Teacher: Split the class in half. Discuss POV (see Chapter 8). How might an alien behave that is different to how a human behaves? What language choices could be made to make the alien sound 'alien'? What unusual behaviours might the alien have that would attract the attention of the human pupil? One half of the class will tell the story from the alien's POV, the other half will tell it from a human pupil's POV.

Wordtamer sample model

Matt's POV: "Listen up, all of you." Miss Hadlow clapped her hands. "Line up by the door in pairs. It's time for assembly."

Matt looked across at Kirsten, his best friend. They always went to assembly together. But she was chattering to the new boy – Norman Smith. Matt got a knot in his tummy. Kirsten seemed drawn to Norman. Matt didn't trust him. He had slanted eyes, like a cat, and it was weird that he was still wearing gloves indoors.

He might be Nor*man* but he wasn't Nor*mal*.

Suddenly Norman looked round, as if he knew Matt was watching him. Matt felt an icy stab of fear.

Wordtamer sample model

Alien's POV: The alien blinked as hoards of the babbling hominids began to gather by the opening in the inner-structure.

"Hey, Norman, would you like to stand with me?" one of them asked.

The alien remembered Norman was its hominid name. "Thank you. I would," it said. It stretched its mouth into the shape that Instructor V had explained was 'The Smile'.

The alien felt a tremble in the mind-sensor on the back of its head, and experienced a knowledge-scan data rush. A male hominid was observing its behaviour from an unseen point in the inner-structure. This observing hominid didn't trust the alien. The alien would have to keep its radar trained on this suspicious male. It didn't want to be discovered. Not yet.

Teacher: Discuss a range of possible endings in terms of impact on a reader (see Chapter 9).

Pupils: Make notes and 'dabble'. Explore ways this first day at school could end. Write a possible last line in draft form.

Pupils: *Go it alone* – start the story, moving from the point where the alien is new to the classroom, and getting the characters through a dramatic first day to the end (see Chapter 11). Consider the alien's superpowers, and the impact this could have in the classroom.

Teacher: Feedback based on backstory, characterisation, point of view and the strength of the ending. How effectively do the original backstory and world-build information inform the plot and the action? Is there a sense of genre in any of the written detail? How convincing are the characters in terms of how they respond to situations they are faced with? Do both characters behave consistently, regardless of the POV? Can the reader feel empathy for the characters, and how has this been achieved? What techniques has the writer used to create drama and suspense? Is the plot viable or are there ways it could be developed?

Non-fiction exercise

Write a report from the alien that will be sent to others of its species who haven't travelled to Earth yet, giving an account of the hominid species, and outlining their unusual behaviours and habits.

How would an alien perceive us?

Identify whether the alien recommends that fellow aliens come to join it on Earth, or not.

State the reasons for the alien's decision.

ACT TEN:
ENDANGERED SPECIES –
WELCOME TO MY WORLD
Anthropomorphic realism and research in writing

This session will appeal to those pupils who feel they aren't creative and don't enjoy stories: those who are not drawn to fiction. Much of the storytelling in this session is inspired by facts. The session also has appeal for those pupils who don't enjoy research and aspects of non-fiction as they can learn how integral these elements can be to a piece of creative work. It is an advanced session involving the analysis of both fact and fiction. Pupils will apply researched facts to collaborative ideas, then incorporate these within an independent story.

Learning and curriculum values

Creative writing skills: Explore ideas, character development, empathy, motivation and voice, setting development, descriptive writing, point of view, first and third person perspectives, past and present narrative styles, continuity in tense and narrative style, embedding research facts with fiction, story writing.

Literacy skills: Reading, reading aloud, note taking, shared writing, independent writing.

Extended topic potential: Animals, animal behaviours, habitats, poaching, endangered species, myths (attributed to animals, in particular those that threaten their survival), ICT – the spread of information, educating the world, geography, pets.

Cross-curricular skills – research: Drama, role play, geography, environmental issues, endangered species Issues, global settings.

Life skills: Discussion, collaboration, purposeful talk, thinking, visualisation, listening.

Outcome: Pupils will produce a piece of creative fictional writing using non-fictional prompts; they will learn how to use researched material as a source for creative storytelling ideas. They will experiment with point of view and consider what it is like to *be* a very different species, and evolve an appropriate narrative voice, and setting, for that species.

Props, prompts and materials

- 'White lion and his facts' (photocopiable resource on p. 201)
- 'Author draws from facts' sample model (ideally transfer onto screen for whole class visual aid – on p. 203)
- 'White Magic' story-starter (to print or read out – photocopiable resource on p. 204)
- Additional prepared endangered species factsheets using 'white lion' model (photocopiable resources on pp. 206–208)
- Flipchart sheets
- Marker pens for each pupil
- Writing paper
- Notebook
- Pens, erasers, sharpeners, etc.

Wordtamer: White lion and his facts

White lions are very rare, and those with blue eyes are even more special. African tribes-people used to believe they were like angels, and brought messages from the Gods.

Where do I live?
I live in Africa, where it is very hot. The grass is often yellow and the lakes and rivers can dry up, which make it hard for me and my family to find water.

Who do I live with?
I live in something called a 'pride' – this is a group of lions who all live together and look out for each other. Because I am a male, my dad will get fed up with me when I am a bit older, and I will have to leave his pride and find new lions to live with.

How do I 'talk' to my family?
Lions are famous for roaring. Our roar is one of the loudest calls in the animal kingdom. We communicate in other ways too, with meows, roars, grunts, moans, growls, snarls, purrs, hums, puffs and woofs. Each sound has a different meaning. We are really quite chatty, in our own 'lion' way.

How do I spend my day?
Lions are part of the cat family, and so we are nocturnal. We sleep by day, but at night we are wide awake. Our eyesight is seven times stronger than humans' and we can see in the dark. We only need a tiny bit of moonlight, or even starlight, and we can see really well. We hunt for food in pairs, or groups. A lion on its own cannot catch a bigger animal.

What do I eat?
I am a carnivore so that means I eat meat. I hunt animals such as zebra, buffalo and even crocodiles. I also enjoy a tasty mouse or a lizard (sorry about that!). I'm not great at catching my dinner though – my sisters are loads better than me.

Humans like to hunt us. Sometimes they want to kill us, and sometimes they capture us and take us to zoos or circuses.

Activity: Welcome to My World

Prepare A4 sheets showing different creatures' factsheets using the white lion style (suggested species below). A more advanced and longer version of this session could involve pupils finding the facts themselves, and creating their own factsheets to use as reference.

Teacher: Introduce the white lion using factsheet and image. Discuss what an author might find interesting in the 'facts' and list them, then demonstrate how the author evolves these facts into a synopsis and the beginning of a story.

Wordtamer sample model: 'Author draws from facts' list

Things of interest to an author, taken from the white lion factsheet:

- Very rare
- Can see by starlight
- Hunted for zoos and circuses
- Has to leave the 'pride' and live on his own
- They are like angels
- The setting is Africa, with long grass
- Hot, starry nights

Wordtamer sample model

Early synopsis of story idea from factsheet points for white lion:

> The time has come for the lion to leave the pride. He goes at night, by starlight. Because he is white he is easy to see, and hunters chase and capture him. Who - or what - can save him?

Teacher: Class discussion – how many aspects of the author's synopsis come directly from the facts?

Wordtamer sample model

Facts that affect the synopsis:

> <u>The time has come for the lion to leave the pride</u>. He goes <u>at night, by starlight</u>. Because he <u>is white</u> he is easy to see, and <u>hunters chase and capture him</u>. Who - or what - can save him?

The author has used four points of interest to create a story synopsis from facts about the white lion.

Teacher: Read out or print 'White Magic' story-starter for pupils to read in groups. (Additional options provided on the following pages.)

'White Magic' story-starter

It was dark. Haider and his family were prowling in circles, getting ready for the hunt. Lena, Haider's sister, chewed his ear playfully. "Gerroff," snarled Haider, but he wasn't really cross. He loved messing about with Lena.

Suddenly he sensed a shadowy figure by his side. It was his father, the leader of Haider's pride. His father's green eyes gleamed out at him. "You have to go," Haider's father growled. "There are too many young lions in this pride, and soon there won't be enough food for me and your mother to feed them all."

"That's right, Haider," his mother said, padding over. "It's time for you to leave us. You need to find new lions, and make a family of your own."

"But Leo is older than me. Why don't you send him first," Haider pleaded. He looked round at his other sisters, Kiona and Sheena. They had all grown up together and he couldn't bear to leave them behind. "It's because of my white coat, isn't it?" he said, turning back to his parents. "You think the humans will see me more easily, and bring trouble to you."

Haider saw his parents' green eyes narrow, and he knew he was right. They thought he would bring danger to them all. They wouldn't change their minds. Haider slunk away through the long grass. There was no moon that night, but a thousand stars glittered above him. He passed a herd of zebra, and growled softly. He was hungry, but he couldn't hunt on his own. He would

have to hope a small lizard or rat ran across his path.

In the distance he could still catch the scent of his family, but it was getting fainter. His heart ached at the thought of never seeing any of them again. Especially Lena. He and Lena had been really special together.

Suddenly, Haider stopped. Two of the stars seemed to have fallen from the sky, and were moving towards him. The stars were so huge he was dazzled by them. Was this a strange new magic? Some humans thought that white lions were messengers from the Gods. Maybe one of the Gods had come to save him.

Then he realised they weren't stars. They were the eyes of the growling beast that the humans rode around in. Haider knew if they saw him, they would capture him. He would never have a pride of his own.

He changed direction, moving towards the rocks, and the river. He knew the beast would struggle to climb the rocks, and it couldn't swim either. If he reached the river he would be safe. As the rocks grew nearer, Haider broke into a run.

The humans had special killing sticks that they might fire at him – his own cousin had been caught that way – but if he ran fast enough the killing stick might not get him.

His paws pounded through the dry grass. Thorns and twigs scratched against him, but he didn't notice the pain. He had to keep running. From behind him, he heard the shouts of the humans, and the growl of their beast. They were getting nearer.

Pupils: Discuss and identify how many aspects of the author's 'White Magic' story are drawn from facts.

Wordtamer sample model

Facts used to support fiction in 'White Magic':

> It is dark: the author had learnt lions hunt at night.
> The lion has to leave: the author had learnt male lions leave to form their own pride.
> There are stars: the author had learnt lions can see well by starlight.
> He is rare: hunters will want him.
> Lions cannot hunt large prey alone.
> Tribal people used to believe white lions with blue eyes were magical.
> The setting reflects details from the factsheet about the lion's natural environment.

Teacher: Discuss point of view and anthropomorphism (see Chapter 8). This story is told through the eyes of a white lion. How has the author captured the sense that it is a lion, and not a human character?

Wordtamer sample model

Aspects related to 'lion' characteristics:

> The lion moves and behaves like a lion. He doesn't understand the concept of a moving vehicle, or a gun.
>> He reacts to his family based on a lion's needs, and not human ones.

Teacher: Place pupils in groups and hand out factsheets for different endangered species.

Wolf

Wolves are very clever and have special friendships with each other, but humans hunt them because they are scared of them.

Where do I live?
I live in Europe, deep in the forest. It gets *really* cold in winter.

Who do I live with?
I live with my family in what is called a 'pack'. My mum and dad are the leaders of our pack. Some of my older brothers and sisters are a bit bossy. I do love them all, but one day I will leave and form my own pack.

How do I 'talk' to my family?
I am a bit like a dog, so I bark and whimper, but my favourite sound is howling. I can send messages to my family when I howl, even if they are a long way away. When one wolf howls, we usually all join in.

How do I spend my day?
We hunt at night, as we can see in the dark. Sometimes our eyes actually glow. We rest in the day, although I sometimes play chase with my brothers and sisters, and we play-fight with each other too.

What do I eat?
If I'm lucky our pack will catch a deer or a moose, and we all share it. I like to go fishing too, and love a big tasty salmon. Sometimes we creep into farms and catch sheep, but that's only if we are *very* hungry. We prefer to stay away from places that smell of humans.

Humans have written lots of stories where we are the 'bad guys' and they are scared of us. This has meant they have hunted and killed a lot of us. We don't like to be near humans but a lot of our forests are being cut down and it is getting much harder to hide.

Grizzly Bear

Grizzlies' main enemies are other bears and humans. It is very rare to see a grizzly bear, because they like to keep out of sight.

Where do I live?
I live in Canada, deep in the forest. It gets *really* cold in winter, so I build a den and go to sleep then.

Who do I live with?
I don't live with anyone, I usually roam about on my own.

How do I 'talk' to other bears?
I groan and growl and if I get *really* cross I bellow. If I lie down, or yawn, other bears know I am not going to bother them. If I flatten my ears and lower my head they had better make a run for it, because that is when I'm angry. I'm not cross all the time though. I'm quite timid really.

How do I spend my day?
I like going fishing and messing about in the lakes and rivers, especially in deserted areas as I am very shy. I like a bit of mountain climbing too. Some days I meet up with other bears and we hang out together, but we usually go off on our own again afterwards. I can run quite fast if I want to, but usually I just lumber about.

What do I eat?
I eat loads in the summer, because I have to store it for my winter sleep. I like salmon, and fruit and berries. I also eat insects, and the odd deer – if I can manage to find one! Oh, and I like honey too!

Even though I am shy I sometimes go into towns and look through the rubbish bins. Some of my friends have even snuck into kitchens and stolen human food before. That's because we get really hungry, and there is less food to eat because humans are cutting the forests down.

I am scared of humans. Some of them would like to hunt me, and shoot me. Humans have even made rugs out of the fur of other bears.

Chimpanzee

Chimps are very clever; they are probably the most intelligent of all animals.

Where do I live?
I live in Africa, in the parts where there are lots of forests as I spend a lot of my time up in trees. I even sleep in trees, which is great as long as I don't fall out!

Who do I live with?
I live in a 'troop' of other chimps. There are fifty of us all together.

How do I 'talk' to my family?
I hoot, scream, grunt and drum on hollow trees with the flat of my hands. I make a loud wroo wroo sound if there is danger about.

How do I spend my day?
I wake at dawn, and go looking for food, or collect drinking water with bunches of leaves. I can walk as well as climb. The younger chimps run about, chase each other and play tag. We also hold hands and groom each other.

What do I eat?
I love fruit, and figs are my favourite. I like berries and apples too. I also snack on nuts, leaves, buds, blossom and insects.

I am wary of humans because they sometimes catch us and train us to do tricks or be their pets. They also cut down our trees and we have nowhere to live.

Alternative possible endangered species for research and development:

Pupils: Read factsheet. Discuss as group and make notes on flipchart sheet around what an author might find interesting. Aim to evolve at least three facts that might be able to be used in a story using the endangered species information.

Pupils: Role play, act out a scene where the animal is in its own environment (see Chapter 8). Nothing bad is happening. The animal is existing peacefully in its own world, and the habitat is one that is familiar to it (see Chapter 7). Try to move like this animal. How will this animal think? What will this animal see? How will this animal feel?

Teacher: Discuss whole class experiences of 'being' this animal – of stepping into its skin. What was different to being human? Did they learn anything new about the animal by moving like it, and thinking like it? How might the animal speak if it had a voice (see Chapter 10)?

Teacher: Establish the differences between first and third person. Establish the differences between writing in the past or present tense.

First person is generally more immediate and engaging, but the writer is restricted by being able to describe only what the character directly experiences. Third person has less impact but offers more scope for descriptive detail, hints, clues and references to information the character doesn't know. Perhaps experiment with both.

Consider the values associated with present versus past tense. Present has more impact and draws the reader into the scene, past enables the reader to gain more of a 'whole view' perspective on the narrative. Perhaps experiment with both.

Pupils: Discuss group ideas and create a synopsis for a story with the endangered animal as the main character.

Pupils: Rewrite synopsis into individual notebooks.

Pupils: Make notes and 'dabble'. Consider the setting as described on the factsheet. What would make a strong beginning (see Chapter 11)? Could the piece start with dialogue (see Chapter 10)? Think about whether this narrative would work best in first or third person.

Pupils: Write the beginning paragraph.

Pupils: Share beginnings with group – listeners try to identify what aspects are drawn from fact, and what aspects are drawn from fiction.

Pupils: *Go it alone* – continue the story, building in tension and conflict, to the end (see Chapter 11).

Teacher: Feedback based on the impact the research has made on the writing. Focus on characterisation: does the overall voice feel like it is an animal's point of view? Is the behaviour of the animal consistent with the factual material *and* fictional characterisation? Has the POV been consistent? Does the setting feel relevant to the animal's factual environment? What techniques has the writer used to create drama and suspense? Has the writer been consistent with tense (past or present) and voice (first or third person)?

Non-fiction exercise

Discuss in groups the value of fiction that informs readers of endangered species.

Research an additional endangered species *or* a creature that is already extinct.

Write an appeal to the public on this animal's behalf.

END OF THE SHOW

A great many subjects begin their lives as fields of study at universities. Specialisms are enhanced by experts, and this knowledge is eventually trailed down through the age groups: colleges, secondary, primary, infant and pre-school.

Complex patterns around process and outputs need to be pruned and simplified, offering re-interpretations for younger and younger learners.

Creative writing, although partly connected to professional writing, reading and literacy, can also be viewed in this context. Initially blossoming at Masters Level in America and the UK, its popularity grew, spreading outwards first to meet requirements at undergraduate level and then stretching its roots down into schools.

Much gets trimmed back in this process, but one bough that it seems important to retain in its original shape is the branch of curiosity; the risk taking qualities that need to be nurtured in order for the subject to properly thrive.

In teaching Creative Writing to adults and undergraduates, one of the fundamental elements I have often observed is that students can be under-prepared for engagement with a creative subject. Many struggle with the notion of taking risks with ideas.

A creative subject evokes a level of freedom in terms of approach and delivery, and this in itself can trigger anxieties. For those who have never been taught creatively, or given the opportunity to explore possibilities around ideas, the (perceived) potential for failure can feel both exposing and limiting. They sometimes beg for concrete guidelines: 'Just tell me what to do and I'll do it. I want to make sure I get it right.'

There is no judgement being served here. These learners have, very often, chosen to follow a dream. A passion. All courses, at any level, make demands on time and money. Of course those enrolled want to do well. The difficulty is that, in applying value to product rather than process, the potential to tap into what is unique and original may never be awoken. And, in a creative subject, learning to be unique and original is as close as it gets to finding the magic key.

To try and counteract this lack of confidence I devised a module called *'Creativity: into the wilderness,'* which encouraged first year undergraduate students to work on a subject they considered they would fail at. Music, art and drama were all brought into the mix and the criterion for students was to find something they believed they had no talent or inclination for, and work their way through it. They were assessed not purely on the output, but on the integrity of their investigation.

The following two extracts (from emails) may do a better job than me at articulating the value of such an experience. Both these extracts have come from exemplary students; one has gone on to study at PhD level, the other is an award winning performance poet. They have both become popular and innovative lecturers in creative writing at university level:

> I really didn't enjoy the Creativity module to start with. What was the relevance of art or meditation when I wanted to be a writer? As far as I could tell, being able to sketch my hand without looking down at the pencil and paper was not a skill that I would be using often throughout the course of my degree, and so what was the point?
>
> The point was, as it turns out, that I didn't *get* creativity (the module or the concept). I didn't understand the fact that creativity is about taking risks, about pushing yourself and about experimentation. Ultimately, creativity, for me at least, is about learning through failure. You try something, it doesn't work, you figure out why and then you try again. You may fail multiple more times, but each time you will learn something new and so you will be failing *better*.
>
> Creativity taught me to take risks with my writing and to embrace the fear that often comes with entering the unknown. It helped to forge my creative identity and to discover my 'voice' as a writer. Without the creativity module I doubt I would have done as well in my degree, and ultimately, I doubt I would now be teaching on the same programme that I once studied.
>
> (Elphick, personal communication)

> The creativity module showed me that I am an artist outside of being a writer. It showed me that I could develop multitudes and platitudes and pathways in terms of negotiating problems, creative, logical and emotional, in order to guide me to the answers, the finished articles I needed the most. It showed me the value system I have in my head; what I hold most important in terms of process and expression. It's the reason I became a performer and removed my shyness, or rather, taught me that my shyness was still an interesting dynamic to pursue in a performance context... It began my risk taking streak; showed me that it's better to put all comfort zones on hold and dive into the areas unexplored, even with the potential of failure, in order to make these accidents part of expressing in a way I hadn't done previously.
>
> (Wojcik, personal communication)

Both of these ex-students make reference to risks and comfort zones, and it seems to me that perhaps this is the quality hardest to feed down, but the core essential ingredient that the subject needs, for both pupils and teachers. Risk, in the context of creative writing, means exploring new approaches. It means experimenting with ideas, and attaching value to the possibility of something being 'wrong'. In some sense it means exposure – to expose feelings and deepest thoughts; these are where the best ideas lay hidden. Once the risks are taken the practice of writing will have more meaning, and when we produce work that is meaningful we have the motivation to keep developing it.

This book has attempted to trim back some of the complexities that tangle up around the teaching of creative writing, yet still embrace the fact that the subject needs to bend when the wind blows. It won't grow straight and it won't always grow at exactly the place where we thought we planted it.

I have taken some risks with this book too. I am aware it doesn't always follow standard academic-publication styles or structures. I may be open to ridicule. I may, even worse, be ignored.

Maybe a book like this isn't needed.

Maybe it is only me who would value a book like this.

I won't, therefore, end this book's conclusion with my own grand statement. Instead, I will stand back and give the role to one of my characters. A red-haired young man who has helped me throughout this endeavour. It's a risk but then, well... you know how I feel about those.

Characters, as we know, sometimes take over from the author. Already I sense myself slipping away. Becoming shadowy and indistinct. While I still have enough voice to be heard, let me re-introduce you to Seb. You first met him on page 16, and he's been hanging around in various chapters all the way through:

Seb slumped down in front of the telly.

"Good day at school?" Mum poked her head round the door.

Seb shrugged and grunted. "OK, I s'pose."

Mum rolled her eyes and headed off to the kitchen.

Seb switched on the remote, his eyes still fixed on the screen, but for once he wasn't watching what was on. Today *had* been OK really. The visiting author seemed a bit weird but Seb didn't mind weird. Weird was a zillion times better than boring, and he'd liked some of the stuff the author said. There had been a bit about characters, and how you could be your own character — sort of live inside your own story. And that group project where they'd made up a whole dragon world was awesome. They'd had to 'become' dragons and Seb was a fire-dragon, mostly due to the colour of his hair. He'd acted out being 'angry fire-dragon' and pictured the anger like a trapped flame. Angry Fire-Dragon lived inside a volcano and had masses of power to make it erupt if anyone annoyed him.

Seb turned the telly off and went to the window.

The leaves lay in heaps of gold and brown and ochre. The colours of rust.

The colours of fire.

The author had said they all had to switch their minds on. "Once you start looking properly, you'll find stories everywhere. It's all about how you tune yourself to see things," the author explained. "Dragons can happen."

The rest of Seb's group started messing about then, pretending they had giant switches on their heads. Seb had done the giant switch thing too, but secretly he wished he'd listened more. He liked the idea of finding stories everywhere. He knew his reading and writing weren't great, but he was good at thinking.

If he thought about a story enough, it might almost write itself. Just then, something caught his eye. For a brief second he imagined he saw something scutter out of the leaves; something small and fast. What if it was a baby dragon? What if he followed it to the land of the volcano? What if he turned out to be The Most Powerful Dragon of All Time?

"What are you staring out of the window for, loser?"

Seb looked round to see his sister Bella watching him, her hands on her hips. As bossy and annoying as ever. He didn't care. He'd put her in his story too, and trap her in a deep dark cave. She'd have to beg him to let her out.

"You're really weird," Bella said. "You're just grinning at nothing."

Seb opened his mouth to tell her she'd be sorry once she was in that cave, but the words didn't come out right. In fact, they didn't come out as words at all.

There was a crack of sound, like thunder. A flame of gold lit up the room. Seb roared.

CREDITS

Teacher, librarian, educational specialists and author discussions via emails and phone; school based research support and/or input through school visits; initial website and ICT support; project referees:

Amy Adams (Teacher) Peel Common Junior School, Gosport; Lucy Adlington (Author); Glynis Alexander (Teacher/Teaching Consultant); Jon Audain (Teacher/Lecturer/ICT Consultant) Monkeeshine Consultancy; Carole Bishop (Headteacher) Peel Common Junior School, Gosport; Beverley Birch (Editor/Author); Paul Bryers (Author/Film Director); Emma Cairns (Teacher) Bridgemary School, Gosport; Liz Chamberlain (Lecturer) Open University; Andy Clark (Deputy Headteacher) Locks Heath Junior School, Locks Heath; Sue Clarkson (Teacher) Locks Heath Junior School, Locks lHeath; Teresa Cremin (Professor of Education/UKLA) Open University; Fiona Crowther (Librarian) The Romsey School, Romsey; Martine Di Paola (Teacher/Student Support) Davison CE High School for Girls, Worthing; Berlie Doherty (Author); Matt Elphick (Lecturer/ Research Officer) University of Winchester, Winchester; Annie Everall OBE (Author Agency) Authors Aloud UK; Amanda Garrie (Author/Teacher/PhD student) University of Portsmouth; Katie Hadlow (Teacher) Redlands Primary School, Fareham; Kevin Harcombe (Headteacher) Redlands Primary School, Fareham; Gill James (Author/Lecturer) University of Salford; Lisa Kelly (Librarian) Isle of Portland Aldridge Community Academy, Dorset; Diana Kimpton (Author); Julie Lawes (Director) CatchUp Literacy, Thetford; Andrew Loneragan (Teacher) Peel Common Junior School, Gosport; Anne Marley MBE (Author Agency) Authors Aloud UK; Sue Moody (Librarian) Mountbatten School, Romsey; Marie Mullins 'Mulholland' (Teacher) Siskin Junior School, Gosport; Sarah Mussi (Author); Mo OHara (Author); Isabelle Pearce (Library Adviser) Hampshire Schools Library Service, Fareham; Dee Reid (Literacy consultant/Trainer) CatchUp Literacy, Thetford; Teresa Rich (Teacher) Locks Heath Junior School) Locks Heath; Jim Rogers (Teacher) Elson Junior School, Gosport; Pru Scott (Teacher) Cantell School, Southampton; Andy Seed (Author); Hayley Sheath (Teacher) Cantell School, Southampton; Helen Smith (Librarian) Brookfield School, Locks Heath; Ali Sparkes (Author); Gary Spracklen (Headteacher) King Barrow School, Portland; Margaret Taylor (Librarian) Henry Cort School, Fareham; Teri Terry (Author); Ann Warwick (Librarian) Davison CE High School for Girls, Worthing; Lisa Willis (Teacher) Siskin Junior School, Gosport; Antosh Wojcik (Poet/Lecturer) University of Winchester.

INDEX